The Window Before

The Window Before

The Politics of Alliance Implementation

BRETT V. BENSON
BRADLEY C. SMITH

OXFORD
UNIVERSITY PRESS

Oxford University Press is a department of the University of Oxford.
It furthers the University's objective of excellence in research, scholarship,
and education by publishing worldwide. Oxford is a registered trade mark of
Oxford University Press in the UK and in certain other countries.

Published in the United States of America by Oxford University Press
198 Madison Avenue, New York, NY 10016, United States of America.

Library of Congress Cataloging-in-Publication Data
Names: Benson, Brett V., 1973- editor | Smith, Bradley (Bradley Carl) editor
Title: The window before : the politics of alliance implementation /
[edited by] Brett V. Benson, Bradley C. Smith.
Description: New York : Oxford University Press, 2025. |
Includes bibliographical references and index.
Identifiers: LCCN 2025027889 (print) | LCCN 2025027890 (ebook) |
ISBN 9780197806722 hardback | ISBN 9780197806739 paperback |
ISBN 9780197806746 epub | ISBN 9780197806760
Subjects: LCSH: Alliances | Combined operations (Military science) | Military readiness
Classification: LCC JZ1314 .W56 2025 (print) | LCC JZ1314 (ebook) |
DDC 327.1/16—dc23/eng/20250828
LC record available at https://lccn.loc.gov/2025027889
LC ebook record available at https://lccn.loc.gov/2025027890

DOI: 10.1093/9780197806760.001.0001

Paperback printed by Integrated Books International, United States of America

The manufacturer's authorized representative in the EU for product safety is
Oxford University Press España S.A. of Parque Empresarial San Fernando de Henares,
Avenida de Castilla, 2 – 28830 Madrid (www.oup.es/en or product.safety@oup.com).
OUP España S.A. also acts as importer into Spain of products made by the manufacturer.

For our families.

Contents

Preface

The inspiration for this book grew out of our observation of the geopolitical turbulence in the years leading up to Russia's 2022 invasion of Ukraine. During this period, support for Ukraine's NATO membership steadily increased among both the Ukrainian public and political elites, even as Russia's vocal opposition grew louder and more intense. The simultaneity of these two developments led us to an important observation: Military alliances are not implemented instantaneously. Instead, leaders in states aspiring to join or build alliances often spend years negotiating, coordinating, and laying the groundwork to combine their military forces.

When that process is complete, alliances can become formidable joint fighting forces capable of deterring adversaries. But before implementation is fully realized, states are in a vulnerable position. Adversaries often discover what these aspiring allies are trying to achieve, but also know their combined military strength is not yet operational. This creates a window of time—"the window before" as we call it in our book title—during which enemies can attempt to disrupt, delay, or derail alliance formation.

As we studied other historical efforts to form military alliances, we were struck by how most alliances take time to implement and by how much political maneuvering—secrecy, threats, diplomatic deal-making both among allies and between allies and adversaries, and even violence—took place not after a formal alliance was signed, but during the ambiguous, unsettled period when one was merely being considered and implemented.

We wrote about these dynamics in the context of the outbreak of the Ukraine war in a *Washington Post* article, and it became clear to us that this pre-alliance window is both analytically rich and underexplored. States don't wait for treaties to be signed before they act. Commitments are floated, tested, and contested long before they are formalized. This book is our attempt to make sense of that window—to understand the political logic, strategic incentives, and risks that arise in the shadow of potential alliances. We argue that what happens before an alliance is formed can be just as consequential as what happens afterward.

Acknowledgments

This book is the product of many conversations, critiques, and collaborations over the course of several years. We have accumulated a long list of people and institutions to thank, and while we cannot fully capture the influence each has had on this project, we are grateful for the community of scholars and students who have engaged with our work and helped us improve it.

We would like to thank our colleagues at Vanderbilt University who work on problems related to armed conflict. In particular, we are grateful to Peter Bils, Andrew Coe, Cassy Dorff, Andres Gannon, Brenton Kenkel, Jenn Larson, Emily Ritter, and Peter Schram for their thoughtful comments and valuable feedback on various stages of this book. We also benefited from the insights, questions, and feedback we received from Alexandre Debs, Matt Furhmann, Jesse Johnson, Ashley Leeds, Jim Morrow, William Spaniel, and Scott Wolford.

We are especially indebted to the undergraduate researchers in the Research on Conflict and Collective Action Lab at Vanderbilt University. These students played a crucial role in the development of our case studies, spending countless hours tracking down documents, compiling timelines, and piecing together complex historical narratives. Their diligence and intellectual curiosity helped us build the empirical foundation of this book.

We also thank General Mark Hertling and Colonel Rick Montcalm for sharing their time and insights with us in interviews based on their deep professional experience in security cooperation. Their perspectives, grounded in years of leadership and on-the-ground work, helped illuminate the practical challenges and strategic nuances of alliance coordination. We are also grateful to members of Security Forces Assistance Brigades and partner forces in NATO countries who generously participated in interviews and offered valuable information that helped us better understand the real-world dynamics of alliance formation and implementation.

We also gratefully acknowledge financial support from a Foreign Policy Research Grant provided by the Stand Together Trust between 2020 and

2023. This support allowed us the time and flexibility to pursue the depth of research required for this project.

Finally, we thank our families. Bradley is grateful to his wife, Sarah, his parents, Jeff and Fran, and his brother, Will. Brett is grateful to his wife, Lacy, and children, Max, Joey, and Remi. Their patience, encouragement, and unwavering support sustained us through the many highs and lows of this process. As any author knows, the toll of writing is often felt most acutely by those closest to us. This book is built not only on our ideas and labor but also on their strength and sacrifice.

1
Introduction

Do military alliances deter or provoke conflict? In today's world, where military alliances bind different coalitions of countries together, this question has profound implications for global geopolitics and security. The answer also sheds light on the role of past alliances throughout history.

Policymakers have long debated this issue. In his 1949 inaugural address, President Harry S. Truman proposed a series of military alliances, including what would become NATO, to foster global peace. He argued that such alliances deter conflict: "If we can make it sufficiently clear, in advance, that any armed attack affecting our national security would be met with overwhelming force, the armed attack might never occur."[1]

This deterrence theory underpins the ongoing justification for NATO. Jens Stoltenberg, NATO Secretary General since 2014, frequently highlights NATO's peace-enhancing deterrence. In an interview conducted at Princeton University's Wilson Center, Stoltenberg explained: "[T]he whole purpose of NATO is to prevent war, is to prevent a military attack. And we have done so successfully for 75 years, even during the most dangerous and the coldest period of the Cold War, where you had hundreds of thousands of combat ready Russian troops on the border of NATO. We had West Berlin in the middle of East Germany. And throughout those decades, we were able to deter any Soviet or Russian aggression against NATO territory, because it was so clearly communicated that an attack on one Ally will be an attack on all Allies."[2]

Leaders from European countries and the United States echo the deterrent value of alliances when expressing support for NATO. For example, former Estonian President Kersti Kaljulaid affirmed: "NATO's deterrence has always been adequate and I'm not worried about the physical security of

[1] Inaugural Address of Harry S. Truman, January 20, 1949, URL: https://avalon.law.yale.edu/20th_century/truman.asp.

[2] Speech by NATO Secretary General Jens Stoltenberg at the Wilson Center Auditorium followed by Q&A, June 17, 2024, URL: https://www.nato.int/cps/en/natohq/226742.htm?selectedLocale=en.

The Window Before. Brett V. Benson and Bradley C. Smith, Oxford University Press.
 DOI: 10.1093/9780197806760.003.0001

my country. Not at all . . . NATO deterrence has always held . . . all through NATO's history."[3] Former Secretary of State Hillary Clinton emphasized NATO's role in maintaining European peace: "The United States, obviously, has a great interest in helping to maintain peace and security in Europe, and we have a formal alliance, NATO, to do so."[4] Reflecting on NATO's 75-year history, Secretary of State Antony J. Blinken asserted: "And what is at the heart of NATO? This extraordinary commitment—that an attack on one is an attack on all—is the strongest possible deterrent to conflict, the best possible way to avoid war, because any would-be aggressor contemplating an attack knows that if they take on one of us, they have to take on all of us."[5]

Belief in the deterrent value of alliances extends beyond NATO. In 2015, US President Obama and Japanese Prime Minister Shinzo Abe strengthened the US–Japan alliance, with Abe asserting that it provides "credible deterrence for the peace in the region."[6]

However, others argue that alliances can provoke conflict. Cold War strategist George Kennan opposed NATO's expansion in 1997, fearing it would provoke Russia.[7] This view is shared by others, including a 1995 letter from retired US diplomats warning that NATO expansion could exacerbate instability in Europe.[8] John Mearsheimer argues that NATO's expansion triggered Russia's invasion of Ukraine in 2022, as Putin sought to prevent Ukraine from joining NATO.[9]

The debate over whether alliances deter or provoke conflict is high-stakes and has major implications for global policy. If alliances deter conflict, expanding them could reduce global tensions. This would support advocating for NATO expansion, bolstering military cooperation in Asia, and

[3] Eestlased Eestis, "'I'm not afraid': The president of tiny Estonia gives a giant lesson in leadership," March 28, 2017, URL: https://www.eesti.ca/i-m-not-afraid-the-president-of-tiny-estonia-gives-a-giant-lesson-in-leadership-wp/article49460.

[4] "Fmr. Sec. Hillary Clinton to Fareed Zakaria: Putin indirectly responsible for MH17," interview with Fareed Zakaria, July 27, 2014, URL: https://cnnpressroom.blogs.cnn.com/2014/07/27/fmr-sec-hillary-clinton-to-fareed-zakaria-putin-indirectly-responsible-for-mh17/.

[5] Remarks given at the 2024 NATO Public Forum, July 10, 2024, URL: https://www.state.gov/secretary-antony-j-blinken-at-the-2024-nato-public-forum/.

[6] https://japan.kantei.go.jp/97_abe/statement/201504/uscongress.html.

[7] George F. Kennan, "A Fateful Error," *The New York Times*, February 5, 1997, Section A, p.23.

[8] Open letter published by Richard T. Davies, "Should NATO Grow? A Dissent," *the New York Review*, September 21, 1999, URL: https://www.nybooks.com/articles/1995/09/21/should-nato-growa-dissent/.

[9] For a summary of the academic debate regarding NATO's role in starting the 2022 Russian–Ukraine War, see Alex Hughes (2023), "Plan Z: Reassessing Security-Based Accounts of Russia's Invasion of Ukraine," *Journal of Advanced Military Studies*, 14:2, pp. 174–208.

forming new alliances. Conversely, if alliances provoke conflict, caution is warranted, suggesting that NATO should not expand further and that strengthening certain alliances might be dangerous.

Our book argues that both views capture part of the truth but miss key aspects of how alliances impact conflict. Alliances can deter conflict by increasing collective power, but they can also provoke aggression when their formation threatens a rival's interests. Understanding the dynamics of military cooperation is crucial for predicting when alliances will foster peace or provoke war.

Some experts acknowledge both the deterrent and the provocative potential of alliances. Jens Stoltenberg, a strong NATO advocate, admitted that NATO's expansion could provoke conflict, stating that "Putin went to war to prevent NATO, more NATO, close to his borders."[10] Fiona Hill, a former Deputy Assistant to the US President, suggested that NATO didn't cause Russia's invasion of Ukraine but created options for countries under pressure from Russia, which Putin wanted to prevent.[11]

These perspectives suggest a nuanced view of alliances: even defensive ones, which may ultimately foster lasting peace, can create provocative pressures at certain stages of their formation by influencing the options available to different actors. This book delves into these complexities by exploring the dynamic process of alliance formation. We argue that the shift in power resulting from an alliance typically unfolds over time, creating a *window of time before* the alliance's full strength is achieved. During this "window before," rivals might take preventive actions, including military conflict, to thwart the alliance. Meanwhile, prospective allies may expedite the formation of the alliance or take other measures to counteract these preventive actions, aiming to secure the anticipated benefits of the power shift.

We analyze why states react aggressively to anticipated alliances and how they can mitigate such reactions. By examining historical cases and developing a dynamic theory of alliances, we provide insights into when alliances will lead to peace or provoke war. This theory not only advances our understanding of historical and current international relations but also

[10] Jens Stoltenberg, "Opening remarks," at the joint meeting of the European Parliament's Committee on Foreign Affairs and the Subcommittee on Security and Defense, September 7, 2023, URL: https://www.nato.int/cps/en/natohq/opinions_218172.htm.

[11] Fiona Hill interview with Rieke Havertz and Martin Klingst, "The World Is Feeding Russia's Imperial Delusions," *Zeit Online*, May 12, 2023, URL: https://www.zeit.de/politik/ausland/2023-05/fiona-hill-ukraine-war-russia-europe/komplettansicht.

offers practical implications for policymakers navigating today's complex geopolitical landscape.

1.1 Overview of the Argument

The formation and maintenance of a military alliance is a complex, gradual process. Initially, prospective allies agree to cooperate militarily, often aiming to formalize their partnership through an official treaty. However, it may take a considerable amount of time before they are prepared to act together with their combined military strength. NATO officers interviewed for this book frequently expressed frustration at the misconception that alliance-making is instantaneous. Many believe that once a country joins an alliance like NATO, it is immediately integrated. In reality, transitioning from an independent nation relying solely on its own defense to a fully integrated alliance member involves significant effort and time.

A crucial, yet often overlooked, phase in forming an alliance occurs between the initial decision to cooperate and the point at which members are fully prepared for joint military action. We refer to this as the *alliance implementation stage*. During this period, prospective allies finalize the terms of their agreement and ensure effective collaboration in combat. The implementation process can be lengthy due to the complexities of resolving differences and overcoming various challenges.

Figure 1.1 illustrates the dynamic process of alliance formation and its associated stages, including the implementation stage. The life cycle of an alliance is divided into three main phases: the pre-implementation stage, the implementation stage, and the post-implementation stage. Throughout, members of the alliance and enemies may bargain with each other in the shadow of conflict with the given distribution of power in each respective stage. In the pre-implementation stage, governments of prospective allies decide whether to join an alliance. In making this decision, they look ahead and anticipate factors in the future stages. At this point, power from the alliance has not yet shifted. If any prospective ally bargains or fights with an enemy, they do so alone without the benefit of the combined power of allies.

Continuing to the implementation stage, if prospective allies decide to form an alliance, then they must work through many time-consuming obstacles before the alliance is finalized. During this stage, the power shift begins but is not yet complete. Here, the advantages of the alliance do not yet translate to bargaining and fighting. In the post-implementation stage the power

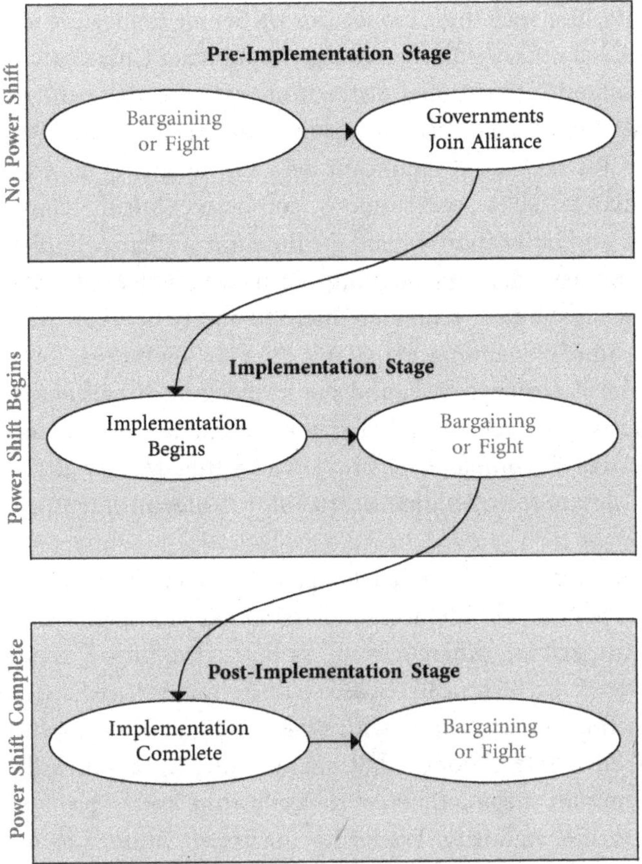

Figure 1.1 Dynamic alliance formation timing

shift is complete and allies enjoy the full benefits of a shift in the distribution of power. Arrows indicate the sequence and interactions between these stages, highlighting how power shifts and strategic decisions evolve throughout the alliance formation process.

What causes variation in the length of the implementation stage? Implementation delays generally fall into two main categories: political and military. Political delays typically arise before the formal signing and ratification of the alliance. Leaders negotiate the scope, terms, and conditions of the alliance, often hindered by logistical issues such as travel distances and language barriers. Disagreements over key issues—such as territory, obligations, and consultation processes—can extend negotiations. Constitutional requirements, such as legislative ratification, further contribute to delays. For example, the mutual defense pact between the United States and the

Republic of China took three months for US Senate ratification after signing, during which tensions with the People's Republic of China escalated.

Domestic and international distractions can also delay the signing and implementation of alliances. For instance, domestic political instability in France and Russia caused significant delays in finalizing the 1894 Franco–Russian alliance. These interruptions, combined with the complexities of negotiation and ratification, extend the timeline of alliance implementation.

On the military side, implementing an alliance involves coordinating joint warfighting capabilities. Achieving interoperability between allied forces is crucial but time-consuming, requiring strategic alignment, joint decision-making, technical integration, and the unification of multinational forces into a cohesive unit. Often, military implementation begins only after the political process is complete, meaning that a ratified treaty does not immediately translate to full operational capability. Achieving interoperability can take months or even years, demanding substantial investment and effort.

Despite its importance, the challenge of military interoperability is frequently overlooked in alliance scholarship. Key obstacles include technological disparities, differences in military training and tactics, and language barriers. Technical issues, such as mismatched weaponry and communication systems, along with varied military cultures, further complicate effective integration. Additionally, unifying command structures involves complex negotiations over leadership roles, promotions, and decision-making authority, extending the time required to achieve full operational capability.

Once the implementation is complete, new allies benefit from aggregated military power. Prior to full implementation, an alliance member possesses only a fraction of the potential fighting capability of a fully implemented alliance, resulting in diminished bargaining leverage in peacetime. After full implementation, alliance members gain substantial bargaining and fighting power.

The anticipation of this power shift, combined with the time required for implementation, drives political action between allies and target states. While allies benefit from increased power post-implementation, targets face reduced bargaining power and potential coercion. This effect extends to defensive alliances as well. Offensive-minded targets may find their plans thwarted by a new defensive alliance.

When the power shift is finalized, targets must accept the new balance of power. Enhanced joint warfighting capabilities increase deterrence, particularly in defensive alliances. If alliances were implemented instantaneously, allies could quickly transition from vulnerability to relative security. However, as discussed in detail in this book, alliances are not implemented instantaneously. During the implementation period, targets anticipate the forthcoming power shift and may engage in aggressive preventive actions to counter it. Following the logic of dangerous commitment problems (Fearon 1995; Powell 2012), if the anticipated power shift is substantial, the target may find it advantageous to act preemptively to prevent the alliance and stop the shift. The implementation window provides targets with the opportunity to foresee the potential downsides of the impending shift and take aggressive measures to counteract it.

Our theory highlights that both the *size* and the *speed* of the power shift influence the likelihood of preventive war. Rapid implementation leaves targets with insufficient time to react, while slower implementation allows for extended negotiation periods. The most threatening scenario arises when the impending power shift is significant enough to prompt a preemptive strike but not so immediate as to outpace a target's ability to respond.

A key finding of our book is that alliances may trigger preventive wars *before* they are fully implemented, even if they enhance deterrence and promote peace *after* they are in place.[12] As demonstrated in Chapter 3, the provocative nature of impending alliances applies to both offensive and defensive alliances. In addition, as we show in Chapter 4, under some conditions targets of alliances will resort to full-scale preventive wars, while at other times they will instead choose to launch small-scale aggressive actions and limited wars to try to block an impending alliance. The primary factors predicting whether an alliance might provoke war, large or small, are the size and speed of the anticipated power shift. We provide a detailed analysis of the relationship between implementation speed and the likelihood of preventive war, noting that this relationship is non-monotonic.

Despite the significant power shifts typically associated with alliances and their oft-threatening speed, historical evidence shows that many alliances are implemented peacefully. This raises the question: Why do we frequently observe peaceful implementations if alliances induce substantial and threatening power shifts? In this book, we extend the baseline

[12] We detail the incentives for preventive wars during alliance implementation elsewhere in Benson and Smith (2021). The theoretical argument presented in this book extends far beyond the baseline theory laid out in this article. Beyond the core insights in that article, we provide novel theoretical analysis, results, and empirical analysis.

theoretical analysis to explore various strategies to avoid the provocative effects of alliances.

The key to peaceful implementation of alliances lies in the incentives for potential allies to avoid provoking attacks while still capturing future benefits from the power shift that come from having an alliance. Leaders have at their disposal various strategies to mitigate the risk of war. On the one end, they might opt to forgo forming alliances to avoid provoking conflict. While such an approach can prevent immediate hostilities, it also results in allies missing out on the potential benefits of alliance formation. On the other end, the allure of the benefits from an alliance may compel allies to risk inciting conflict. In these cases, forming an alliance becomes a calculated gamble. If an alliance is peacefully implemented, it is often because allies finalize their provocative partnership before the target has time and opportunity to launch a preventive attack. Conversely, unsuccessful attempts occur when this gamble does not pay off. In this book, we examine numerous historical examples where attempts to form alliances led to armed aggression. In some cases, this aggression successfully thwarted the alliance; in others, the allies secured the alliance before aggression escalated to the point of abandonment.

Between the extremes of abandoning an alliance or fully accepting the risks of a provocative alliance, prospective allies often employ various strategies to balance the risks of war with the benefits of the alliance. These strategies, which are further explored in Chapter 5, significantly increase the likelihood that a preventive war will be avoided. A strategy often adopted by allies is to design treaty terms and implementation processes to minimize provocation. One method involves limiting the power shift by drafting a treaty that limits allies' commitments of military capabilities, as demonstrated by the US and NATO's approach to East Germany's NATO membership in 1990. Another strategy is to expedite implementation by simplifying treaty requirements and avoiding lengthy military integration. The aim of the 1894 Franco–Russian alliance, for example, was to force the enemy to divide its forces across two fronts rather than achieving superiority through combined allies' capabilities. This strategy simplified implementation by sidestepping the need for allies to work through the costly and time-consuming process of integrating military forces and achieving interoperability.

Another effective strategy for facilitating rapid implementation is to minimize the time targets are aware of an alliance. By keeping negotiations and other implementation steps secret, the process can be accelerated, as demonstrated by the 1894 Franco–Russian alliance and the 1955 US–ROC mutual defense pact, both of which concealed critical details to achieve a favorable power shift without alerting the target. We explore the use of secrecy to expedite implementation in Chapter 5 and present historical examples where this tactic was deliberately employed to achieve strategic advantages.

In addition to designing the treaty terms and implementation process to facilitate peaceful implementation of alliances, prospective allies and adversaries also often engage in negotiations to prevent preventive wars. Allies may offer compensation to the target to induce them to accept the alliance, as was done to persuade the Soviet Union to allow East Germany into NATO. Conversely, targets might offer compensation to one or more allies to discourage the formation of the alliance. As discussed in Chapter 6, such strategies are common. Historical examples include France's sale of the Louisiana territory to the United States and various neutrality agreements, such as the Molotov–Ribbentrop Pact, which illustrate how compensation can influence alliance dynamics.

In sum, this book explores the intricate dynamics of military alliance formation and implementation, focusing on the nuanced phases between the initial agreement and full operational readiness. It examines the political and military delays that can hinder this process, emphasizing the challenges of achieving interoperability and the various strategies used to mitigate risks and speed up implementation. The book argues that while alliances can enhance deterrence and peace once fully operational, their formation can provoke preventive wars due to the significant power shifts they create. By analyzing historical examples and theoretical models, the book reveals how both the size and speed of these power shifts affect the likelihood of conflict and explores the strategies employed by prospective allies and adversaries. It shows how these strategies can either sustain peace or lead to preventive wars, depending on how they navigate the risks and opportunities presented by the impending shifts in power.

1.2 Implications of the Theory

There are four questions that naturally follow from our argument. First, what are the implications for the study of military alliances, especially the debate regarding the effect of alliances on conflict. Second, what are the future opportunities for researchers? Third, when should we expect to observe, in practice, the different outcomes that we predict in theory? Fourth, what does our theory imply for current challenges and tensions in the world? We address these questions in Chapter 7.

How does our research in this book contribute to scholarly debates about the relationship between alliances and war? Alliance scholarship mirrors the broader policy debate on whether alliances deter or provoke conflict. Some studies suggest that alliances have a deterrent effect, reducing the likelihood of war (Leeds 2003; Benson 2012; Johnson and Leeds 2011; Leeds and Johnson 2017). In contrast, other research highlights that alliances can increase the risk of war, particularly around their formation and immediately afterward (Kenwick, Vasquez, and Powers 2015; Kenwick and Vasquez 2017). This dichotomy is captured in Morrow (2017)'s formal model, which integrates both provocation and deterrence. According to Morrow, the key variable is the level of uncertainty about the conflict of interest between the alliance's target and its recipient. This uncertainty influences whether the alliance is deterrent or provocative.

Our theory complements this dual perspective by focusing on the dynamics of alliance implementation. We argue that while alliances can deter conflict in the long term, they may provoke preventive actions during their implementation phase due to the commitment problem. This insight aligns with Kenwick, Vasquez, and Powers (2015)'s observation of the heightened risks around alliance formation. Our model provides a unified framework for understanding these conflicting findings, highlighting the critical role of timing in the alliance–war connection.

Given the theory laid out in this work, what are the future research opportunities to build on the overall body of alliance research to date? We see opportunities for a research agenda, including new theoretical and empirical work on alliance implementation. As we discuss in the conclusion of the book, future research should explore how well cases fit the informational logic offered by Morrow (2017) versus the commitment–problem logic we offer and develop targeted tests to further investigate these mechanisms. In addition, there are opportunities to integrate informational theories of alliances with the dynamic framework that we have constructed here. Moving in a more granular direction, future research might also drill down on the bureaucratic politics of military integration, as our research uncovers many industrial organization questions about the inner workings of alliance institutions, and NATO in particular. Finally, the process of alliance implementation is an area that can be further evaluated and measured. In Chapter 7, the Conclusion chapter, we discuss these possible pathways for theoretical work and data collection.

In Chapter 7, we also address an additional question implied by our research: When should we expect to observe the different outcomes predicted by our theoretical model? Specifically, we explore when large-scale wars versus smaller conflicts aimed at preventing alliances are likely to occur, and when prospective allies might design implementation processes to accelerate rather than delay actions. We also examine when negotiations between allies and adversaries might be favored over preventive wars. Our analysis reveals that these distinctions are influenced by both the theoretical conditions outlined in this book and real-world constraints. In essence, our theory not only clarifies differences in comparative statics related to the size and speed of power shifts but also highlights practical limitations that can either hinder or facilitate certain strategies. Overall, our theory offers a fresh perspective on understanding empirical patterns of alliances and war, providing a nuanced approach to analyzing the alliance–war connection in empirical studies.

Finally, the subject matter of this book is also highly relevant for understanding current events. The Ukraine War and ongoing discussions about NATO expansion elevate the critical nature of the arguments that we make. In Chapter 7, we discuss the application of our theoretical insights for these and many other ongoing challenges in the world, such as the tensions in the Taiwan Strait and emerging alliances between Russia and China and North Korea. Our findings have important implications for policymakers looking to expand or initiate military cooperation. For example, we argue that the rules of NATO's membership process are deliberately designed to slow implementation speed, which facilitates peaceful expansion to include new members in some cases, but might invite conflict in others. By laying out explicit membership requirements during its "membership action plan" process, NATO unintentionally provides a roadmap for adversaries to disrupt the process of alliance expansion. Our findings indicate some possibly productive reforms, including a more private, deliberative process for determining when to include new members in the alliance.

We also discuss the relevance of our theory for current initiatives to form, strengthen, or expand security partnerships in Asia. We offer cautionary insights on the prospective partnership between Russia and China, as well as talks intended to broaden US alliances throughout Asia and calls to clarify and strengthen the United States' defense commitment to Taiwan. Our findings shed light on some of the most worrisome security issues today.

Finally, in addressing the third question, we discuss the contributions that our theory makes to existing research. One main implication is that our dynamic theory of alliance implementation helps reconcile some gaps in the theoretical and empirical research on military alliances and conflict. However, our contributions do not only provide implications that help to understand previous work. Rather, in the concluding chapter we outline the next steps in a research program that focuses on alliance implementation, and its implications. We point to important questions in both theoretical and empirical research that are raised by the new perspective we bring to bear in this book.

1.3 Organization of the Book

The book has four parts. **Part 1**, which includes Chapters 2 and 3, introduces the concept of an implementation window and presents a theory of alliance implementation, power shifts, and provocation. The introduction of what is involved in implementing a military alliance is novel in the literature on military alliances. In Chapter 2, we describe the political and military steps that prospective allies typically take to bring an alliance to fruition. We rely on our own research as well as interviews with military officers who have expertise in the area of alliance implementation. The emphasis throughout this chapter is on the amount of time it takes to work through various steps in the implementation process. In addition to information gathered through expert interviews, we also provide historical case evidence to show how prospective allies work through the challenges of implementing an alliance and eventually realizing the benefits of having an allied relationship.

In Chapter 3, we present a dynamic theory of alliance implementation. To understand when and why alliance-driven power shifts cause war, we need a dynamic model that incorporates the process of alliance formation and implementation. This theory is captured in a formal theoretic argument. Alongside the formal presentation of the theory, we provide an extensive prose description and interpretation of the theoretical argument. In particular, we tie the microfoundations and assumptions of the theory to concrete historical cases, building on the discussion in the previous chapter. We formalize our theory in a dynamic three-player crisis bargaining model. The distinguishing feature of this model is that we treat security cooperation as a dynamic process. As such, our model grows naturally out of the previous chapter's focus on the implementation of alliances. In the model, a pair of friendly states attempt to implement an alliance. At the same time, they are locked in a dispute over some issue with an enemy state. That state chooses whether to peacefully bargain, or to engage in a preventive war to settle the issue before the opposing alliance can be implemented.

Part 2 of the book explains when military partnerships provoke wars. In Chapter 4, we lay out our theory of preventive wars. Our theory identifies two key factors: the size of the power shift caused by an alliance and the speed with which an alliance can be fully implemented. Building up this theory, we show that allies may knowingly risk provoking an enemy under some conditions. Simply put, under the right conditions alliance formation may represent a rational gamble in which allies try to implement a new agreement before an adversary can attack to interfere.

This chapter details the conditions under which the anticipation of a new alliance provokes war. It also explores the different approaches taken by adversaries to block alliances, providing an explanation for why in some cases large-scale wars are initiated, while in other cases only minor incursions are used. We argue that alliance implementation provokes war when the power shift caused by an alliance is sufficiently large relative to the speed with which the alliance can be implemented. We also extend our analysis to defensive alliances and discover that the logic of the argument applies whether the intent of the alliance is offensive or defensive.

We also show that the size of a war is related to the cost-effectiveness of small-scale wars as a blocking strategy. We explain how the availability of small-scale aggressive options makes the implementation window especially volatile, as opponents of an alliance may resort to a range of relatively inexpensive hostile actions if there is even a small chance of frustrating the impending action. Yet, there is also an upside to small-scale aggression: It may substitute for large-scale conflict and thus reduce the overall level of violence when large-scale war would otherwise break out.

With these theoretical conditions are established, we turn to the historical record. We trace a number of cases, showing that the logic embodied in our formal model of alliances is present there. In particular, we draw on the 2008 Russian invasion of Georgia, the 1954 Taiwan Strait Crisis, and the ongoing Russian invasion of Ukraine for evidence consistent with our arguments. Finally, we provide quantitative evidence that is consistent with our theory's predictions about the connection between alliances and war. In particular, we show that our theory provides insight into the timing of war initiation in the data; wars are significantly more likely to begin in the time just prior to an alliance's implementation, compared to the time after.

Part 3 of the book, which consists of Chapters 5 and 6, demonstrates that some wars to block partnerships can be avoided with clever tools of statecraft. We focus on two of these tools: concessions in deals between allies and adversaries and adjustments to the design of an alliance's treaty terms and implementation process. We show that though allies willingly risk war under some conditions, in others they intentionally manipulate the terms of cooperation to avoid provocation. Furthermore, concessions—either from an ally to a shared enemy or in the other direction—can pave the way for peace.

Chapter 5 builds on the previous chapter's analysis to detail the conditions under which provocation can be avoided. Our theory points to the size and speed of the power shift from a new alliance as the key factors determining whether provocation occurs. Consequently, we argue that allies sometimes knowingly manipulate these factors to avoid provoking an enemy.

This chapter first details the conditions under which such manipulation is preferred by the allies to a stronger alliance that carries a risk of war, and then provides historical evidence to illustrate the dynamics. We show that allies have historically sought to place limits on the military threat an alliance poses, as well as to draw out the timeline of implementation. As our theory suggests, both of these decisions serve to make the alliance less threatening to a shared enemy. We draw on a diverse range of historical cases to illustrate these dynamics, including German unification, NATO expansion in the late 1990s, US Security Cooperation with Israel, and contemporary discussions over the inclusion of Sweden and Finland in NATO.

In Chapter 6, we detail an alternative strategy to avoid provocation: taking peaceful actions to prevent an alliance from being implemented. While states targeted by alliances may lash out aggressively to block implementation, this is not the only available strategy. Rather, targeted states may strike quid pro quo "deals," offering concessions to potential allies in exchange for their foregoing the alliance. As a result, war is avoided because the threat of a new alliance is eliminated through peaceful means. As in the previous chapters, we illustrate these dynamics by tracing the logic in documentation from the historical record. In particular, we argue that this logic was present in the Cuban Missile Crisis. We also argue that such deals need not be all-or-nothing affairs. In many instances, targeted states strike deals to place limits on the terms of an alliance to render it less threatening. We argue that this dynamic was present in the Louisiana Purchase, the Cuban Missile Crisis, and many nineteenth-century neutrality pacts.

Part 4 is the final section of the book and includes only Chapter 7. This chapter offers some implications for both academics and policymakers. For academics, we argue that our theory points to the importance of understanding security cooperation as a dynamic process. In doing so, our theory has delivered new insights into the connection between alliance politics and war. For policymakers, our findings point to the danger of careless security commitments. Our theory suggests that, without care, alliances may provoke war. We tie this implication to debates about NATO expansion, arguing that NATO should reconsider its membership protocols, as they serve to invite conflict by providing a window of opportunity for enemy states like Russia to strike before implementation succeeds. We further discuss the danger of careless security commitments by drawing policy implications for security in East Asia. In particular, we argue that US policymakers should take care in designing packages of support to Taiwan, as the dynamic considerations our model points to are highly relevant in determining whether future conflicts will occur.

We also draw some conclusions to guide future work, pointing to historical patterns in the frequency and design of military alliances. Policymakers sign fewer formal military alliances today than in the past. Instead, countries engage in various kinds of informal military cooperation arrangements. Today's formal military alliances also differ significantly in content from those signed before World War II. The alliances of the past were often secret and did not include specifics about how to integrate military forces. We discuss what these changes imply for how countries today cooperate militarily. We also highlight the dangers that come from the fact that modern alliances are harder to implement and harder to keep secret, and military technology is far more sophisticated today than in the past.

1.4 Methodological Approach

The book includes both analytical theory and empirical evidence, including historical case evidence and quantitative data analysis. To impose analytical rigor on our theoretical arguments, we develop them using formal, game-theoretic tools. However, although we use this rigorous, mathematical framework to impose logical discipline on our arguments and to generate a number of counterintuitive insights, we also take steps to ensure that our arguments are transparent and accessible to readers with no technical background or no interest in engaging with the technical details. Most importantly, we accompany all of the main theoretical arguments with full, plain-language prose descriptions. Throughout the book, we also provide a running table of main theoretical results. As a result, some readers may elect to skip the technical arguments in favor of the prose descriptions and summary of results. In addition, this Introduction chapter also provides broad outline of the argument and some of key intuition that can be found worked out in greater detail in the formal analysis.

In taking these steps, we aim to provide compelling explanations of topics dominating today's headlines while keeping them accessible to a broad audience without loss of nuance or rigor.

The book also provides a significant amount of novel empirical content. We include historical comparisons between Russia's efforts to block NATO expansion after German reunification in 1991, in Georgia in 2008, in Crimea in 2014, and presently in Ukraine. Our qualitative evidence moves beyond NATO to explore the relevance of our argument for other situations. We examine the efforts by the United States and Great Britain to implement their World War II wartime alliance. We develop a full-case analysis of the attempt by the People's Republic of China to use force to block the 1954 military alliance between the United States and the Republic of China on Taiwan. We also provide new historical analysis of situations such as the 1894 Franco–Russian alliance and the 1954 US–Taiwan alliance, in which new allies manipulated the alliance terms or compensated the target of the alliance to permit the alliance to form peacefully. We also analyze historical cases where targets of impending military partnerships offered concessions to prevent the new partnership from forming, or to shape the terms of the partnership. These examples include France's sale of the Louisiana Territory to the United States in 1803 to prevent an alliance between the United States and Great Britain, the US agreement to remove nuclear missiles from Turkey to bring about an end to Soviet–Cuban military partnership in 1962, and Molotov–Ribbentrop Pact as a deal to neutralize the Soviet Union.

Our empirical evidence does not stop with the analysis of historical cases. We also conducted extensive interviews with both former and active duty

NATO officers. The bulk of this interview content appears in Chapter 5, which details the difficulties of alliance implementation.

Finally, we use quantitative analysis of hundreds of military alliances to assess our theory. In particular, we investigate a nuanced prediction of our theory: that alliances are most likely to provoke conflict just before they are brought into force. While some quantitative analyses are often inaccessible to non-scholarly audiences, we are careful to present the results in a way that can be followed by those with no statistical background. The nature of our analysis allows us to present much of the evidence graphically, without the use of convoluted regression tables, which many readers have trouble deciphering.

2
Implementation and the Logistics of Military Assistance

A military alliance alters the balance of power, improving the partners' chances of winning a war against a common enemy. In this book, we build on existing scholarly conceptions of military alliances. Following earlier research, if an alliance member becomes involved in an armed conflict to resolve a policy dispute, then the other alliance partners may be obligated to intervene in the conflict on behalf of their ally. An alliance treaty specifies the obligations of allies during conflicts (Leeds et al. 2002; Benson 2011). The combined strength of allies fighting together improves their chances of winning the war. According to existing theories, this capability aggregation has benefits: It deters aggression from enemies. This logic implies that alliances cause enemies to make more policy concessions to allies and deter them from taking military action against allics.[1]

Our study augments these insights with a critical feature of security cooperation that has not been previously modeled: The military benefits of an alliance may not arrive immediately. Rather, various factors often cause a delay between the decision to form an alliance and the point at which the joint military benefits of the alliance are realized. Common in most alliances, this delay creates opportunities for states to take action *after* states are aware that a power shift is impending but *before* the alliance has had time to cause a shift in the distribution of power. Throughout this book, we call the period

[1] Throughout this book, we build on existing formal theories in international relations. Formally speaking, we build on models in which alliances affect war payoffs of alliance members and targets of the alliance. See, for example, Smith (1995); Morrow (2000); Benson (2012); Benson, Meirowitz, and Ramsay (2014). Following conventions, we also model alliance members' payoffs for peaceful settlements as being related, capturing the idea that the allies value the same policy goals (Fang, Johnson, and Leeds 2014; Benson 2012; Benson, Meirowitz, and Ramsay 2014; Wolford 2014), and that alliance formation is subject to a participation constraint (Benson 2012; Benson, Meirowitz, and Ramsay 2014). Finally, the third party may act to shape the outcome of war through intervention or alliance formation, but does not act to initiate conflict itself (Smith 1995; Morrow 2000; Fang, Johnson, and Leeds 2014; Benson 2012; Benson, Meirowitz, and Ramsay 2014; Wolford 2014). Thus, our model incorporates standard features of previous theoretical work.

The Window Before. Brett V. Benson and Bradley C. Smith, Oxford University Press.
 DOI: 10.1093/9780197806760.003.0002

during which allies are working on the alliance, up to and including the moment that its military benefits are realized, alliance implementation.

This period represents a window of opportunity for leaders to engage in political maneuvering to influence the impending power shift. Actions that leaders choose during this time include war, diplomatic negotiation, and creative treaty design. As we will show in subsequent chapters, the speed of alliance implementation and the size of an alliance-induced power shift jointly influence what kinds of political maneuvers leaders choose. Thus, studying alliance implementation sheds light on the process of alliance formation and is key to understanding wars, deals, and treaty outcomes.

Dynamic alliance implementation is a novel concept in the study of military cooperation. In this chapter, we explore the factors that determine the length of implementation time. We consider two kinds of delay: political and military. The political dimension of alliance implementation begins when political leaders from different countries begin to discuss a shared goal of military cooperation. Before an alliance is signed, political elites negotiate its intended scope and depth, as well as the terms specifying who does what under what conditions (Benson, Meirowitz, and Ramsay 2014; Benson and Clinton 2016). A great deal of research has been dedicated to understanding the variation in content of alliance treaty terms that stems from this political process (Leeds et al. 2002; Benson 2011), and some work has been done on intra-alliance negotiations (Snyder 1997; Poast 2019). However, little has been done on the causes and consequences of delays in these processes.

What are the sources of delay during the political process of alliance implementation? One source, especially historically, is simply the time it takes to move diplomats, military personnel, and information back and forth between countries that may be thousands of miles apart. Before the advent of modern communication technologies, negotiations could take weeks or months as messages were exchanged between leaders and their intermediaries (Mattingly 1988).

A second cause of delay is negotiating alliance terms before signing and then working through the ratification process (Poast 2019). Delays in such negotiations may result from significant disagreements between prospective partners, the institutional steps required for ratification, and factors beyond the control of prospective partners. For example, from the time that Dwight Eisenhower became president in 1953, his secretary of state, John Foster Dulles, began to discuss the possibility of a military alliance that included the Chinese Nationalists on Taiwan. The alliance was eventually ratified by the US Senate at the beginning of 1955. The United States and the Republic of China (ROC) spent nearly two years discussing and negotiating the US–ROC Mutual Defense Pact. Deep disagreements slowed and sometimes stalled negotiations. Both sides explored whether the alliance might be multilateral or bilateral, and whether there needed to be a formal alliance or perhaps just an executive order. They debated the geographic area of defense coverage as well as the final alliance treaty terms that would trigger *casus foederis*. In addition to having to resolve these deep-seated disagreements, finalization of an alliance in the United States requires ratification by the Senate. Consequently, the Eisenhower administration kept one eye on these domestic constraints as they worked through negotiations with the Chiang Kai-shek regime.[2] In another example, in late 1891 and early 1892, before they could finalize their alliance, the governments of France and Russia spent months hammering out the logistics of troop commitments, including how many troops each side would commit to a hypothetical conflict (Snyder 1997, 117–120).

Another source of delay is domestic or international political distractions unrelated to the alliance itself. Implementing the 1894 Franco–Russian alliance took approximately three and a half years. In addition to long-distance travel and disagreements over treaty terms, unexpected domestic turmoil in both Russia and France caused both sides to pause their pursuit of the alliance for an extended period (Snyder 1997, 121).

The terms of membership of an existing alliance might also slow implementation of a new one. NATO membership rules are an excellent example. Prospective NATO members must take costly measures to meet NATO's Membership Action Plan criteria, and these efforts may not immediately succeed. In the following section, we discuss all of these political causes of delay in implementing military alliances.

The second dimension of alliance implementation concerns military factors. Coordinating joint warfighting power enables allies to capture maximum benefit from an alliance relationship (Weitsman 2014). Coordinating joint military power to the point of force interoperability takes time. It hinges on the coordination of strategic planning, implementation of joint decision-making, technical integration of material capabilities, and uniting multinational forces into one joint fighting force. Often steps towards military implementation do not begin until the political process is complete.

[2] See Stolper (1985); Christensen (1996); Benson (2012).

This means that in many cases, a military alliance is not fully implemented at the point of signing and ratification. This is important, as it means that the mere presence of a ratified alliance treaty does not provide a meaningful signal that the process of implementation is complete. Military interoperability is a time-consuming process that requires substantial investment and effort. Months or years often pass between the finalization of a treaty and the time that allied military forces achieve a level of interoperability such that the joint gains from aggregating capabilities are fully realized.

The importance of military interoperability has been almost entirely overlooked in scholarship on alliances. Because interoperability is crucial to achieving the power-aggregating benefits of an alliance, we commit space in this chapter to the difficulties of achieving it. We briefly preview some of these factors here. Technology is one hurdle. Differences in munitions and other weaponry, disparities in technological advancement and fluency, and incompatible communications systems must be brought into line before military cooperation can be effective in the event of war. Such concerns were one roadblock to rapid NATO expansion in the 1990s (Goldgeier 2010, 76).

In addition to technical differences, soldiers from diverse partner countries seldom have the same military education, training, culture, or warfighting tactics. These differences result in procedural frictions when integrating forces. Allies may speak different languages, which can introduce friction even when the alliance has an official language, as NATO does. And translation and language training take time.

Finally, to fully gain a joint warfighting advantage, alliance partners may wish to unify command. This is a time-consuming multi-step process that involves negotiating which leaders from which countries take the lead, how officers get promoted, where command headquarters are located, and what decision-making authority each leadership post has.

Importantly, resolving all of these political and military issues takes time. Efforts to overcome them in the short term may fail in unexpected ways, leading to delay that is not perfectly predictable. To capture delay of this nature formally in the theoretical analyses presented in subsequent chapters, we model alliance implementation via the parameter r, which may be interpreted as the expected speed of implementation of an alliance. Conceptualized as such, r impacts the amount of time between the moment when prospective allies decide to form an alliance and the moment when the military benefits of the alliance are realized: the point of implementation.

2.1 Political Delay

It is well known that the formation of a new alliance requires negotiation. Snyder's classic 1997 work on alliances places this at the forefront, pointing out that negotiations among potential allies are an important part of the multilateral conflict process. Negotiating the terms and conditions of an alliance treaty plays an important role in enhancing the credibility of allies' commitments to one another. Morrow (1994) details this logic, arguing that alliances generate credible commitments by altering the incentives of member states to intervene on behalf of one another.

Per Morrow (2000), these incentives can be placed into three categories. First, an alliance may enhance joint warfighting capability, making intervention more attractive by increasing the probability of joint victory. Second, an alliance may specify individual rewards for a state that fulfills its commitment; these "spoils of war" in turn create incentives for members to follow through on their commitments. Third, an alliance may alter the costs of fighting, either reducing the cost of intervention through burden-sharing or increasing the cost of abandonment through an audience-cost mechanism. Both of these mechanisms make intervention more attractive, enhancing the credibility of alliance commitments.

These factors are crucial for enhancing the credibility of alliance commitments. However, they do not arise automatically or instantaneously. Rather, measures that alter member states' incentives must be negotiated and agreed on by potential alliance partners. As with all international agreements, this negotiation process is complicated by the fact that such agreements must be self-enforcing, given the anarchic nature of international relations, with no governing authority to enforce these agreements. Importantly for our purposes, negotiating the terms of an alliance treaty takes time in practice. In the remainder of this section, we discuss how the intricacies of alliance negotiation may delay implementation.

2.1.1 International Negotiations

Intra-alliance bargaining is an important topic in its own right, and accounts for significant delay in the implementation of a new alliance. Prospective alliance partners have different preferences and different capabilities. Naturally, working out differences between countries' security interests requires diplomatic engagement. Diplomatic travel by itself is time-consuming. And the political process of navigating competing preferences among alliance partners takes time. As mentioned, the terms of the 1955 pact between the United States and the ROC took many months to resolve. The ROC preferred a blanket defense commitment from the United States. The United States preferred to impose conditions on the ROC because of concerns about moral hazard (Benson 2012). And the United States wanted to limit the territorial scope of the pact to the island of Taiwan, while the ROC wanted it to extend to several ROC-held islands in the Taiwan Strait. These differences were the primary cause of delay in the implementation of that alliance.

Likewise, negotiations over the 1954 Southeast Asia Treaty Organization took time. One of the early sticking points was whether this multilateral treaty should include the ROC and the island of Taiwan. Initially, Dulles was enthusiastic about the possibility, but it was a deal-breaker for other members, especially the British.

Along with their varying preferences regarding the scope and depth of the treaty terms, allies have different capabilities and varying views on the extent and nature of their commitments to the alliance. Some of these differences emerge as a result of equity concerns, such as former US president Donald Trump's contention that the United States contributes more than its fair share to NATO and East Asian alliances. Other disagreements emerge over how political leaders view the security threat. In many extended deterrence alliances, the threat of an enemy target is felt much more acutely by one ally. That ally will likely push for greater levels of commitment than other allies. As a result of such differences, political leaders will often negotiate the level of burden that each side will bear. The Franco–Russian alliance is an example of a treaty that included in its terms specific troop levels that each side promised to commit under specific conditions.

Allies also negotiate how spoils will be divided. Benson, Meirowitz, and Ramsay (2014) show formally that alliance negotiations may include agreements over how to split a peace surplus that emerges from deterring wars that would otherwise occur. Allies may also anticipate a war and negotiate how to divide the spoils when it's over. One of the points of discussion in early talks between Roosevelt and Churchill was what the post–World War II international order might look like and who might have influence in what region (Reynolds 1981).

Then there are intra-alliance negotiations that are even more political. As Morrow (1991) argues, capability aggregation is not the only purpose alliances serve. The promise of a military alliance acts as a bargaining chip. Powerful states offer security in exchange for policy concessions from their less powerful partners. Thus, in alliances where there is an asymmetry of power, powerful states win concessions from partners, achieving greater autonomy at the price of providing security to their less powerful allies. Thus, it is no surprise that the creation of a new military alliance often involves a flurry of negotiation.

These negotiations, if they succeed, can serve to strengthen an alliance. By creating linkages across security and non-security issues, potential allies enhance both the probability that alliance negotiations eventually succeed as well as the credibility of their promises to one another (Poast 2013). However, such negotiations have a drawback: They lead to delay in the early stages of alliance implementation.

Sweden's recent path to NATO membership illustrates how international politics can stand in the way of quickly implementing a new alliance commitment. In the days following Russia's invasion of Ukraine on February 22, 2022, discussion of Swedish membership in NATO suddenly accelerated. This was a stunning reversal of two centuries of Swedish neutrality. From January to May 2022, support for NATO membership among the Swedish population increased from 37% to 62%.[3] Despite initial opposition from the ruling Swedish Social Democratic Party, this huge swing in public opinion led Sweden to formally apply for NATO membership on May 17, 2022. But despite this newfound enthusiasm, Sweden's membership was not granted immediately. In fact, 18 months passed before the unanimous ratification required for entry into NATO.

International politics was a roadblock. In particular, though 28 of the 30 NATO members (at that time) quickly ratified Sweden's membership, Turkey and Hungary held out, each conditioning its ratification on a series of demands. Importantly, none of these demands centered directly on opposition to Sweden's fitness to be a NATO partner. Rather, both Turkey and Hungary used their veto power to engage Sweden on other international political issues, winning concessions in the process. Turkey's opposition centered on accusations that Sweden had not done enough to crack down on Kurdish groups that Turkey classified as terrorist organizations. The reason for Hungary's opposition was less clear-cut; in fact, the Hungarian

[3] Ipsos, und Novus. "Do you think Sweden should join the military alliance NATO?" Chart, January 30, 2024. Statista. Accessed July 19, 2024. https://www.statista.com/statistics/660842/survey-on-perception-of-nato-membership-in-sweden/.

government never publicly stated a reason. However, many speculated that it was related to President Viktor Orban's history of sympathy for Russian leader Vladimir Putin.[4]

Ultimately, both of these roadblocks were overcome. The Swedish reforms succeeded at alleviating Turkey's concerns. And after Sweden promised to sell Hungary 14 additional Gripen fighter jets, Hungary also agreed to allow the NATO accession.[5] The length of the delay in this case—18 months—is striking. In many ways, Sweden is an ideal candidate for speedy accession to NATO. Unlike other recent aspirational members, such as Georgia, Sweden easily met NATO's membership criteria, which center on upholding democratic standards as well as military preparedness. Yet its accession was still delayed. This is one example of how international political forces can drive a wedge between budding allies at the negotiation stage of an alliance.

2.1.2 Domestic Veto Players

Domestic politics are another source of friction in the implementation of a new alliance. As mentioned, alliances can be understood as coordinating states' expectations about what will occur in the event of war. Coordination of these expectations necessarily brings domestic politics into the fray. In this section, we discuss how domestic politics complicates the process of implementing a new alliance. In doing so, we highlight the prevalence of domestic considerations in the alliance implementation process. We also demonstrate that these factors persist across regime types: both democracies and autocracies experience alliance implementation delay as a result of domestic frictions.

The possibility of a new military alliance often leads to domestic dissent. In fact, in the early stages of alliance negotiations, partners often seek to hide their plans from their own domestic publics to avoid opposition (Ritter 2004). Opposition arises because military alliances, especially defensive ones, present domestic populations with a trade-off. On the one hand, membership in an alliance may have significant security benefits. On the other hand, it has costs, both in peace and war. This inherent trade-off often sparks

[4] https://www.voanews.com/a/nato-allies-pressure-hungary-over-blocking-sweden-accession/7478430.html.

[5] https://www.theguardian.com/world/2024/feb/23/sweden-inches-closer-to-joining-nato-after-budapest-talks.

domestic political friction, as these costs and benefits create domestic winners and losers. Though the alliances occur in the realm of international politics, domestic opposition can pose a real problem for policymakers.

These challenges are most pronounced in democratic states, where domestic institutions often require ratification of new international treaties by an elected legislature. But they are not limited to democracies. Though in principle autocratic leaders face fewer constraints than their democratic counterparts, in practice, they must also find a way to prevent insurrection. The possibility of the opposition organizing to overthrow an autocrat's hold on power thus always puts constraints on policymaking. To avoid such overthrow attempts, successful autocrats must win the cooperation of opponents, and they often do so by allowing the opposition to formally participate in nominally democratic institutions (Gandhi and Przeworski 2007). Thus, domestic political opposition to a new alliance provides a nearly universal constraint on a leader's ability to enter into new treaty relationships, though the severity of this constraint varies with regime type.

Japan's alliance relationship with the United States throughout the 1950s provides one useful illustration of how domestic politics can stand in the way of attempts at cooperation. In particular, this case illustrates how domestic forces often act in opposition to the existence of an alliance itself.

When the US occupation of Japan ended, on April 28, 1952, the two nations faced important questions about what their security relationship would look like going forward. Though the US occupation had ended, a security treaty ratified by the United States earlier in 1952 allowed indefinite stationing of US troops in Japan. Unsurprisingly, this arrangement met opposition from both left- and right-wing domestic groups in Japan, sparking the Bloody May Day protests, which resulted in two deaths and hundreds of injuries.

Recognizing this discontent, as well as the need to move troops stationed in Japan to support the war effort in Korea, US officials sought to enable Japanese rearmament. Perhaps surprisingly, given the domestic opposition to US troop presence, rearmament was not universally popular among the Japanese public. Rather, there was a distinct desire, especially among left-wing groups, to avoid an alignment with either the United States or the Soviet Union. This slowed US pushes for Japan to rearm, with Japanese prime minister Shigeru Yoshida resisting US demands to do so in 1954 (Kim 2016, ch. 6). And the domestic opposition continued to grow, peaking in 1960, when the alliance treaty was substantially revised. While the US security relationship with Japan has received much attention in the literature, for present purposes, this anecdote suffices to illustrate how domestic opposition can slow the process of cooperation between allies.

Egypt's security partnerships in the early 1970s also illustrate how domestic opposition can sidetrack a budding alliance. In particular, this case illustrates two important points that complement the example of Japan we have just seen. First, it shows that domestic opposition can constrain a state's alliance relationships in an autocracy. Second, it shows that opposition may not center around the alliance itself. In Egypt, domestic political economy considerations that were not directly related to the alliance complicated the process of negotiation, standing in the way of deeper cooperation.

By 1971, Egypt's open warfare with Israel had given way to a period of relative peace. This resulted in a lack of urgency on Egypt's behalf for security partners, opening the way for Anwar Sadat to reevaluate Egypt's alliances. In May 1971, Egypt signed the Soviet–Egyptian Treaty of Friendship and Cooperation. The treaty was prompted by Soviet concerns about losing control following Sadat's purge of relatively pro-Soviet elements of his cabinet (Barnett and Levy 1991, 387). It aimed to formalize existing patterns of cooperation while shoring up the Soviet gains in light of the cabinet realignment. The Soviet concerns were well founded, as Egyptian domestic pressures led to a cooling of the partnership in the following years. This cooling was accelerated after the Soviets demanded in 1972 that Egypt pay for all weapons deliveries in full, which had the effect of quadrupling the amount Egypt paid for Soviet arms (Shazly 1980, 143).

This price hike exacerbated domestic tensions within Egypt, requiring Sadat to take action. A major source of domestic dissent was the public perception that Egypt was overly reliant on the Soviets for security, and that people were being asked repeatedly to make sacrifices for little gain (Barnett and Levy 1991, 388). To placate domestic dissent, Sadat reduced the number of Soviet military advisers allowed in Egypt from 15,000 to a mere 1,000, retaining only crucial personnel such as those who had technical and weapons expertise and could not be quickly replaced (Shazly 1980, 164–165). This caused a major rift in the Egyptian–Soviet security partnership. Although the withdrawal of Soviet advisers was done in a way meant to minimize the disruption of joint war planning, it still had a meaningful impact on Egypt's ability to perform effectively in joint military operations. Further, the Soviets responded by placing further restrictions on the type of weaponry on offer to the Egyptians. Ultimately, this illustrates the sometimes negative effect of public opinion on alliance cohesion, even under an autocracy. Fearing domestic unrest and a loosening of his grip on power, Sadat took steps that undermined the efficacy of his security partnership with the Soviets.

While these cases illustrate how domestic opposition to aspects of an alliance can cause friction, domestic political distractions unrelated to the alliance itself can also pose problems for budding partnerships. For example, in 1891, France entered into negotiations with Russia that would eventually culminate in the Franco–Russian alliance of 1894. The negotiations proceeded relatively smoothly at first, but then France fell into crisis. The crisis arose in 1892, when accusations of bribery emerged that involved vast swaths of the French government, including then-Prime Minister Georges Benjamin Clemenceau. The accusations dated back to 1888, with French ministers accepting bribes in exchange for their silence about problems with the Paris-based Panama Canal Company, which had received heavy private investment. As the company quickly failed and was liquidated, details emerged about the impropriety that had resulted in losses for French investors. Although this scandal was entirely unrelated to the possibility of a Franco–Russian alliance, it stalled the negotiations, dominating headlines in France and occupying the attention of the French government well into 1893 (Snyder 1997, 171). As this illustrates, direct domestic opposition to an alliance is not the only possible source of friction. Unexpected events can arise, which then monopolize the finite attention and resources of government officials.

2.2 Delay from Implementing Military Interoperability

The ability of allied militaries to work and fight together plays a critical role in determining whether an alliance aggregates power beyond the independent fighting abilities of individual countries. If allies are not able to cooperate to align strategy, doctrine, logistics, and operating procedures, then the warfighting benefit of an alliance may fall short of its potential. Fully aggregating capabilities for joint fighting depends on the effectiveness with which the partner militaries operate together.

Military interoperability varies across alliances. Many alliances fail to integrate, and complete interoperability is rare. NATO is an example of an alliance that expends significant resources to help new members' militaries integrate and to sustain interoperability among existing members. At the other end of the spectrum are alliances without military integration, either because their purpose is to divide the capabilities of their opponent or because the target of the alliance is so prepared and ready that the allies cannot coordinate a joint military force before the target resorts to violence. An example of a capability divider is the military alliance between Germany and Japan in the Tripartite Pact of 1940. Because the goal of the alliance was to tie down US military forces in two parts of the world, Germany and Japan did not join forces. Germany would pursue its goals separately in Europe and Russia, while Japan separately fought against the Allied Forces in China and the Pacific. Given the goal of dividing US capabilities by independently pursuing their own military objectives in separate parts of the world, neither Germany nor Japan made an effort at interoperability over the life of their alliance.

The second scenario in which allies do not integrate militaries occurs when the target of the alliance is militarily more prepared to launch an attack against one or more members of the alliance before the allies can coordinate a joint military force. One example is Great Britain's defense commitment to Poland in 1839. Hitler knew that the British lacked the short-term ability to extend sufficient military force to Poland. Full implementation of the commitment would entail not just the promise but also the ability to carry it out, which Hitler reasoned was limited in the short term but likely forthcoming in the future. Knowing that Britain's commitment to Poland lacked teeth in the short term influenced Hitler's calculation of the timing of aggression. He announced to his generals, "The power of the initiative cannot be allowed to pass to others. The present moment is more favorable than in two or three years' time. ... We are faced with the harsh alternatives of striking or of certain annihilation sooner or later" (Alexandroff and Rosecrance 1977, 418). In this case, Great Britain was insufficiently powerful, relative to Germany, for an alliance to be implemented within a short time frame.

When countries seek to integrate joint warfighting capabilities, interoperability depends on how effectively the allies resolve challenges. At the high end of an interoperability continuum, integrated Allied Forces operate together effectively. NATO is the prime example. At the lower end, Allied Forces may coordinate allied war plans by assigning wartime theaters to separate allies but lack a joint military command. Where interoperability falls short, allies often fail to standardize equipment and do not share operational procedures. Lack of a common language often poses communication challenges, causing militaries to use translators or silo forces by language facility. An example of an alliance where forces fell short of realizing joint warfighting capability because of interoperability challenges is the World War I French–English alliance. Language and military-culture differences limited the joint military potential of the alliance. In another case, during World War II, German and Romanian military forces were unable to overcome language, cultural, and procedural barriers. These obstacles inhibited joint cooperation and led to failures for the alliance on the Eastern Front (DiNardo 1996).

What factors cause variation in military interoperability? In this section, we discuss barriers to interoperability and demonstrate that allies' efforts to overcome these challenges lengthen the time it takes to implement the full force of the potential power shift of the alliance. A useful way to organize a discussion of the process of implementing interoperability is to adopt the analytical categories developed by NATO. Per NATO doctrine, there are three dimensions of interoperability: technical, procedural, and human (NATO AJP-01 2017). Each of these dimensions includes factors that may delay implementation.

In general terms, the technical dimension includes the ability of allies to use compatible technological systems at the tactical level, including communications systems and operational fighting equipment. Resolving equipment incompatibilities requires temporary bridging patches, as well as more permanent bridging solutions and costly systems-acquisition decisions. Procedural interoperability resolves questions about *how* allies will fight together. Effective coalitional fighting includes agreement on doctrine and standard operating procedures pertaining to how the Allied Forces will jointly conduct operations.

To illustrate procedural interoperability friction, an exercise with the US Army's Joint Multinational Readiness Center in Germany, which included US and NATO partner commanders, revealed disagreements between officers about the tactical definition of "seize" stemming from different national military doctrines (CALL N.d.). To execute joint tactical operations, allied militaries must unify their understanding of such procedural terms and come to an agreement on operational objectives and the procedures for accomplishing those objectives.

The third dimension of interoperability is human. It includes leadership structure for issuing commands to a multinational force, an ability to overcome language barriers to facilitate communication across forces, and functional resolution of cultural and relationship differences that create interpersonal frictions.

In discussing obstacles to interoperability in these three areas, we will refer to evidence from historical alliances as well as interviews with NATO officers. We conducted interviews with 15 former and current officers, some American and others from NATO partner countries, who have the responsibility for facilitating defense cooperation among NATO allies. Some officers have experience working through the challenges of bringing a new alliance member up to speed with NATO standards, operations, and procedures. We also interviewed a team of US Army Security Force Assistance Brigade (SFAB) advisors, whose primary objective is to facilitate interoperability between the United States and its allies. SFAB teams assess, advise, and support allies' military operations. These in-person interviews have provided insights into and firsthand experiences with the challenges of interoperability. In this section, we will reference these interviews by name when permission to quote has been granted but keep our informants anonymous when that was specifically requested.

The main point of this section is to demonstrate that barriers to interoperability slow alliance implementation. This is important because it illustrates that the implementation process does not end at the moment an alliance treaty is signed. Interoperability requires time and effort, and is a constantly evolving process. We will discuss specific challenges according to the three categories of interoperability: technical, procedural, and human.

2.2.1 Technical Interoperability

Standardization of equipment is a crucial aspect of interoperability. Fighting together effectively requires that the technical systems used by different partner states interact smoothly. Failure to address the challenges of technical interoperability has plagued attempts at coalition warfare throughout history. Both the Axis and Allied powers in World War II experienced these challenges. The Axis powers' difficulties on the Eastern Front have been traced to radical differences in the level of technology of the members' armies (DiNardo 1996, 713). And the Allied powers experienced similar challenges. For example, in 1941, the United Kingdom began to replace the US-manufactured Thompson submachine gun with the British-manufactured Sten. While the Sten could be quickly manufactured domestically, it had a significant drawback: It used a 9 mm round, while the Thompson had used a .45-caliber round. This meant that in areas where British forces used the Sten, they were unable to rely on US supply assistance, as the United States was not prepared to provide 9 mm rounds in large quantity (Zhou 2016, 7).

Though ammunition standards are just one of many technical barriers to interoperability, tracing their history in NATO illustrates the difficulty of solving a technical problem that, on its face, appears straightforward. In principle, all that is required is that allies adopt a common standard for small-arms ammunition. In practice, however, this raises a political problem. Though allies have a common interest in establishing a common standard, precisely *what* this standard is and *who* has a say in setting it can lead to tension.

As Kapstein (1991) argues, states typically prefer to produce arms domestically, with international collaboration on arms production a "second-best" solution, all else equal. In the wake of World War II, arms production in Europe had been drastically set back by the bombing of many manufacturing facilities. Therefore, NATO cooperation on ammunition standards at this time is in some sense a best-case scenario, as the European members of the newly founded NATO suffered from diminished domestic production capacity. Even so, adopting and enforcing NATO ammunition standards has been difficult.

The process began in 1951, following the creation of the NATO Standardization Agency. Its primary objective was to develop and promote standardization agreements, which specify the processes, terms, and equipment that member nations should adopt to ensure interoperability.

Though NATO member states tested a variety of small arms ammunition starting in 1949, two options rose above the rest by 1951. The first, the 7.62 × 51 mm round, grew out of refinements to the .30–06 round used in the United States' standard-issue rifle from World War II, the M1. At the same time, the British military had developed an alternative small arms round, the .280. The American-proposed round was larger and had more stopping power, but it produced a greater recoil, reducing accuracy when fired from a fully automatic rifle. The British-preferred .280 was smaller, and had the advantage of greater accuracy in automatic rifles, but failed to meet American armor-penetration standards in tests (Zhou 2016, 27–35).

Importantly, the practical battlefield trade-offs between these two options were not the only source of disagreement. Political and economic considerations also played a role (Fast 1981). As the United States began to move towards advocacy of the 7.62 × 51 mm round, British Defense Minister Emanuel Shinwell broke from the Americans, declaring that the UK would adopt the .280 cartridge in April 1951. Though technical justifications were given for this decision, there is evidence that national pride played a significant role (Zhou 2016, 31). In response, the United States campaigned to bring the rest of NATO to its side. This campaign, combined with newly reelected Winston Churchill's desire to place NATO standardization over domestic political-economic considerations, eventually led the UK to concede, accepting the US-preferred standard. Ultimately, in 1954, NATO adopted its first rifle ammunition standard, settling on the 7.62 × 51 mm cartridge.

As this example illustrates, equipment standardization is a time-consuming and ever-evolving process. Further, it has no natural endpoint. Although the 7.62 × 51 mm round was adopted in 1954, this standard did not endure forever. Following decades of research and battlefield experience, NATO further revised its ammunition standard, adopting the 5.56 × 45 mm round through a standardization agreement in 1980. Acknowledging the necessity of constant maintenance of these standards, NATO has also adapted its organizational structure to become more agile in the realm of standardization. For example, in 2014, the NATO Standardization Agency underwent a significant transformation and was restructured into the NATO Standardization Office (NSO). This change was part of a broader effort to streamline NATO's standardization activities and improve efficiency. The NSO's mission is to enhance the interoperability of NATO forces by developing, coordinating, and promoting the implementation of standardization agreements and related documents. The NSO works with national standardization offices, NATO commands, and other stakeholders to ensure that standards are up to date and meet the operational needs of the alliance.

The NSO's efforts are ongoing, and it has issued hundreds of standardization agreements since its inception. They cover not only traditional areas like weapons and communication systems but also newer domains such as cyber defense and unmanned systems. This illustrates an important point: Technological coordination is not a static process. Innovation in military technology and emerging threats combine to drive changes in the security landscape, and allies must constantly address these challenges to take advantage of the capability-aggregating benefits of an alliance.

The ever-present nature of technological challenges was a consistent theme in the interviews we conducted with NATO officers. Several examples stand out. First, many NATO members procure Abrams tanks from the United States. However, these tanks pose logistical challenges. In some European partner states, bridges cannot accommodate their weight and size. This prevents full standardization of this equipment across NATO partners, requiring partner states to invest in a variety of equipment, which itself further complicates training and personnel development. Further, transportation of tanks to delivery sites is complicated by nonstandardized rail gauges in partner countries; tanks have to be transferred from one train to another, a time-consuming and costly process that delays arms acquisition.

Radio communications technology is another example. Multiple NATO officers commented on the difficulty of integrating radio systems from former Soviet states into the NATO apparatus. Soviet radio technology was incompatible with standard NATO equipment, which posed difficulties when partners such as Hungary eventually joined NATO. Even three decades after the dissolution of the Soviet Union, one NATO officer remarked that communication technology differences among NATO partners are a "huge problem." The problem is so persistent that NATO officers in the field have developed their own shorthand term for it: "swivel chairing." That is, incompatible technology often requires someone to sit between two different radio or computer systems in a swivel chair, manually transferring information from one system into the other. As with other sources of technological incompatibility, this leads to inefficiency and delay in the process of coordinating interoperability among NATO partner states.

2.2.2 Procedural Interoperability

Differences in Military Doctrine and Culture

Differences between allies in military doctrine and culture also slow interoperability. Interviews with military officers from NATO member countries that originally belonged to the former Warsaw Pact, as well as interviews with NATO officers responsible for training troops and officers from those countries, revealed that differences in military education have created significant frictions between partner countries. As a simple illustration, a NATO commander from a former Warsaw Pact country told us, "I was trained to believe that red represents my friends and blue represents my enemy, and suddenly overnight blue is supposed to be my friend and red my enemy. This transition in thinking was not easy for older-generation commanders." Such a small difference in military education may lead to a sticky transition in uniting fighting doctrines.

A key holdup in interoperability is the differences between partner countries in how enlisted personnel are trained. These differences lead to divergent perceptions and treatment of noncommissioned officers (NCOs). US military training, which is now shared by many long-standing NATO allies, emphasizes the professionalization and development of enlisted personnel and NCOs. It inculcates a broad skill set for enlisted personnel, covering warfighting abilities, technical skills, and leadership decision-making autonomy. NCOs are trained and entrusted to assume authority and make decisions for small units. Advantages of this educational approach include the ability of fighting forces to readily adapt to different battlefield environments, enhanced small unit discipline, and well-rounded soldiers. A well-developed NCO corps also enhances interoperability with alliance partners, because the large supply of well-rounded enlisted personnel enables multinational forces to effectively adapt to each other. Because NCOs are entrusted with command authority, information flows up and down the chain of command. This feature contributes significantly to the effectiveness of joint military exercises, which play a crucial role in developing and routinizing joint warfighting between allies. In addition to training allies to move and fight together, military exercises expose gaps in interoperability if NCOs are entrusted to make decisions and to provide and accept feedback. When allies share a culture of NCO leadership, learning and adaptability can occur between partner countries and up and down the chain of command.

By contrast, Soviet/Russian-trained NCOs are trained to operate within narrower boundaries. Relying on mass conscription of large enlisted armies and with a military tradition that emphasizes large-scale, high-speed maneuvers, the Russian military saw no need for autonomous decision-making at the level of NCOs. As a result, Soviet-style military education did not foster leadership or autonomous decision-making in enlisted soldiers. Instead, professionalization of enlisted personnel typically focused on technical training for specific equipment, weapons systems, and functions. Only elite officers were trained for and granted decision-making authority. This approach was useful for a one-dimensional style of fighting but inflexible for a variety of warfighting environments, including adapting to allies' command doctrines.

Combining these two different doctrinal backgrounds within an alliance poses challenges to interoperability. Commissioned officers' distrust of NCOs is one obvious source of tension that limits the flow of information between allies and thus limits the ability of multinational forces to train up to the same level of readiness. As an example, NATO SFAB advisors, some of whom are NCOs and nearly all of whom are outranked by the partner officers they advise, are trained to monitor joint exercises and then to provide specific feedback to NATO allies. In our interviews, some SFAB advisors noted that Soviet-trained NATO officers sometimes resist advice from lower-ranked SFAB officers and often refuse to listen to NCOs altogether.

Another area where this difference in military culture causes problems with interoperability is when lower-ranked officers and enlisted personnel from different countries need to make decisions and operate together. Several interviewees shared their frustration with partners being unwilling to act even on relatively trivial action items until a high-ranking officer from their own country ordered it. Such a lack of autonomy slows joint operations to the pace of decision-making by a limited number of superior officers.

Again, overcoming such differences in military culture and education takes time. Completely transitioning to a unified military culture requires the retirement of officers from different training backgrounds. Short of turning over a generation of leaders, allies have other options, which are nevertheless time-consuming. In NATO, several venues are designated to teach joint doctrine. NATO maintains 34 Partnership Training and Education Centres across NATO and partner countries. Their goal is to "improve professionalism of national personnel, increase international troop interoperability, and conduct education and training activities related to NATO partnership programmes and policies."[6]

The US military also runs its own programs to facilitate interoperability between multinational NATO forces. The Army SFAB is one example. Another prominent program is the Joint Multinational Readiness Center, operated by US 7th Army in the Oberpfalz region of Bavaria. The JMRC hosts ongoing joint forces training. Retired general Mark Hertling, former commander of US Army Europe, commanded the 7th Army and ran the

[6] https://www.nato.int/cps/en/natohq/topics_187359.htm.

joint training programs in Germany. In an interview, he emphasized that differences in doctrine inhibit interoperability and joint readiness. The key, according to Hertling, is constant training and joint exercises. He explained that elite Soviet-trained officers invariably struggle with NATO doctrine, but that enormous strides towards interoperability can be achieved by training multinational partners at the sergeant level. Once they have the skills for autonomous decision-making, they are better able to command small units and function effectively in a multinational chain of command.

2.2.3 Human Interoperability

Command Structure

A high priority for a new military alliance in which allies expect to fight alongside each other is to establish the military leadership and a command structure. Without a coherent command structure, the advantages of aggregating joint warfighting capabilities will be limited, and the joint objectives of the alliance cannot be carried out to their maximum potential. A command structure includes a shared plan of leadership hierarchy that specifies who commands and controls the allies' military operations, a format for selecting leadership, and a location for command headquarters.

Reflecting on the barriers to greater Anglo–French War cooperation to prevent France's occupation by Germany in World War II, Hastings Ismay, secretary of Britain's Committee of Imperial Defence in the lead up to the outbreak of war between Britain and Germany and later Churchill's chief staff officer during the war, emphasized the importance of the location of the headquarters. "The one lesson that stands out sharply from the history of Anglo-French war collaboration in 1939-1940 is that since the Allied headquarters must necessarily be in one or the other of the two capitals, there must unavoidably be a home team and a visiting team. Hence the partners, however closely they work together, cannot be quite on the same footing."[7]

Alliance command structures vary in sophistication depending on the extent to which alliances are designed to aggregate warfighting capabilities. The 1940 Tripartite Pact that resulted in the Axis alliance between Germany, Japan, and Italy did not set up a command structure. Formed primarily to

[7] Ismay Hastings, "Anglo-French War Collaboration 1939-1940," 4, WO 193/305, NA. Quoted in Bamford (2022, 188).

deter US entry into the war by threatening to stretch and divide enemy forces rather than to aggregate ally capabilities, the alliance did not try to structure military cooperation through integrated command. In fact, there was little attempt at all to coordinate military activities between the allies (Carley 1999). Implementation of such alliances is not slowed by the challenges of negotiating and putting into practice joint command structure and establishing a command headquarters. However, the gains of a beneficial shift in aggregated power are also limited, because, without a coherent command structure, allied militaries cannot act together as effectively and efficiently.

On the other hand, alliances that aim for joint gains from military interoperability require the establishment of an integrated command structure. NATO is a prime example, with a sophisticated military command structure designed to aggregate and coordinate the joint fighting capabilities of multiple member countries. At the top of NATO's command structure sits the NATO Military Committee, located in Belgium, which consists of the defense chiefs of all member countries. The committee's main function is to provide military advice to and execute orders from the North Atlantic Council, which is the principal decision-making body of the alliance. The committee coordinates and directs NATO military policy and strategy. Below the Military Committee are two strategic commands: Allied Command Operations, which is responsible for planning and executing all NATO military operations, and Allied Command Transformation, which is responsible for promoting interoperability throughout the alliance. All together, the command structure includes thousands of personnel from member countries across multiple posts and offices under these main authorities.

The process of establishing a command structure for a new alliance can be complicated and time-consuming. In existing alliances, such as NATO, new members join an established command structure. While less time-consuming than forming an alliance *de novo*, joining an existing command structure may nevertheless require time to subordinate one's existing military command to the established structure of the alliance. To facilitate this process in NATO, the defense chief for a new alliance member is invited to sit on the Military Council, and NATO operations begin to include commanders of the new member in joint military exercises. Eventually, military commanders from the new member country assume posts in the NATO command structure.

To facilitate interoperability, NATO supports specific programs, such as the Connected Forces Initiative defense cooperation offices in countries' embassies, and projects like the SFABs. An SFAB is a specialized US Army unit responsible for assessing and advising allied and partner nations. The work of SFABs elevates partner commanders' roles and effectiveness in NATO command by helping commanders get up to speed with NATO operational objectives, procedures, and standards. Though highly trained and knowledgeable, SFAB advisors are usually outranked by the partner commanders they are assigned to critique and advise. Consequently, the effectiveness of integrating partner commanders into NATO command depends on the diplomatic skills of SFAB advisors and, critically, the willingness of partner commanders to welcome expert feedback and criticism from lower-ranked and occasionally NCOs. Interviews with SFAB advisors revealed that this process requires careful and time-consuming relationship building by officers on both sides.

Individual personality differences can cause serious setbacks and significantly delay cooperation. In one example described by a NATO commander from a relatively new member country, an outside NATO expert who was invited to speak to NATO commanders unwittingly insulted the commander of a NATO country. This one interaction slowed SFAB cooperation significantly, even though the expert had no formal association with the SFAB.

While integrating command into an established alliance is difficult enough, it is especially challenging when new allies come together without an existing structure for aligning command. The Anglo–Franco alliance targeting Nazi Germany serves as a useful example. In 1938–39, the British and French shared the objective of countering the emerging Nazi Germany. But implementation of their alliance was delayed because of complications in their relationship regarding how to coordinate command and joint fighting strategy. The British were reluctant to subordinate themselves to the French because of painful memories of being locked into costly French mission objectives in World War I; similarly, the French distrusted the British (Alexander and Philpott, 1998). These relationship challenges stalled efforts to work out the logistical details of command, control, and strategy necessary to mount a cooperative defense of France, let alone make good on defense commitments in Eastern Europe.

These lessons motivated sincere efforts at mutual accommodation when it came to the Anglo-American World War II alliance. After France fell in 1940, the British, desperate for assistance, began earnestly courting a partnership with the United States. In the space of two years, the partnership grew from mostly an arms trade relationship to a tightly integrated wartime alliance (Bamford 2022).

At the urging of General George Marshall and after overcoming initial British objections, the allies agreed to form a unity of command, the Combined Chiefs of Staff (CCS), which directed all Allied strategy and operations. The CCS comprised American joint chiefs of staff and British chiefs of staff, and its headquarters were set up in Washington, DC, which required the British to have a Joint Staff Mission there. With the chief decision-making command for Allied operations located in DC and only a British staff in permanent residence to represent British interests, the Americans became the *de facto* leaders of the alliance. The CCS controlled Allied Forces in every theater and named Dwight Eisenhower the Supreme Allied Commander of Europe, with operational control over all American and British forces involved in the invasions of France and Germany. The Anglo-American alliance in World War II is an illustration of how the military command of partners in a new alliance can become tightly integrated when motivated by a common enemy in intense warfighting conditions. And yet, even so motivated, the establishment of command structure was nevertheless a time-consuming process, as Americans and British spent significant time working on their joint relationship before finalizing the formal command structure after the United States joined the war (Bamford 2022).

Language

A common barrier to interoperability within an alliance is language. Because British and American allies shared a language, there was relatively little difficulty communicating between officers and integrated forces. By contrast, language barriers stymied coalitional cooperation among the Axis powers in World War II. Many Hungarian and Finnish officers spoke German, but communication between German, Italian, Japanese, and Romanian forces was limited. German, Japanese, and Italian militaries never reached the level of cooperation where gains from force integration could be realized. On the Eastern Front, German and Romanian forces did try to collaborate, but inability to communicate caused problems. The bridge solution was to recruit and assign interpreters to military units. However, there was a shortage of interpreters who could communicate technical military words and concepts.

How severe is a language barrier to interoperability, and how long does it take to overcome this obstacle? As in the German–Romanian case, language barriers were a well-documented primary cause of failure of Axis coalition forces during World War II (DiNardo 1996). Even in NATO, where English is the primary language, language barriers interfere with interoperability. Interviews with NATO commanders revealed that acquiring enough language proficiency in English for seamless officer-to-officer or soldier-to-soldier communication is one of the main hurdles for many new NATO members.

One NATO commander, who was an officer in the Hungarian military when Hungary joined NATO in 1999, mentioned that at the time of accession, only a small handful of officers, himself included, in the entire Hungarian military had any background in the English language. He and other officers were assigned to intensive language training in the United States and with instructors in their NATO units so that at least some officers in the Hungarian military would have a passing ability to communicate with officers in NATO partner countries. He said that this language barrier was a major hurdle to interoperability and that it took a couple of years before the two militaries could effectively communicate with each other.

2.3 Alliance Implementation in Practice

How long does it take to implement an alliance? In this section, we examine the 1942 Anglo-American alliance in greater detail to get a sense of how the political and military factors we have discussed combine to cause a temporal lag from the time that prospective allies begin to cooperate to the time that those allies are able to realize the joint gains from a military alliance.

The Anglo-American alliance already had many advantages, and yet it still took almost four years to reach the full joint force on display in the land, air, and sea assault on Normandy that began on July 6, 1944. Before this, the allies had fought together in other theaters, such as North Africa, but they were not ready to launch the coordinated cross-Channel assault necessary to defeat Germany until mid-1944. Much of the groundwork for this power shift was laid in the 18 months prior to the formal Declaration by the United Nations of January 1, 1942. But after the declaration, realization of the gains from the alliance still required much more work.

In this section, we provide a timeline of military cooperation between the United States and Great Britain. This case is especially illuminating for our purposes. It is hard to imagine an alliance better positioned for rapid implementation. The allies were motivated by a common threat, they shared a language, and after Japan's attack on Pearl Harbor, neither confronted significant domestic or international resistance that slowed implementation of the alliance. And yet, even with the stars so aligned, complete realization of the power shift still took several years. The reasons for the halting pace correspond to the political and military dimensions of implementation laid out earlier in the chapter. We set forth the implementation timeline and highlight the challenges along the way.

2.3.1 The Anglo-American Coalition

When Britain declared war on Germany in September 1939, more than two years before Japan's attack on Pearl Harbor would draw the United States into the conflict alongside Britain, both the British and US armies were inadequately prepared to confront Germany on their own, or even together. The British army had 1,065,000 personnel, while the US Army had a mere 188,565 (Skinner, 1950, 16). Given the United States' lack of readiness to impact a modern European war, the British had little expectation of anything beyond American neutrality at that time (Reynolds, 1981, 78). During this period, Britain turned to the United States primarily for war supplies and weaponry (Bamford, 2022, 158–159). Politically, the American public was isolationist, with the idea of engaging in overseas conflicts seeming distant both to the average citizen and to policymakers. Consequently, military cooperation between the Americans and the British was restricted to communication through military attachés, with minimal sharing of sensitive intelligence (Bamford 2022, 160).

In mid-1940, American attitudes shifted dramatically following Germany's conquest of Western Europe, including Poland, Denmark, Norway, Belgium, the Netherlands, and France. This startling turn of events significantly heightened the perceived German threat among Americans and led many to question whether Britain could endure. But even so, the US public remained largely opposed to involvement in the war, with 59% favoring isolationism. This reluctance was not unfounded; during the summer of 1940, Britain itself debated whether to resist German expansion or seek a peaceful settlement that could safeguard its colonial interests outside Europe (Reynolds 1981, 104–108). The alarm triggered by France's fall spurred a desire for closer military cooperation between the United States and Britain. The fall of France marked the beginning of an implementation phase, as British and American leaders began to set themselves on a footing for enhanced military cooperation. However, substantial cooperation was delayed by six months due to US concerns that Britain might also succumb to Germany and because President Roosevelt was facing reelection in an isolationist, anti-interventionist climate.

Domestic opposition in the United States to entering the war was a major factor that delayed early military cooperation between the United States and Britain. As noted earlier, domestic politics can impede the formation of new alliances. In the United States, strong antiwar sentiments, influenced by the experience of World War I, were prevalent. A November 1939 Gallup poll found that 68% of Americans believed it was a mistake for the United States to have entered World War I (*Gallup and Fortune Polls* 1949). While they sympathized with Great Britain, they were largely opposed to getting involved in this new conflict. Consequently, there was an ongoing debate about how, or even whether, to assist Britain. This was a central issue in the 1940 US presidential contest between Franklin D. Roosevelt and Wendell Willkie. Both major parties had significant isolationist and noninterventionist factions. Reflecting this sentiment, the party platform adopted at the 1940 Democratic Convention declared, "We will not participate in foreign wars, and we will not send our army, naval, or air forces to fight in foreign lands outside of the Americas, except in case of attack." Roosevelt further pledged during his campaign that he would "not send American boys into any foreign wars." Despite the alarming speed with which the Nazis were conquering Western Europe and the significant concern that Britain might be the next target, domestic public opinion and the impending presidential election limited the United States' willingness to commit more substantially to aiding Britain.

Before the United States' November presidential election, British leaders saw it as a significant delaying factor. In June 1940, Prime Minister Winston Churchill informed Jan Smuts, the prime minister of South Africa, that the United States would likely join the war after the election.[8] Many other leaders

[8] Churchill to Smuts, tel. 209, June 10, 1940, quoted in Reynolds (1981, 107).

were similarly frustrated by the slow pace of US involvement due to domestic politics and shared the belief that the situation would improve once the election was over and antiwar sentiment no longer hindered the Roosevelt administration (Reynolds 1981, 107–108).

Towards the end of 1940, cooperation between the United States and Britain began to increase. Public opinion had started to shift, showing growing support for aiding Britain. By October 1940, a majority (59%) were in favor of assisting Great Britain, even if it risked US involvement in the conflict. This support continued to build over the next year. Furthermore, Roosevelt's substantial reelection victory allowed him greater flexibility in foreign policy. As domestic political obstacles gradually eased, the United States progressively enhanced its military cooperation with Britain, although most of these efforts remained confidential and were conducted exclusively between the military leaders of the two nations.

As an initial measure, the United States increased weapons sales to Britain, expanded its own large-scale rearmament program, and began plans to enlarge its armed forces. In August 1940, the United States sent secret delegations of naval, air, and army representatives to Britain to discuss military cooperation, marking the beginning of a new era of continuous American military observation and intelligence sharing (Bamford, 2022, 172–173). By September, the British and Americans reached a secret agreement for a "full exchange of military information" (Bamford 2022, 184), which included highly confidential details of weapons systems, munitions, aeronautical instruments, and manufacturing processes. After Roosevelt's reelection, he authorized a covert military staff conference in January 1941 and advocated for the passage of the Lend-Lease Bill. This legislation allowed him to transfer defense materiel to any nation in exchange for payments deemed appropriate by the president. Under Lend-Lease, the United States significantly increased the shipment of essential weapons to Great Britain.

Roosevelt also authorized a covert military staff conference, which was held in January 1941 in Washington, with American, British, and Canadian military leaders (ABC-1). The leaders established an informal, hypothetical alliance. They essentially outlined plans for an allied fight should the United States enter the war. This meeting represented the first formal coordination among the leadership of the three armies, as they discussed confidential matters and developed joint strategies for potential involvement. Civilian leaders were not yet involved. From the outset of the ABC-1 discussions, it was evident that the United States was reluctant to combine command structures, while the British pushed for closer cooperation (Wilson 1994, 83). Although the possibility of a "supreme war council" was mentioned, little else was concretely established regarding the structure of integrated command, as it was still too early for the Americans to expedite the implementation of the alliance.

In addition to delays caused by domestic political friction, this chapter has also explored how cultural, doctrinal, and other differences between allies can impede implementation. Some of these differences became apparent during the ABC-1 conference and were only largely resolved a year later, at the Arcadia Conference involving Roosevelt and Churchill. One major point of contention was general strategy: The British prioritized their colonial holdings in the Mediterranean and North Africa, while the United States focused on direct engagement in the European theater. This strategic divergence was rooted in differing military doctrines, which, as we have seen, can significantly challenge interoperability. The British preferred indirect warfare, whereas the United States favored direct engagements with overwhelming force. These and other disagreements required negotiation and resolution before the allies could effectively collaborate. There were also disputes over whether and how command might be unified. Even during the secret ABC-1 meetings, where cooperation was contingent on a hypothetical US involvement in the conflict, deep disagreements between the prospective allies were already evident.

A preliminary joint war plan emerged from the ABC-1 conference. It included a sketch of a joint strategy for fighting the Axis and "Principles of Command," including a division of strategic areas and which countries would take the lead in which theaters. One actionable agreement that came out of the conference was an agreement to establish British and American military staff missions in DC and London "to ensure the machinery of collaboration is ready should the US come to war" (Bamford 2022, 190–191).

Another point of contention that slowed negotiations between the Americans and the British was the concern that Britain might, like France, soon fall to Germany. This prospect complicated American decisions regarding the supply of war materials to the British. The possibility of Germany dominating all of Europe generated sympathy for Britain and arguments for increased support. British leaders played on these fears and sympathies among many, including Roosevelt himself (Reynolds 1981, 116–117). On the other hand, Americans also worried that excessive support to Britain could ultimately harm US interests if Britain were to fall, with American-supplied weapons potentially being taken over by German forces (Bamford 2022). These concerns escalated to the point where not only was the discussion of further US support to Britain postponed, but the United States began to press Britain to consider transferring the guardianship of the British fleet and empire to the United States (Reynolds 1981, 117–120). At the same time, the growing German threat spurred US leaders to advocate for strengthening the US military. Consequently, US interests superseded sympathy for the British position, and many US leaders prioritized arming American forces over directing resources to Britain.

In the long term, the strategy developed to resolve this negotiation impasse improved weapons interoperability between the United States and Britain. Once the Americans were satisfied that the British would not easily fall to the Germans, support for arming Britain increased. But there was no question that the United States also needed to ramp up its own armament production. Instead of retooling factories to produce equipment specifically for British needs, the United States opted to develop systems both countries could use. They invited the British to provide input on adapting US machinery for their use, leading the British to purchase equipment that was already largely compatible with US specifications. Desperate for weapons, the British accepted the final modified designs, which became the standard for Anglo-American tank equipment in the years that followed (Bamford 2022, 174–175). And in September 1940, the United States agreed to send 50 World War I destroyers to Britain in exchange for territorial concessions in the Caribbean and the western Atlantic, where the United States intended to establish military bases (Reynolds 1981, 121) and take the significant step of stationing US military personnel on British soil.

In addition to arms support, interactions and exchanges of personnel between the United States and Britain increased. In August 1941, military leaders from both nations convened for the Atlantic Conference aboard the US cruiser *Augusta* and the British battleship *Prince of Wales* in Placentia Bay, Newfoundland. The attendees included General George C. Marshall, US Army chief of staff; Major General Henry H. Arnold, newly appointed chief of the Army Air Forces; Admiral Harold R. Stark, chief of naval operations; and Admiral Ernest J. King, commander-in-chief of the US Atlantic Fleet. On the British side were General Sir John Dill, chief of the Imperial General Staff; Admiral Sir Dudley Pound, first sea lord; and Air Vice Marshal Wilfrid Freeman, vice chief of the Air Staff. The conference led to the joint issuance of the Atlantic Charter, outlining Roosevelt and Churchill's vision for the postwar world. While no new military agreements were reached, the principles established at the ABC-1 conference were reaffirmed (Bamford 2022, 196).

By the end of 1941, the United States and Great Britain had set up joint staff talks, stationed US military personnel in British territories, ensured a steady flow of US arms to Britain, and established a free exchange of intelligence. However, there was still no agreement on a unified joint military command, and no joint military training or exercises had been conducted to address differences in doctrine and procedures. In this regard, the process of achieving interoperability remained in its early stages.

After the United States entered the war, following the attack on Pearl Harbor, Roosevelt and Churchill quickly arranged a joint conference. The Arcadia Conference, held from December 22, 1941, to January 14, 1942, in Washington, DC, brought together Roosevelt and Churchill, along with top American and British military leaders. This conference marked the formalization of the US–British alliance. However, significant work remained to effectively combine forces and alter the balance of power. During the conference, notable strategic disagreements arose. General Marshall advocated for a cross-Channel attack and the United States prioritized focusing on Japan. In contrast, Britain wanted the United States to prioritize Europe and pushed for joint efforts in the Mediterranean to reinforce British colonial holdings (Wilson 1994, 86), rather than a direct cross-Channel attack.

The differences in strategic approaches took considerable time to negotiate and resolve, not to mention the challenging task of integrating the military capabilities of the two nations. The primary outcome of the Arcadia Conference was an agreement that targeting Germany would be the top priority, although not through a direct approach. By 1942, it was evident that the alliance was still not in a position to execute a successful cross-Channel amphibious assault together. In the fall of 1942, the allies established a "system of communication and deliberation" that would guide their coalition efforts for the rest of the war (Wilson 1994, 93). Even after they formally solidified their alliance, it took another year and a half to set up the Anglo-American military communication and coordination system. It wasn't until 1944 that the allies were ready to launch a direct cross-Channel assault, a delay due more to early challenges in interoperability than to strategic disagreements.

Another significant issue addressed at the Arcadia Conference in January 1941 was the question of unifying command. The allies agreed to establish a CCS based in Washington, DC. Reaching consensus on how to unify command involved intense negotiations, and implementing the agreement took many months, in some cases lasting for the entire duration of the war. As mentioned, having the headquarters in Washington, DC, was a difficult concession for the British, as it meant bringing hundreds of British officers and staff to the United States, making the United States the primary partner in the alliance (Wilson 1994, 89). Another discussion point was how to address the roles of other allies, such as Russia, China, and the Netherlands. The British insisted on maintaining a special Anglo-American relationship. Ultimately, the United States and Britain decided to exclude these other allies from the CCS.

In addition to finalizing strategy and the chain of command, US and British military commanders needed to negotiate several other critical matters affecting interoperability. They had to establish a process for approving military decisions by both nations, determine lines of command for different theaters, and create systems for integrating land, air, and sea forces within a multinational alliance. This included addressing logistical issues such as coordinating the shipment of war materials, managing the treatment of the wounded, and encrypting communications.

The close working relationships between American and British officers also revealed cultural differences that occasionally hindered cooperation. Bonner L. Fellers, an American attaché in Cairo who observed the British campaign in North Africa, felt that the US Army would require "its own separate theater of operation, separate line of communication, [and] separate base," criticizing British methods as too lax for modern warfare (Bamford 2022, 196). Although not universally shared, such sentiments reflected broader concerns among many officers about the effectiveness of American and British forces working together and apprehension about potential compromises of US security (Bamford 2022, 198). But after months of working and training together, the allies gradually worked through such cultural frictions.

The Anglo-American alliance provides a valuable case study for understanding the factors that can delay the implementation of an alliance and the time required to realize its full potential. Even though the partners had a common enemy, common goals, and a common language, the process of fully harnessing the alliance's potential to shift the balance of power unfolded gradually. Several key factors contributed to this delay.

First, domestic constraints in the US political environment played a significant role. Anti-interventionist public sentiment and the presidential election of 1940 caused US leaders to delay military cooperation with Great Britain. While some of these domestic constraints eased after the election, it was not until the Japanese attack on Pearl Harbor that both countries were freed from these internal obstacles. Second, technical barriers to integrating military equipment needed to be overcome. These challenges were addressed through the production process, as US manufacturers retooled to supply both the US and British militaries. Third, procedural and human barriers to interoperability required resolution. The allies needed to establish a unified command structure and train their forces to move, communicate, and fight together effectively. Cultural differences between the British and Americans also had to be navigated. Overall, it took nearly three and a half years for the Anglo-American alliance to fully realize its potential for shifting the balance of power.

2.3.2 Scope of Implementation Delay

As the history of the Anglo-American coalition illustrates, political and military factors often combine to delay the implementation of a new security partnership. Though this case provides evidence of the relevance of implementation delay, broader application of these concepts requires care. No two security partnerships are the same. Given this, how does implementation delay operate in a diverse set of contexts? Before we develop our dynamic theory of alliance implementation in the following chapters, we offer an important consideration to guide scholars in understanding the wide variety of forms that implementation delay might take. In particular, we highlight how the primary source of implementation delay depends upon the goals of an alliance.

We have argued that implementation delay arises from friction in two arenas: political and military. Political barriers to implementation are omnipresent. When states come together to negotiate over the terms of joint military action, disagreement is inevitable. For example, in the course of building an international coalition prior to the Gulf War, US officials negotiated with dozens of stakeholder countries. These negotiations culminated in the support of 42 countries, with many providing troops and material support for the eventual war. These negotiations were time-consuming, beginning in September 1990 with US Secretary of State James Baker's "tin cup trip" and culminating with the passing of UN Resolution 678 on November 29. When allies have competing goals, such negotiations often bog down as diplomats seek to align competing war aims (Poast 2019). And even when they agree on war aims, negotiations persist over side payments and the distribution of joint gains (Smith 2021). In sum, political challenges arise in every security partnership, and act as a force to slow alliance implementation.

In contrast to the omnipresent nature of political challenges to implementation, integrating military capabilities is not always necessary to accomplish the objective of a security alliance. When military interoperability is not required, the power shift from an alliance might occur as early as signing and ratification. When should we expect military integration not to be an issue? The answer lies in how states intend to cooperate to enjoy the benefits of their joint military power. In some alliances, integration and interoperability are not necessary to realize these gains.

More precisely, there are two situations when military integration and interoperability are not necessary. This happens when alliances are capability dividers rather than capability aggregators, and when the relative ally–enemy disparity in force readiness is so large that the security objectives do not depend on military integration. This latter circumstance is especially applicable in asymmetric alliances with a superpower targeting a relatively weak enemy.

What is a capability divider? In contrast to alliances that are formed to aggregate capabilities to enhance the joint warfighting ability of the alliance partners, capability-divider alliances are designed to split the military capabilities of the alliance's target. An alliance may divide the target's capabilities if it forces the opponent to fight multiple opponents on multiple fronts. Because members of such alliances do not intend their militaries to fight together, interoperability challenges are not a cause of delays in implementation. The German–Japanese alliance in the Tripartite Pact is a prime example. It was formed primarily to deter US entry into World War II, by threatening to stretch and divide enemy forces rather than to aggregate ally capabilities.

Another example of a capability divider is the 1894 Franco–Russian alliance. Dividing German capabilities was the primary motivation of

French–Russian security relations from 1894 through 1940, when Germany attacked and occupied France (Clark 2012). Although the terms of the 1894 alliance specified troop-level commitments and military plans, the "capability-division" objective of the alliance did not require the militaries to fight together. The objective was to force Germany to divide its forces to defend both the Eastern and Western Fronts. The alliance took many years to implement, but this was due to political reasons, not military interoperability challenges.

In the lead up to the outbreak of World War II, dividing German power was still the shared Franco–Russian strategy. Policymakers in France debated whether they should abandon their security commitments on the Eastern Front so as to avoid getting entangled with ongoing German aggression. Ultimately, the French decided that the Eastern alliances were too important, because they served to divide German power and gave France the best chance of deterring Nazi aggression against their homeland. As premier Edouard Herriot summarized this point at the time, "I consult the map. I see only one country, which can bring us the necessary counterweight and create a second front in case of war. That is the Soviet Union" (Scott 1962).

Capability-divider alliances bring about a relative power shift, but not through integrating allied fighting forces to create a more powerful combined military force. Rather, the objective is to weaken the enemy target's ability to fight each of the allies separately. To accomplish this objective, allies coordinate the timing and locations of their respective fighting commitments and sometimes also their force-level commitments. These matters are often negotiated in advance and incorporated into the language of the alliance before it's signed. Thus, most military matters in capability-divider alliances are subject to the politics of implementation and can be resolved prior to signing and ratification.

The second situation in which factors related to the integration of allies' military forces do not delay implementation is when one of the allies is so powerful relative to the target of the alliance that integration is unnecessary. Many asymmetric alliances with superpowers that target relatively weak enemy countries fit this model. An example is the 1955 mutual defense pact between the United States and the ROC. In 1955, the United States was a superpower, and the ROC was militarily weak after losing a civil war to the People's Republic of China (PRC) and retreating to the island of Taiwan. The PRC was significantly weaker than the United States, especially in naval and air capabilities, both of which would be required for an amphibious takeover of Taiwan. Having just fought a war on the Korean Peninsula, the United States had troops stationed in South Korea and in Japan. And the Seventh Fleet, against which the PRC was defenseless in naval and coastal operations, could be deployed to the Taiwan Strait.

The PRC would seem to have a geographic advantage, making the implementation of a US–ROC military defense of Taiwan problematic. Taiwan is only 90 miles from PRC forces on China's mainland, and to defend Taiwan, the United States would need to transport planes and thousands of troops to Taiwan from Korea and Japan. It would also need to send in the Seventh Fleet. All this would take time. But at the time, the PRC was not able to launch a speedy amphibious assault across the Taiwan Strait. ROC forces were strong enough to hold out until US naval and air forces could disrupt such an assault.

Because of this military asymmetry between the United States and the PRC, the United States and ROC militaries did not need a joint force on Taiwan or NATO-style interoperability to meet the obligations of the mutual defense pact. Even a slow US military response from remote locations would have been sufficient to defend the territory of Taiwan. The United States did not need to worry about developing interoperability with Chinese Nationalist forces, because the PRC was not ready to launch a full-scale attack on the mainland of Taiwan. Such alliance commitments, if credible, can be implemented at the time of signing and ratification.

Over time, with the modernization of PRC forces, this dynamic has changed. In 2024, US forces trying to move to Taiwan and the Taiwan Strait would encounter significant resistance from advanced PRC forces. The PRC has also developed advanced naval, air, and ground forces capable of launching a speedy amphibious operation. The shift in relative readiness and reaction time has altered what would be required for a successful allied counterforce. Hypothetically, if the United States and Taiwan decided to formalize an alliance today to defend Taiwan, the military dimension of alliance implementation would be more involved and would take significantly longer today than it did in 1954–55.

In sum, these considerations point to two lessons for applying the concept of implementation delay to the historical record. First, political barriers to implementation are omnipresent. Regardless of the alignment of allies' goals, the fact that war is costly and risky implies that questions about the distribution of costs and benefits will arise. Resolving these questions requires time and effort, preventing the instantaneous implementation of an alliance. Second, the presence of military barriers depends on the nature of a partnership. If an alliance is designed to divide the capabilities of an adversary, partners need not fight on the same battlefield, and interoperability is therefore not a major concern. Similarly, in the case of an asymmetric alliance, a junior alliance partner's military force plays a relatively minor role, and so the need for interoperability presents a relatively minor hurdle. These considerations imply that though implementation delay is nearly always relevant, its degree and nature vary significantly across partnerships.

2.4 Conclusion

In this chapter, we have introduced a novel concept in the study of military alliances: the implementation phase. This is the time that will elapse between the formation of an alliance and the full realization of its benefits. The process of alliance implementation opens a window for political maneuvering and can significantly influence the effectiveness of the alliance. The length of this phase is determined by various political and military factors.

Political factors that may delay implementation include diplomatic negotiations, domestic and international distractions, and institutional hurdles related to ratification or the membership rules of existing alliances. Military factors that often slow implementation pertain to force interoperability. Achieving military interoperability involves integrating strategic planning, technical capabilities, and command structures. Allies must also reconcile technical, procedural, and human differences.

We noted that military interoperability challenges do not slow implementation when alliances, like the Tripartite Pact or the Franco–Russian alliance, are designed to divide targets' capabilities. In addition, in some asymmetric alliances in which one ally is significantly more powerful than the adversary, as with the 1955 US–ROC Mutual Defense Pact, military integration may not be necessary. The powerful ally's mere presence can be sufficient to deter or counter the enemy, making swift military interoperability less critical. In these two types of alliances, signing and ratification often mark the end of the implementation phase.

Understanding the variation in the length of alliance implementation is crucial for analyzing the timing and nature of political maneuvering during the alliance formation process. In the next chapter, we will develop a theory of dynamic alliances that incorporates this concept of implementation timing.

To formalize this idea, we introduce the parameter r, which represents the expected speed of implementation. This parameter influences the duration between the decision to form an alliance and the moment when the alliance's military benefits are fully realized—the point of implementation. By incorporating r into our theoretical framework, we aim to capture how delays and varying implementation speeds affect the strategic behavior of states during the alliance formation process.

3

A Theory of Alliance Implementation, Power Shifts, and Preventive War

Time and again, the process of creating new military alliances sparks political turmoil and even war. However, the mechanism connecting impending alliances to aggression is not well understood. One reason for this lack of clarity is that throughout history, leaders have taken many different actions in anticipation of impending alliances. New alliances, whether with offensive or defensive purposes, have provoked hostility in some cases but not in others. In 1990, despite initial Soviet opposition and threats of escalation, NATO expanded to include the former East Germany, which had been covered by the Warsaw Pact. In contrast, Georgia's quest for NATO membership, which gathered steam at a 2008 NATO summit, triggered a Russian invasion.

This variation carries over into the present day. As the war in Ukraine continues, there is growing evidence that Russia's invasion of Ukraine in February 2022 was motivated, at least in part, by Russian president Vladimir Putin's goal of preventing Ukraine from taking further steps towards NATO membership. In the weeks leading up to the attack, Putin said that Russia needed guarantees beyond word-of-mouth assurances that Ukraine would never be permitted to join NATO. Days after the attack, Putin told French President Emmanuel Macron that guarantees of Ukrainian neutrality were key to any peace agreement.

Yet, other ongoing efforts to expand NATO have not sparked similar aggression. Neither Finland's recent successful bid for NATO membership nor Sweden's ongoing membership process triggered military action from Russia. Russia issued a sequence of diplomatic condemnations, but did little else to interfere. This contrast illustrates precisely the variation we are interested in explaining: Why did Ukraine's aspirations to join NATO lead to military conflict, but Sweden's and Finland's prompt only empty threats?

We aim to explain why, in general, anticipated alliances provoke varying responses. Since 1990, NATO has added 14 member states, expanding

The Window Before. Brett V. Benson and Bradley C. Smith, Oxford University Press.
 DOI: 10.1093/9780197806760.003.0003

from 17 to 31 countries, with the most recent being Finland. Most prospective member countries joined without violent opposition. Russia attacked preemptively twice: Georgia in 2008 and Ukraine in 2022. In 2014, Russia stoked small-scale military aggression in Ukraine. It issued military threats in three cases—accession of the reunified Germany in 1990, and during the run-up to the formal bids of Finland and Sweden in 2022—but none of these threats were carried out, and they did not slow the bids for membership. In 2023, evidence also came to light of a Russian plan to destabilize Moldova, partly to prevent its joining NATO.[1]

This is not merely a story about NATO. Though not all alliances provoke preventive war, attempts to use aggression to block the formation of new alliances have occurred throughout history. In some cases, such as the 1954 defense pact between the United States and Taiwan, alliances are successfully brought into force in spite of military attacks from targeted states. Further, the expectation of aggression from a targeted state may deter the formation of a new alliance. Many potential alliances may not have formed because of the threat of preventive conflict. For example, a large SEATO-style military alliance in Northeast Asia was considered but then scrapped because of the risk that an attempt to include Taiwan in a multilateral alliance would trigger a broader military conflict with China.

As these examples illustrate, potential new alliances may stir a range of political activity in the window of time before final implementation. Targets may engage in small-scale aggression, or full-on armed attacks, to discourage prospective allies from joining forces. The historical variation in how countries react in anticipation of a new enemy alliance suggests the need for a theory to explain whether and under what conditions the prospect of a new or expanding alliance is provocative. The remainder of this chapter lays out such a theory.

The key innovation of our theoretical approach is that we conceive of military cooperation and alliance formation as a dynamic process. Existing theory misses this central aspect. Though, in principle, a new alliance can be formed in an instant, this is not how military cooperation unfolds in reality. Meaningful military cooperation that yields results on the battlefield takes time and effort. As we discussed in the previous chapter, myriad hurdles stand between potential security partners and a meaningful relationship that

[1] https://www.cnn.com/2023/03/16/europe/russia-moldova-secret-document-intl-cmd/index.html.

acts to shape the balance of power. Put simply, implementing alliances takes time. Examining the alliance process in this way yields novel insights about the variation we observe in aggression in anticipation of new alliances.

In this chapter, we first discuss the dynamic process of forming an alliance. We then develop a theory that shows how the timing of alliance implementation provides a window for opponents to meddle in the alliance process.[2] In this step, we establish a baseline theory of a generic alliance without regard to defensive or offensive stipulations. This baseline theory generates basic results and serves as a foundation for a number of extensions throughout the book. After developing the baseline theory, we discuss the main results. We then offer an extension of the theory that examines specifically defensive alliances. The purpose of this section is to see whether the incentives in the baseline theory carry over to the special case of defensive alliances. Throughout the chapter, we maintain a running list of the main theoretical results in a summary table.

3.1 The Dynamic Process of Alliance Formation

In constructing a dynamic theory to understand preventive conflict in anticipation of impending alliances, what key features should be considered? First, military alliances aggregate the martial power of the allies. This results in a shift of warfighting power in favor of the allies, disadvantaging their enemies. Second, implementing an alliance and fully realizing the resulting power shift takes place over time. From the moment that two or more states begin working together on a plan to combine military forces, the plan proceeds through multiple stages, and the benefits of the power shift are typically not fully realized until later in the process.

With these two features in mind, we construct a theory that accounts for routine interactions between allies and enemies throughout the stages of the alliance formation process. The main dynamic that we capture is strategic bargaining before, during, and after the underlying shift of power. At each stage in this process, actors' strategic thinking is informed by the history of interactions, the state of the power shift, and the prospects for future bargaining. That is, the adversaries think both prospectively and retrospectively, in some cases acting preemptively to threaten, negotiate, or sometimes even attack in anticipation of a shift that has not yet occurred—and in other

[2] Portions of this chapter appear in Benson and Smith (2021).

cases engaging with each other while the power shift is occurring or after it is complete.

The dynamic process of alliance formation unfolds in three stages.

1. Pre-implementation stage: This initial stage occurs when prospective partners decide to form an alliance, without any power shift having occurred yet. During this period, the focus is on reaching an agreement on the formation of the alliance.
2. Implementation stage: This stage involves the actual hard work of implementing the alliance. This stage can be prolonged due to various political and military factors. During implementation, the alliance is vulnerable to attempts by enemies to disrupt the process and prevent the anticipated power shift.
3. Post-implementation stage: Once the alliance is successfully implemented, the power shift is fully realized. At this point, the new dynamics and relationships established by the alliance become effective.

Throughout these stages, adversaries may engage in bargaining or conflict. In the pre-implementation stage, disputes may lead to bargaining or fighting before a decision is made to join an alliance. During the implementation stage, the ongoing bargaining or fighting is influenced by the anticipated benefits of the power shift that will accrue to the prospective ally once the alliance is completed. In the post-implementation stage, with the power shift now realized, the new ally and the target may again engage in bargaining or conflict, leveraging the advantages gained from the completed alliance.

How do actors' incentives change in each stage of this process? In the pre-implementation stage, prospective allies look down the road of the process to determine whether the future benefits outweigh the immediate costs and the longer-term risks of trying to implement an alliance. There are two main benefits they might consider. First, their joint warfighting capability will improve. Second, this greater warfighting ability will improve their peacetime bargaining strength. However, implementation is not instantaneous or guaranteed. These benefits will only be fully realized at some point in the future, if and when the alliance has been completely implemented and the power shift fully realized.

Along with the benefits of an alliance, the prospective partners will have to consider the downsides. There are direct costs, which can be higher or lower, depending on factors such as differences between the allies, domestic opposition, and bureaucratic hurdles. Then there is the risk of attempts by enemies to try to stop the alliance. These costs and risks may convince the prospective partners that the alliance is not worth pursuing.

If they decide to move forward, then they begin the implementation stage, a critical phase because it exposes them to interference from enemies. Implementing, including negotiating terms and integrating military forces, can be a lengthy process. When the prospective allies can control the speed of the implementation process, they can speed it up or slow it down as necessary. But factors beyond their control may delay it, and they and their enemies cannot typically precisely predict how long implementation will take. Successful implementation on a tight timeline is by no means guaranteed. Sometimes the effort dies under the weight of normal diplomatic and domestic pressures—but occasionally alliances fail because enemies successfully interfere.

As allies work to implement an alliance, targeted states may realize that the window of opportunity—the chance to settle outstanding disputes before power shifts out of their favor—is closing. They may try to settle the disputes peacefully, but doing so risks allowing the alliance to come into force before they can achieve a favorable resolution. If and when the alliance is fully implemented, the power shift may mean that the new allies can no longer be pushed around by the targeted state. Consequently, negotiated settlements that advantage the state targeted by the alliance cannot be sustained after the alliance is fully implemented. And so, anticipating this future disadvantage, targeted states sometimes take action to prevent the alliance from coming into force at all. Two options exist here: The targeted state may try to negotiate to prevent the alliance; or it may attack one or both allies.

If an alliance is successfully implemented, the new allies enter the post-implementation stage. At this point, power has shifted in favor of the allies and to the disadvantage of the enemy. The allies now have greater military power, and this joint warfighting capability also strengthens their peacetime bargaining position. With their new clout, the allies can expect to receive more favorable settlements during negotiations with the enemy.

At all stages of this dynamic alliance formation process, allies and adversaries may negotiate or fight. They might do so before implementation begins, while implementation is proceeding, or after it is complete. Most theories of alliances conceive of this crisis-bargaining interaction between allies and adversaries as a one-time engagement that takes place after the alliance is formed. In reality, prospective allies and their adversaries are usually already engaged in explicit or implicit crisis bargaining before the alliance is even pursued—this is often the primary motivation for that pursuit. But the possibility of political or military coercion continues while the alliance is being implemented, and it doesn't go away once the implementation is complete.

As we have noted, bargaining differs between these three stages because of what has happened in the past and what actors anticipate will happen in the future. In the pre-implementation stage, bargaining occurs bilaterally between an enemy and one of the allies. Prospective allies have to decide whether to take on the expected costs and risks of trying to implement an alliance. During the implementation stage, other actors know that these countries have decided to try to implement an alliance. Bargaining occurs with the same distribution of power as in the pre-implementation phase, because the combined warfighting capabilities of the alliance have yet to be realized. But there is a difference: All the actors anticipate a time when the allies will be advantaged in both war and peace. In the post-implementation stage, actors know that an alliance has been fully implemented and the balance of power has shifted. Now, targets of the alliance must bargain against the combined strength of the allies. Because the alliance process unfolds dynamically over time, enemies and allies alike make calculations by thinking retrospectively and prospectively about the impact of the power shift on their current circumstances relative to another point in time, whether because the power shift is forthcoming or because it has already happened.

In spite of the importance of these dynamic forces in the historical record, they are largely absent from canonical theories of alliance politics and war. Rather, existing theory has largely focused on what Morrow (2000) has called the "credibility problem" inherent in alliances. Credibility is key to functional and effective security cooperation. After all, a primary goal of alliances is to deter aggression from adversaries. Successful deterrence requires that an adversary believe that the allies' promises to aid one another in war are *credible*. This is precisely the credibility problem: Deterrence requires credibility, and allies must find a way to make their promises credible to one another. Broadly, the literature points to two mechanisms tying alliances to credibility.

First, alliances allow members to convey their willingness to intervene on behalf of one another *before conflict breaks out*. This is the "signaling value" of alliances. Research focusing on this mechanism has pointed to the important role alliances play in allowing states to credibly signal to enemies their interests and, by extension, their willingness to fight. Military coordination within alliances of the kind discussed in the previous chapter is the mechanism of such signaling. Because military coordination entails costs, willingness to pay these costs provides a meaningful signal to adversaries that an ally is willing to act on behalf of its partners. Thus, alliances are one avenue through which states may credibly signal their intentions to both friends and foes by taking costly actions (Morrow 1991, 1994; Fearon 1997).

Second, alliances may change the incentives of states to intervene *once conflict has already occurred.* This is "commitment value" of alliances. NATO, and the force integration it requires (which we described in the previous chapter), is a prime example of this effect. By increasing the effectiveness of multilateral warfare prosecuted by the members, NATO makes combined military operations more attractive, increasing the probability that the members will fight together (Morrow 2000, 71). The commitment mechanism is also related to the logic of "tying hands" in international relations (Fearon 1997). Because leaders may be punished by domestic or international audiences if they fail to live up to their alliance commitments, alliances alter the cost–benefit calculation of intervention by adding "audience costs" for failing to come to the aid of a partner.

In focusing on the credibility problem, both the theoretical and empirical literatures have delivered many important insights about the connections between alliances and war. However, this work has largely focused on comparing situations in which an alliance is present to ones in which there is no alliance. As a result, it has largely abstracted away from the operational realities of implementing military cooperation that we discussed in the previous chapter. And that means that it has focused on static, one-shot interactions rather than dynamic considerations. In the following section, we present a dynamic theory of alliance formation, bargaining, and preventive war. This theory formalizes the discussion of this section, folding the process of alliance implementation into a dynamic model of multilateral crisis bargaining.

3.2 Formal Description

The dynamics of the alliance formation process naturally lend themselves to formal analysis. In this section, we construct a formal model to evaluate the prospective and retrospective considerations that affect the incentives of prospective allies and enemies of alliances throughout the process. Readers who wish to bypass the formal description of the model and technical analysis can skip to Section 3.4, where we provide a prose description of the main theoretical results.

Consider a world with three states. State 1 and State 2 repeatedly bargain over a disputed issue. State 3 has interests in the peaceful settlement of this issue that are aligned with those of State 1, though the allies may have differential payoffs from war.[3] In every round of bargaining, States 1 and 3 may attempt to implement a military alliance, at some cost.

This interaction occurs over an infinite number of periods, indexed by $t \in \mathbf{N}$. In each period t, the interaction is characterized by a commonly observed state variable, s^t, which can have only two values: A if an alliance is presently in force, and N if no alliance is presently in force. Both the sequence of actions in a period and the players' per-period payoffs are a function of s^t. Throughout, we focus on the case in which there is no alliance at the outset of the interaction: $s^1 = N$.

The timing of the stage game is as follows. In a period in which $s^t = N$, State 3 makes the first move, choosing whether to offer an alliance commitment to State 1. If State 3 offers, then State 1 chooses whether to join. If State 3 offers and State 1 joins, then the alliance is implemented with probability r (and thus implementation fails with probability $1 - r$). If State 3 chooses not to offer or State 1 chooses not to join, the alliance is not implemented. In all cases, once States 1 and 3 have made their decisions, bargaining occurs, with State 1 proposing a settlement of the issue, $x^t \in [0, 1]$ for the period. After observing this proposal, State 2 chooses to accept it or reject it. If State 2 rejects, players receive their war payoffs in all future periods. If State 2 accepts, play proceeds to the next period, with s^{t+1} determined by whether an alliance was implemented in the current period. In a period in which $s^t = A$, play proceeds with State 1, proposing $x^t \in [0, 1]$ or attacking, and State 2 choosing to accept or reject. After an alliance has been implemented in period t, $s^{t'} = A$ for all periods $t' \geq t$.

States discount future period payoffs by $\delta \in (0, 1)$, and we normalize states' dynamic payoffs by $1 - \delta$. If State 2 accepts an offer of x^t in period t, then States 1 and 3 receive period payoffs of x^t and State 2 receives a period payoff of $1 - x^t$.

[3] Our modeling of settlement preferences is standard in the literature, with allies having identical policy preferences as in Fang, Johnson, and Leeds (2014), Benson, Meirowitz, and Ramsay (2014), and Wolford (2014). For models in which allies may have differential preferences over peaceful settlements, see Benson (2012), Smith (2021), and Phillips and Wolford (2021).

If a war occurs, then each player receives its (discounted) war payoff in all future periods. If $s^t = N$ and an alliance failed to be implemented in the current period, then state i's war payoff is w_i. If an alliance was implemented in the current period or in any previous period, then state i's war payoff is w_i'. To model the inefficiency of war, we assume that $w_2 + \max\{w_1, w_3\} \leq 1$ and $w_2' + \max\{w_1', w_3'\} \leq 1$. To capture the effect of alliances on the players' war payoffs, we assume that $w_2' \leq w_2$, $w_3' \geq w_3$, and $w_1' \geq w_1$. This reduced-form representation of the effect of alliances on war payoffs can be microfounded in a number of ways, some depending on an alliance influencing State 3's intervention decision and some not. One possibility is that the alliance changes State 3's incentives for war participation, encouraging it to provide support that it would not provide without the alliance in place. Another possibility is that the alliance enhances coordination and improves States 1 and 3's joint fighting capability, holding fixed State 3's choice to intervene.[4] Using these war payoffs, we can characterize the size of the anticipated power shift from an alliance between States 1 and 3 that impacts State 2's decision to accept or reject State 1's bargaining offers. From State 2's perspective, the size of the power shift is $w_2 - w_2' \geq 0$. We simplify this expression by referring to $w_2 - w_2'$ as Δ throughout.

Finally, we assume that the process of implementing an alliance is costly. In any period in which the alliance has not yet been implemented, State 3 pays a cost of $a > 0$ if it chooses to offer an alliance. Similarly, in a period in which the alliance has not yet been implemented, State 1 pays a cost $a > 0$ if it accepts State 3's invitation. Throughout, we assume that the cost of alliance implementation is lower than the inefficiency generated by war: $a < 1 - w_2 - w_1$.

3.3 Formal Results

As is standard in the analysis of dynamic games, we focus on stationary, Markov perfect equilibria (Maskin and Tirole 2001).[5] Here this amounts to subgame perfect equilibrium with two additional restrictions. First, the

[4] In the interest of parsimony, we do not explicitly model State 3's intervention decision here, though we demonstrate in the appendix that our results carry over to a richer model where State 3's choice of intervention is endogenously determined by the alliance's implementation.

[5] If we extend our consideration to non-Markovian equilibria, it is possible to construct equilibria with non-stationary behavior in which history-dependent off-path punishment strategies by State 2 induce the allies to forego alliance. Such equilibria are the focus of Chapter 6. Whenever such a non-stationary equilibrium exists, the stationary equilibria we focus on also exist. Further, for sufficiently large $\delta < 1$, non-stationary equilibria relying on off-path punishments of the type described here

players condition their behavior in period t only on the payoff-relevant state of the world, s^t. Second, for any t, t' such that $s^t = s^{t'}$, the players use the same strategies. Henceforth, we refer to such a strategy profile as an "equilibrium." Proof of all propositions appears in the appendix.

We begin by considering the obstacles to alliance formation. We do this to establish a baseline for comparison with cases in which an alliance does materialize in equilibrium. Further, the results of the current section illustrate an important feature of equilibrium play in our model: If an alliance does not occur, then neither does war.

The decisions of prospective partners to offer or join an alliance depend on how quickly it can be implemented, relative to the cost of implementation. When implementation is difficult or slow, State 3 will not extend an invitation, and if it does, then State 1 will not accept it. This is because the expected difficulty of implementation makes the cost of such an alliance prohibitive. In this case, alliances do not materialize in equilibrium, the distribution of power remains fixed, and bargaining proceeds peacefully. Proposition 3.1 lays this out formally.

Proposition 3.1. *If* $a > r\Delta/(1 - \delta)$*, then there is a unique equilibrium. Strategies in this equilibrium are as follows:*

- *If* $s^t = N$ *and an alliance has not been successfully implemented in the current period, State 1 offers* $x^t = 1 - w_2$*. Otherwise, State 1 offers* $x^t = 1 - w_2'$.
- *State 2 does not join after State 3 invites. If* $s^t = N$ *and an alliance has not been implemented, State 2 accepts any* $x^t \leq 1 - w_2$ *and rejects otherwise. If* $s^t = A$*, State 2 accepts any* $x^t \leq 1 - w_2'$ *and rejects otherwise.*
- *State 3 never extends an alliance.*

The equilibrium described in Proposition 3.1 has two important features. First, the allies never attempt to implement an alliance along the path of play. Second, as a result of the stability in the distribution of power, the path of play remains peaceful.

The prospective partners' decision whether to offer or join an alliance depends on the comparison of what they can receive with certainty by not

fail to exist. To establish the baseline results tying alliance implementation to incentives for conflict, it is useful to begin with a focus on stationary equilibria.

allying and what they can expect to receive by offering or joining—a costly "implementation lottery." If implementation is too costly (the value of r is small compared to a), it is likely that successful implementation will require repeated efforts, each of which will also be costly. In this case, prospective partners are better off not offering or joining the alliance, instead taking the bargaining payoff equal to their non-allied war payoff. This is what they would receive anyway by trying and (likely) failing to implement an alliance. By not offering and joining the alliance in the first place, however, they save the repeated costs of trying to implement the alliance.

Accordingly, if the cost of alliance implementation (a) is high relative to the speed of implementation (r), an alliance is simply not justifiable based on the expected costs. As a result, State 3 never offers and State 1 never joins, and the war payoffs of all players remain fixed throughout the interaction. Because the allies never attempt to implement, bargaining peacefully today does not entail a risk of alliance, and there is no resulting loss of bargaining power for State 2. Consequently, State 2 has no incentive to make an unreasonable demand or to launch a preventive strike. This behavior matches what we know about crisis bargaining models generally: Absent information asymmetries or commitment problems, peace obtains.

This initial result provides a baseline: If no alliance occurs in equilibrium, then war does not occur either. However, we are primarily interested in comparing this to cases in which an alliance *does* come about on the equilibrium path of play. Because of our interest in the relationship between alliances and conflict, the remainder of our analysis focuses on the conditions under which States 1 and 3 attempt to form an alliance in equilibrium.

What are these conditions? The implementation of an alliance brings substantial advantages in bargaining with a shared enemy. By contrast, attempting but failing to implement an alliance results in either a preventive attack by the target or a peaceful bargaining settlement. Either way, the prospective partners pay the cost of the attempted implementation in the present.

Alliances occur in equilibrium when the benefits justify the cost. The following result establishes that this trade-off is borne out in equilibrium.

Lemma 3.1 *If $a \leq r\Delta/(1 - \delta)$, then in every equilibrium, State 3 extends an alliance in every period in which $s^t = N$, and State 1 always joins if State 3 offers.*

Table 3.1 Summary of theoretical results

	Result	Description
Chapter 3		
Lemma 8.2	Alliance Gamble	Governments try to implement provocative alliances if expected benefits are large and implementation is speedy.

Intuitively, if alliance formation is cheap enough, States 1 and 3 will always attempt to implement an alliance in equilibrium. The cut-off value of a indicated in the expression $r\Delta/(1 - \delta)$ is also informative; as the benefits of the alliance become larger or are expected to arrive more quickly, the allies become more tolerant of large costs of alliance formation.

Before moving on, we emphasize two facts that emerge from the analysis. First, if the cost of alliance implementation is such that an alliance does not occur, then war does not occur either. Second, if alliance implementation is cheap enough, then in equilibrium the allies will always be willing to attempt to implement an alliance. We summarize this result in Table 3.1. As the chapter proceeds, we will continue to collect additional results, augmenting this table to track the results we have derived from our analysis.

Choosing to form an alliance is a rational gamble, because the alliance may be implemented peacefully, but an unhappy target might also use violence to prevent it. In the remainder of this chapter, we analyze the model with an eye towards the following question: Under what conditions can an alliance be brought into force peacefully, and when might it provoke preventive violence?

3.3.1 Peaceful Alliances

We first demonstrate that careful bargaining can allow alliances to come into force peacefully without provoking preventive action. To avoid provocation, States 1 and 3 become generous in all periods prior to successful implementation, making generous offers to State 2. These offers serve to compensate the target of the alliance for the expected future loss of bargaining power. If the power shift resulting from the alliance is not too large, these generous offers suffice to render bargaining more attractive for State 2 than launching a preventive attack.

Proposition 3.2. *If $a \leq r\Delta/(1-\delta)$ and $\Delta \leq (1-\delta)(1-w_2)/\delta r$, then the following strategy profile constitutes the unique equilibrium:*

- *State 1 joins if State 3 offers. If $s^t = N$ and an alliance has not been successfully implemented in the current period, State 1 offers $x^t = 1 - w_2 - \delta r\Delta/(1-\delta) \equiv x^N$. Otherwise, State 1 offers $x^t = 1 - w_2'$.*
- *If $s^t = N$ and an alliance has not been implemented, State 2 accepts any $x^t \leq 1 - w_2 - \delta r\Delta/(1-\delta)$ and rejects otherwise. If $s^t = A$ or if an alliance was implemented in the current period, State 2 accepts any $x^t \leq 1 - w_2'$ and rejects otherwise.*
- *State 3 extends an alliance in every period in which $s^t = N$.*

Proposition 3.2 indicates two conditions for the peaceful implementation of an alliance. First, implementation costs cannot be too high; otherwise, allies are better off without the alliance. Second, the resulting power shift needs to be large enough to justify the costs of implementation but not so large that the allies cannot adequately compensate the target for its expected bargaining loss.

The equilibrium strategies detailed in Proposition 3.2 have two important features. First, the outcome is always peaceful. State 2 never chooses a preventive strike and instead is willing to accept the equilibrium settlements proposed by State 1 in all periods. Second, an alliance is implemented with certainty in the long run, because State 2 never takes preventive action on the path of play. Peace obtains in this scenario because State 1 is willing to "buy off" State 2 by making generous offers in pre-implementation periods. In this case, the concessions State 1 is willing to make are sufficient to compensate State 2 for the loss of bargaining power that occurs once the alliance is successfully implemented.

This incentive to avoid war and bide its time for alliance implementation renders State 2 willing to accept settlements that it would reject if it did not expect an alliance to be implemented in the future. Indeed, State 2 is willing to accept settlements in the present that award it less than its expected value of a pre-implementation war. This allows States 3 and 2 to continue working towards implementation of the alliance.

Figure 3.1 illustrates the logic. The horizontal line in the figure represents the set of possible settlements. State 2 prefers outcomes closer to 0, while State 1 prefers outcomes closer to 1. By rejecting an offer in a period before successful implementation, State 2 receives its most favorable war payoff

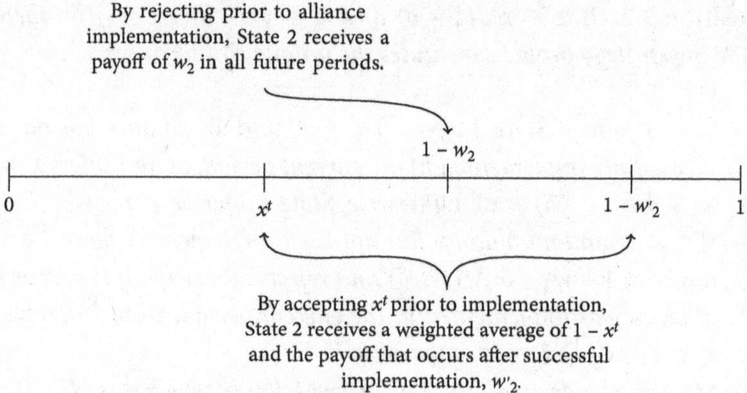

Figure 3.1 Pre-implementation offer in Proposition 3.2.

Note: Figure 3.1 illustrates how State 1 uses generous offers prior to alliance implementation to pacify State 2. By rejecting, State 2 is able to lock in a favorable war payoff, capturing all to the right of $1 - w_2$ in expectation. However, once implementation occurs in a future period, State 2 knows that it will have no choice but to accept less favorable offers, only capturing all to the right of $1 - w_2'$. By making a generous offer x^t, State 1 balances this trade-off, rendering State 2 indifferent in the present between fighting and allowing an alliance to form in the future.

in all future periods, receiving all to the right of the point $1 - w_2$. However, accepting a settlement offer in a pre-implementation period means that States 1 and 3 will have another attempt at implementing the alliance in the following period. If this attempt succeeds, the alliance leads to a shift in bargaining power, and State 2 receives all to the right of $1 - w_2'$ in all future periods.

Following this logic, accepting x^t prior to successful implementation of an alliance carries a significant drawback for State 2: It risks the realization of an alliance in the next period, and the subsequent loss of bargaining power. Accordingly, State 2's expected dynamic utility of accepting x^t in a pre-implementation period is a weighted sum of $1-x^t$ and the payoff of waiting, represented by everything sitting to the right of $1 - w_2'$. As in the figure, this means that x^t must award State 2 more than its pre-implementation war payoff to render it willing to accept.

Thus, State 1's concessions in pre-implementation bargaining create a disincentive for State 2 to launch a preventive strike to block the alliance. If the expected power shift is not too large, these concessions fully compensate State 2 for its expected post-implementation losses and undermine the incentive for a preventive strike. The outcome is peaceful implementation of the alliance.

Table 3.2 Summary of theoretical results

	Result	Description
Chapter 3		
Lemma 8.2	Alliance Gamble	Governments try to implement provocative alliances if expected benefits are large and implementation is speedy.
Proposition 3.2	Peaceful Alliances	Alliances will form peacefully if the resulting power shift is large enough to justify the costs of implementation but not so large that the allies cannot adequately compensate the target for its expected future bargaining loss.

This implies that the dynamic shifts in bargaining power that result from alliance implementation need not encourage aggression. However, this result rests on a critical condition: that the power shift caused by the alliance is not too large. We add a statement summarizing this result to Table 3.2. In the following section, we consider the case in which the alliance results in a more substantial shift in bargaining power.

3.3.2 Dangerous Alliances

If the power shift from an alliance is sufficiently large, careful bargaining may not be enough to stop State 2 from launching a preventive strike to block the alliance. In spite of this, the alliance members will still choose to offer/join the alliance. Hence, under some conditions, alliance members will knowingly attempt to form alliances that increase the probability of war. While the risk of war lurks in the background in this case, war is far from guaranteed. The conditions indicated by our equilibrium analysis suggest why wars provoked by the anticipation of an alliance are rarely observed empirically.

Proposition 3.3 formally states the conditions under which anticipation of an alliance provokes war.

Proposition 3.3. *If $a \leq r\Delta/(1-\delta)$ and $\Delta > (1-\delta)(1-w_2)/\delta r$, then all equilibria are equivalent in outcome distribution to the equilibrium in which players use the following strategies:*

- *State 1 joins an alliance after State 3 invites in every period in which $s^t = N$. State 1 offers $x^t = 0$ in every period in which $s^t = N$ and* *an alliance has not been implemented. Otherwise, State 1 offers* $x^t = 1 - w_2'$.

- *If* $s^t = N$ *and an alliance was not implemented in the current period, State 2 rejects all offers* x^t. *Otherwise, State 2 accepts* x^t *if and only if* $x^t \leq 1 - w_2'$.
- *State 3 extends an alliance in every period in which* $s^t = N$.

Why would States 1 and 3 attempt to implement an alliance that they know will risk war? A key feature of State 2's equilibrium strategy is that it only attacks if it has a window of opportunity to strike before the alliance is implemented. Even if the conditions for a dynamic commitment problem are met, war is not guaranteed, because there will be no war if this window closes quickly enough. In this equilibrium, the formation of an alliance is a rational gamble, with the benefit of alliance weighed against the risk of provoking a preventive war.

How do the potential allies weigh these risks and benefits? Two factors are key. First, if the alliance can be implemented rapidly enough, then the probability of a preventive strike from State 2 is low. Second, the larger the power shift from the alliance, the more valuable its long-term bargaining benefits. The risk of trying to implement the dangerous alliance is worthwhile if it is likely to be successful and the payoffs are high. In this case, States 1 and 3 gamble on the possibility of bringing the alliance into force before a preventive strike can block it. Understanding how potential allies evaluate this risk–reward trade-off is key to our explanation of the rarity of wars provoked by the anticipation of an alliance. As a prerequisite for this discussion in the section that follows, we complete our equilibrium analysis by outlining specifically how the equilibrium probability of war reacts to changes in these two factors.

Propositions 3.2 and 3.3 indicate that the risk of provocation depends on the size of the power shift Δ. In particular, war occurs if

$$\Delta > \frac{(1-\delta)(1-w_2)}{\delta r} \equiv \Delta^*, \tag{3.1}$$

and otherwise the alliance comes into force peacefully as in Proposition 3.2. Equivalently, this condition can be stated in terms of r:

$$r > \frac{(1-\delta)(1-w_2)}{\delta \Delta} \equiv r^*. \tag{3.2}$$

Table 3.3 Summary of theoretical results

	Result	Description
Chapter 3		
Lemma 8.2	Alliance Gamble	Governments try to implement provocative alliances if expected benefits are large and implementation is speedy.
Proposition 3.2	Peaceful Alliances	Alliances will form peacefully if the resulting power shift is large enough to justify the costs of implementation but not so large that the allies cannot adequately compensate the target for its expected future bargaining loss.
Proposition 3.3 (a)	Dangerous Alliances: Power Shift	Targets launch preventive attacks if the resulting power shift is so large that the allies cannot adequately compensate the target for its expected future bargaining loss.
Proposition 3.3 (b)	Dangerous Alliances: Implementation Speed	Higher implementation speeds are more provocative but also more likely to be implemented before a preventive attack can occur.

Inequalities 3.1 and 3.2 indicate the size and speed (respectively) of the power shift resulting from an alliance as key to whether war occurs. These factors are familiar to scholars of conflict, operating to shape the prospects for peace across a variety of contexts (Powell, 2004). We state these results informally in the table that collects a running summary of our theoretical results (Table 3.3).

We next explain how these two factors affect the likelihood that the target will use violence to prevent an alliance. The following two formal results show how the size of the power shift and the speed of implementation determine the equilibrium probability of war.

Proposition 3.4. *Suppose that $a \leq r\Delta/(1 - \delta)$. The equilibrium probability of war is*

- *0 if $\Delta \leq \Delta^*$*
- *$1 - r$ otherwise.*

All else equal, as the size of the power shift from alliance formation grows, war becomes more likely. This follows from a comparison of Propositions 3.2 and 3.3. If an alliance causes a relatively minor shift in the balance of power, bargaining may allow the alliance to come into force peacefully. However, as the alliance causes a larger shift, concessions may be insufficient to pacify State 2. In this case, peace only occurs if States 1 and 3 are able to bring the alliance into force before State 2 can fight, which occurs with probability r.

Less straightforward is the relationship between the speed of the alliance's arrival and the equilibrium probability of war. An increase in r leads to two countervailing effects in equilibrium. On the one hand, as inequality 3.2 suggests, increasing implementation speed may induce a commitment problem and lead to war where peace would have been obtained otherwise. On the other hand, an increase in the speed of an alliance's arrival means that implementation is more likely to succeed quickly, closing the window of opportunity before a preventive strike can occur. How do these competing effects interact?

Proposition 3.5. *Suppose that* $a \leq r\Delta/(1 - \delta)$. *The equilibrium probability of war is*

- 0 *if* $r \leq r^*$
- $1 - r$ *otherwise.*

First, note that whether war occurs at all depends upon the crucial value of r indicated by inequality 3.2. Below this level, bargaining incentives allow an alliance to materialize peacefully in equilibrium. As r rises above it, the equilibrium probability of war jumps from 0 to a strictly positive value. But as r continues to increase, the equilibrium probability of war begins to decrease, reaching 0 in the limit as $r \to 1$.

This nonmonotonic relationship arises because when r is high, the creation of an alliance represents a rational gamble. If immediate implementation fails, State 2 exploits the resulting window of opportunity to launch a preventive strike to block States 1 and 3 from reaping the benefits of the alliance in a future period. If implementation succeeds immediately, State 2 has no choice but to peacefully adjust to the new reality that its bargaining position has been undermined.

Because of this, under the strategies in Proposition 3.3, the probability of delay in the implementation of an alliance, $1 - r$, mirrors the equilibrium probability of war. Equilibrium behavior introduces an endogenous correlation between the speed of alliance implementation and peace. Delay in implementation represents a window of opportunity for State 2 to attack and block a future alliance. In line with Proposition 3.3, if the resulting shift in bargaining power is large, seizing this opportunity is irresistible. As a result, war follows failed implementation in this case. We summarize both of these results about the probability of war in Table 3.4.

Table 3.4 Summary of theoretical results

	Result	**Description**
Chapter 3		
Lemma 8.2	Alliance Gamble	Governments try to implement provocative alliances if expected benefits are large and implementation is speedy.
Proposition 3.2	Peaceful Alliances	Alliances will form peacefully if the resulting power shift is large enough to justify the costs of implementation but not so large that the allies cannot adequately compensate the target for its expected future bargaining loss.
Proposition 3.3 (a)	Dangerous Alliances: Power Shift	Targets launch preventive attacks if the resulting power shift is so large that the allies cannot adequately compensate the target for its expected future bargaining loss.
Proposition 3.3 (b)	Dangerous Alliances: Implementation Speed	Higher implementation speeds are more provocative but also more likely to be implemented before a preventive attack can occur.
Proposition 3.4 (a)	Probability of War: Power Shift	The probability of war jumps at the point that the anticipated power shift is so large that the target cannot be peacefully compensated and then further increases in the size of the power shift.
Proposition 3.5 (b)	Probability of War: Implementation Speed	The probability of war jumps at the point that the target cannot be peacefully compensated, then decreases as implementation speed further increases because implementation is increasingly likely to be finalized before an attack can occur.

3.4 Comparing Peaceful and Dangerous Alliances

Our dynamic theory of alliance formation and provocation answers several questions. First, when will prospective partners decide to join an alliance? We offer a simple and intuitive explanation that helps us ultimately understand a more complicated question: Why would potential partners try to implement an alliance that they know may provoke war from an enemy? Second, we ask: When do targeted states perceive alliances as provocative? Answering this question allows us to understand why some alliances are implemented peacefully, however long it takes, while others trigger aggressive military actions by the target. We isolate two main factors that explain this variation: the size of the expected power shift from the alliance, and the speed of implementation. We then address a third question: If a target perceives an alliance as provocative, will the target always resort to armed conflict to try to stop it? The short answer to this question is a predictable "no." However, there is a counterintuitive reason. Targets often would like to attack to block the most provocative alliances, but the more provocative alliances are those that will be implemented quickly. This countervailing effect means that the most provocative alliances are also the most likely to be successfully implemented quickly, achieving deterrence before the target has a chance to attack.

We begin by discussing the first question. Under what conditions do prospective partners decide to try to form an alliance? The simple answer is that countries join together to embark on a path of military cooperation when the benefits outweigh the costs. This is not, however, a trivial calculation, because the process of forming an alliance is long and risky. Thus, deciding whether to try it entails looking into the future and weighing the anticipated benefits against the short-term implementation costs. Prospective allies do not benefit from the alliance until it has been implemented and the benefits from the power shift have been fully realized in warfighting or peacetime bargaining. The larger the power shift and the faster an alliance can be implemented and those benefits realized, the more the interested countries will be willing to pay the costs of implementation. So, prospective allies will try to form an alliance when the implementation costs are low relative to the size of the future power shift and the speed of implementation. Alliance seekers are willing to pay more for implementation the greater the benefits from the future power shift and the faster those benefits can be realized.

Once prospective partners decide to begin to implement an alliance, that alliance may provoke the target to respond with aggression, or it may be implemented peacefully without an attack. We highlight the size of the future power shift and the speed of implementation as the two main factors that determine whether an alliance is perceived as provocative. As the size of the future power shift grows, the target understandably expects to fare worse in a potential war against the allies. This expectation translates into less peacetime bargaining clout for the target after the alliance is fully implemented. Therefore, the larger the expected power shift and the sooner it will be realized, the worse off the target expects to be. When the expected power shift is above a certain threshold, the target may begin to consider using force to stop the alliance and the power shift.

However, all hope is not lost for the prospective allies. During the implementation window, before the alliance is fully implemented, allies and the target can bargain with each other. If the power shift is not too large and the implementation not too rapid, the allies can offer compensation to the target in the short term that just induces the target not to start a war. In other words, if the future world in which there is an enemy alliance does not look too bleak for the target, then the allies may be able to "buy off" the target with short-term concessions so that the target will allow the alliance to come into being.

On the other hand, if the expected power shift is too large and it is expected to be realized too quickly, there may not be sufficient compensation available to offset the losses the target expects from the power shift. Under these circumstances, the target perceives the impending alliance as provocative in that it threatens the target's ability to secure future political and military benefits. The target then may try to attack to stop the alliance.

Figure 3.2 depicts this intuition graphically. If the speed of implementation is so slow that it isn't worth the costs of implementation for the allies, then they will have no interest in the alliance, and they will not pursue it (*far left*). However, if the speed of implementation is reasonably high, then the allies will decide to try to implement the alliance no matter what. Whether it is implemented peacefully depends on both the speed of implementation and the size of the future power shift.

The bottom-right corner of the figure represents the region in which implementation is speedy enough to bring the reality of an impending and disadvantageous power shift to the fore for the target. However, in this region, the power shift is not large enough to provoke the target into

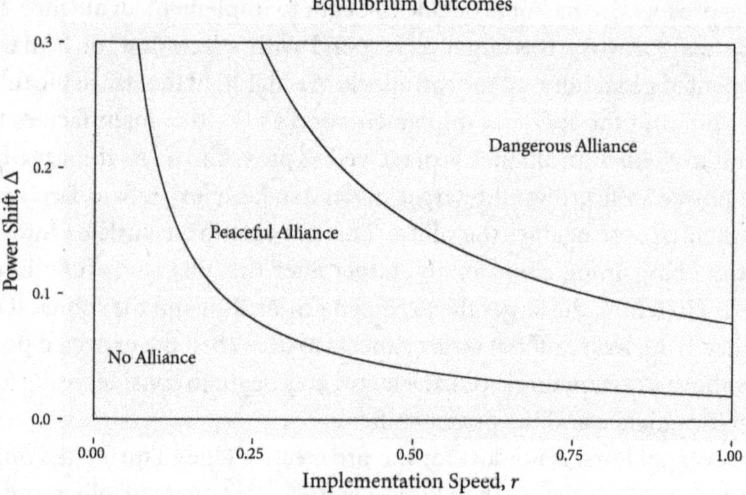

Figure 3.2 This figure presents equilibrium outcomes as a function of the size of the power shift, $\Delta = w_2 - w_2'$, along the y-axis and the speed of implementation, r, along the x-axis. The figure was generated using the parameter values: $w_1 = 0.35$, $w_2 = 0.3$, $\delta = 0.9$, and $a = 0.2$. For low values of these parameters, corresponding to the bottom-left of the figure, no alliance is pursued and peace prevails. For middling values, in the central portion of the figure, an alliance comes into force peacefully in equilibrium. For large values, in the upper-right corner of the figure, the alliance provokes preventive attack and war occurs with positive probability in equilibrium.

aggressive action to prevent the alliance. Why? The key to peaceful implementation in this region, when the expected power shift is large but not too large, consists in the generosity of concessions by prospective allies to the target before the power shift occurs. In the short term, allies can compensate the target beyond what the target could expect to get from fighting. The amount of additional short-term compensation depends on the size and speed of the expected power shift. The faster the implementation and the bigger the power shift, the more allies will be willing to concede for the purpose of placating the target. In 1990, NATO allies compensated Russia to allay its concerns about allowing a unified Germany into NATO. In the first Taiwan Strait crisis, John Foster Dulles and Chiang Kai-shek conceded several offshore islands to Mao Zedong in the lead-up to the signing of the US–ROC defense pact. We discuss each of these cases in detail in later chapters.

What happens when the expected power shift is so large that no amount of short-term compensation can appease the target? Then the attempt to implement an alliance becomes provocative. The region in the top right of Figure 3.2 represents this theoretical expectation. If the expected power shift from the alliance is large enough, the target will expect to fare significantly worse in the future if a war breaks out. The allies' combined wartime strength will be greater, and that clout will enable them to resist threats from the target. They will concede less to the target's demands. They might even use their clout to extract greater concessions from the target. And thus, anticipating a shift of power so large that it will produce political and military circumstances that are even more undesirable than a war, the target will try to use military aggression to block the alliance before the power shift can become a reality. In Figure 3.2, the downward-sloping curve separating provocative from peaceful alliances reflects the fact that the size and speed of the alliance interact to determine whether it is provocative. The larger the power shift and/or the faster the implementation, the more provocative the alliance.

Does a provocative alliance guarantee preventive military conflict? In answering this question, our theory offers a novel subtlety about the relationship between the speed of implementation and the probability of war. We have seen that alliances are more provocative the faster they can be implemented. Whether a target attacks to block an alliance depends on whether it can do so before the alliance is implemented. The target would like to use its military to stop any alliance that it considers provocative. The faster the implementation, the more the target will want to use its military to stop it—but also, the less chance the target will have to stop it before it is implemented. In other words, the more provocative the alliance is because of its implementation speed, the less likely it is that there will be war over the alliance.

Figure 3.3 illustrates this relationship between the speed of implementation and the probability of war. The x-axis represents the speed of implementation; the y-axis represents the probability of war and the probability of implementation. The black line is the probability of implementation, and the gray line is the probability of war. Below $\bar{r}$ both are zero, because if the implementation is slow enough then the prospective allies will decide that it is not worth the cost.[6]

[6] Note that the value $\bar{r}$ is simply the condition from Proposition 3.1 stated in terms of r, so $\bar{r} = a\Delta/(1 - \delta)$.

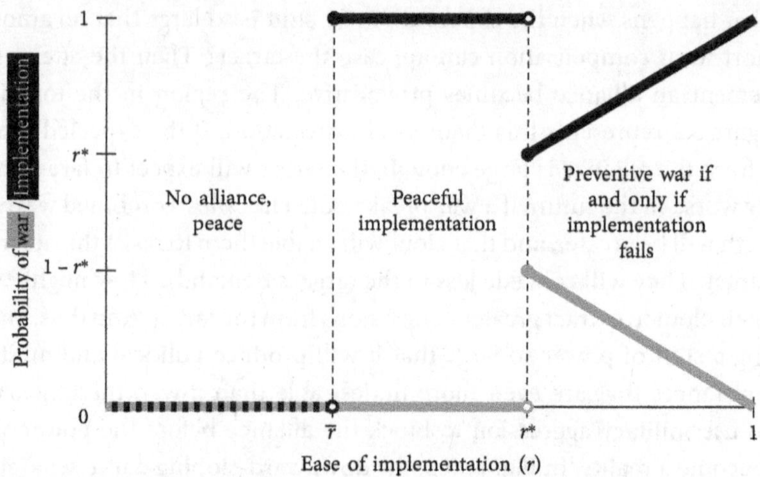

Figure 3.3 Equilibrium probability of war and implementation. For low values of these parameters, corresponding to the bottom-left-hand of the figure, no alliance is pursued and peace prevails. For middling values, in the central portion of the figure, an alliance comes into force peacefully in equilibrium. For large values, in the upper-right corner of the figure, the alliance provokes preventive attack and war occurs with positive probability in equilibrium.

Note: Figure 3.3 illustrates the equilibrium relationship between alliances and war. If $r < \bar{r}$, an alliance is too difficult to implement. The resulting stability of bargaining power ensures peace. If $r > r^*$, then attempts to implement an alliance represent a costly but rational gamble. Success leads to peace and a favorable bargaining position; failure leads to preventive war. If $\bar{r} < r < r^*$, then the ease of implementation lies in a "sweet spot." The alliance is attractive, but is not sufficiently threatening to induce war. In this range, the alliance is implemented along the path of play over rounds of repeated peaceful bargaining.

As the speed of implementation increases above $\bar{r}$, allies will decide to try to implement, and for small enough anticipated power shifts, the target will allow this. Thus, the probability of war is zero, and implementation is guaranteed. Alliances are provocative when the implementation speed is slower than a given value, r^*, for fixed sizes of the power shift. In the region to the right of r^*, the probability of war is nonzero but so is the probability of implementation. That is, alliances are perceived as provocative, but sometimes the target will be able to attack before the alliance is implemented; sometimes it will not. As implementation speed increases, the probability that the target can attack before the alliance is implemented goes down. Therefore, many of the most provocative alliances form peacefully, because targets are not in a position to use military force to stop the alliance from developing.

Even though the probability of war decreases in implementation speed, which suggests that many provocative alliances do not result in preventive war, according to our theory the use of war to stop an alliance is nevertheless possible—and, as we show in the next chapter, it does occasionally happen in the real world. Given the risk of attempting to implement a powerful alliance, why would prospective partners even try it? When the potential power shift is too large, they can prevent war altogether by not even trying to join forces. Yet, allies may go for it anyway.

Our theory highlights the logic of such risky decisions. Trying to implement a provocative alliance amounts to a rational gamble. Because the probability of war depends on how fast the alliance can be implemented, potential partners must weigh the upsides of implementing quickly enough and receiving the future benefits of the power shift against the downsides of the target beating them to the punch and attacking before implementation is complete. When the power shift is sizable enough and the speed fast enough, allies will calculate that trying to form the alliance is worthwhile, despite the risk.

3.5 Defensive Alliances

Our baseline model abstracted away from the conditional, defensive nature of many alliances. We now examine defensive alliances to determine whether the formation of security agreements that are designed to protect the status quo can nevertheless provoke preventive war. Because defensive alliances only require that members come to one another's support if a shared enemy attempts coercion, they do not allow members to exploit the gains of military cooperation in coercive bargaining. Do the preventive-war results of our baseline theory hold up under a specification in which the alliance gives State 1 more power only if State 2 initiates coercion? If these results hold even with the formation of a defensive alliance, then our theory has broad application to many, if not most, alliances formed throughout history.

We extend the model such that State 2 begins the game by choosing either to provoke a crisis and enter into coercive bargaining with State 1 or to maintain the status quo. If State 2 maintains the status quo, then the game ends with players receiving their status quo payoffs in all future periods. However, if State 2 attempts coercion to revise the status quo, then it enters into coercive bargaining with State 1, and States 1 and 3 may attempt to form a defensive alliance in response to this aggression, as in the baseline model. This captures the idea that a defensive alliance only benefits State 1 if State

2 initiates coercion, and that State 2 can maintain a favorable status quo by abstaining from coercion in the first place. In this extension, conditions exist under which State 2 still initiates a crisis that results in a preventive strike to block the formation of the alliance.

Why might a defensive alliance provoke aggression from State 2? As in the baseline model, the strategic logic centers on State 2's expectations about the future. If State 2 is dissatisfied with the status quo, it faces a dilemma. On the one hand, engaging in coercive bargaining may allow it to favorably revise the status quo. On the other hand, it risks prompting States 1 and 3 to form a defensive alliance. If such an alliance forms, State 2's ability to favorably revise the status quo through coercion is significantly weakened. For this reason, if State 2 is dissatisfied with the status quo, it may attack to revise the status quo before States 1 and 3 can coordinate defensively to effectively resist. Hence, if State 2 wishes to revise the status quo in the future, then the qualitative results of our analysis hold for the defensive alliance extension.

Formally, we extend the model as follows. At the outset of the game, the issue under dispute by States 1 and 2 has a status quo outcome, $q \in [0, 1]$. Prior to period $t = 1$, State 2 chooses whether to engage in coercive bargaining with State 1. If the choice is no, then the status quo prevails in all future periods, with States 1 and 3 receiving per-period payoffs of q and State 2 receiving a per-period payoff of $1 - q$. If State 2 does choose to enter into coercive bargaining, then the players begin play as in the baseline model discussed in the previous section.[7]

First, note that if we consider this extension without the possibility of an alliance (i.e., removing State 3 from the model), peace always obtains. To see why, first note that standard arguments for repeated bargaining models can be applied to show that if no alliance is possible and State 2 chooses to revise the status quo, State 1 will offer $x = 1 - w_2$, and State 2 will accept this on the path of play. This is because without the possibility of alliance, the distribution of power is fixed, and so if State 2 attempts to revise the status quo, the distribution of benefits reflects the distribution of power. Therefore, two outcomes are possible in equilibrium when there is no alliance. If $q \leq 1 - w_2$, then State 2 prefers the status quo to the outcome of coercive bargaining, and so State 2 does not use coercion, rather maintaining the status quo. If $q > 1 - w_2$, then State 2 anticipates that it can revise the status quo favorably by

[7] The bargaining protocol does not affect our results. We have also solved a version of the model in which State 2 makes offers to State 1, and the qualitative results are unchanged.

engaging in coercive bargaining with State 1, resulting in peaceful bargaining as described above. Importantly, both outcomes are peaceful.

With the possibility of a defensive alliance, however, war can result. The following result provides the formal argument for preventive war.

Proposition 3.6. *In the defensive alliance extension, an equilibrium in which State 2 engages in coercive bargaining and initiates a preventive war with positive probability on the path of play exists if (1)* $q \geq 1 - w_2 + r\Delta$ *and (2)* $\Delta > (1 - \delta)(1 - w_2)/\delta r$.

This formal result shows that the same provocative finding in the baseline model is also at work with defensive alliances. The condition on the effect of the size of the power shift on preventive war is identical to the condition in Proposition 3.3 (in the baseline model) demonstrating that defensive alliances may indeed provoke preventive wars when the anticipated power shift is sufficiently large.

What is the intuition for provocation when states seek an alliance designed to deter conflict and to preserve the status quo? The key is the effect of a defensive alliance on a revisionist target's *future* ambitions. If q is high, then the status quo favors the allies and disadvantages the target. Typically, this is precisely the circumstance that motivates a defensive alliance: to protect a territorial possession or a status quo policy from a revisionist enemy. The second condition in Proposition 3.6 states the condition for a revisionist target: If q is sufficiently high, the target will try to change the status quo in a favorable direction.

How might the target go about revising the status quo? If it can be done through bargaining, then it would prefer that, either now or in the future. Waiting is unappealing if the allies will successfully implement a defensive alliance. Then both of them will have greater bargaining strength, which the target knows will reduce its ability to alter the status quo in the future.

The target's other option is to engage in bargaining in the present, before an alliance is implemented. However, all actors know that any concessions made in short-term bargaining are only temporary. Attempts by the target to change the status quo while the other states are implementing an alliance will likely be defended and restored by the allies once their forces are ready. Allies may offer short-term compensation to try to induce the target to accede to the alliance. These concessions, however, may only be consumed in the present, because they will stop as soon as the alliance is formed. As merely temporary payments, such concessions do not result in lasting changes to the status quo.

If the anticipated power shift is big enough, then short-term payments cannot satisfy the revisionist target. When this happens, the target will attack to try to prevent the alliance from being implemented. With sufficiently large defensive alliances, revisionist targets expect never to be able to take what they want in the future. In the present, the most they can expect is a temporary payoff to stay peaceful. If this is not enough, then attacking becomes a more attractive option. Thus, defensive alliances can provoke revisionist targets to launch preventive wars if the anticipated power shift is large and if the target is sufficiently revisionist. We add this result to Table 3.5.

3.6 Conclusion

This chapter develops a theory of alliance implementation, power shifts, and preventive war. We have demonstrated that the anticipation of a sufficiently powerful military alliance can trigger a preventive attack. This finding holds even with defensive alliances. Several additional results follow from our theoretical analysis, including predictions about conditions for peaceful implementation of alliances and the probability that preventive wars will break out when alliances are being formed. Table 3.5 summarizes all the main findings demonstrated in this chapter.

Our baseline theory in this chapter serves as a foundation for the motivations and incentives in the dynamic process of alliance formation. Several questions remain. Our baseline theory may be extended in various ways to address these questions. First, what does a war to prevent an alliance look like? Second, when designing an alliance, can allies manipulate its content to avoid preventive wars? Third, can enemies negotiate to prevent or allow alliances?

In answering the first question, we investigate the types of aggressive actions targets take to try to prevent alliances from being implemented. Sometimes targets use small-scale acts of aggression and limited attacks that risk failing to block an alliance. At other times, they launch large-scale wars as a way of both blocking alliances and resolving disputed issues once and for all. We take on the question of why targets use different types of preventive action in the next chapter.

Table 3.5 Summary of theoretical results

	Result	Description
Chapter 3		
Lemma 8.2	Alliance Gamble	Governments try to implement provocative alliances if expected benefits are large and implementation is speedy.
Proposition 3.2	Peaceful Alliances	Alliances will form peacefully if the resulting power shift is large enough to justify the costs of implementation but not so large that the allies cannot adequately compensate the target for its expected future bargaining loss.
Proposition 3.3	Dangerous Alliances: Power Shift	Targets launch preventive attacks if the resulting power shift is so large that the allies cannot adequately compensate the target for its expected future bargaining loss.
Proposition 3.3	Dangerous Alliances: Implementation Speed	Higher implementation speeds are more provocative but also more likely to be implemented before a preventive attack can occur.
Proposition 3.4	Probability of War: Power Shift	The probability of war jumps at the point that the anticipated power shift is so large that the target cannot be peacefully compensated and then further increases in the size of the power shift.
Proposition 3.5	Probability of War: Implementation Speed	The probability of war jumps at the point that the target cannot be peacefully compensated, then decreases as implementation speed further increases because implementation is increasingly likely to be finalized before an attack can occur.
Proposition 3.6	Defensive Alliances	Impending defensive alliances provoke preventive war if the anticipated power shift is sufficiently large and the target is sufficiently dissatisfied with the status quo.

The second question addresses various strategies that countries might take to manipulate the content of alliances to avoid preventive wars. Prospective allies have a great deal of control over both the size of the power shift from an alliance and the speed of its implementation. They might also have incentives to eliminate the implementation stage by keeping the formation of an alliance secret. Do states deliberately control the design of alliances specifically to reduce the risk that they will lead to a preventive war before the alliance can be implemented? We address this question in Chapter 5.

The third question is related to negotiations between enemies. Before an alliance is formed, do the potential partners have incentives to negotiate with targets of the alliance either to prevent or to permit the alliance? In Chapter 6, we extend our baseline theory to cover this.

4

Provocation and Preventive War

In January 1894, a peasant uprising in Korea set off a chain of events that would spark the First Sino-Japanese War. The Japanese responded with force, and their navy soon clashed with a Qing naval vessel heading to Korea to intervene on behalf of the Korean state. The ensuing conflict, which lasted over eight months, resulted in more than 50,000 casualties (Jowett 2013). The immediate catalyst that triggered Japan's aggression was a peasant rebellion opposing Japanese influence (Paine 2002, 113). However, the deeper cause lay in the long-standing rivalry between Japan and the Qing dynasty in China over dominance in Korea. The Qing had long held sway in the region, and Japan, concerned about losing its foothold, was alarmed when 3,000 Qing troops were sent to Korea to restore order during the uprising (Paine 2017, 18–19). This deployment signaled a potential peak of Qing influence in Korea in the latter half of the nineteenth century.

The strengthening of Qing influence had set the stage for the implementation of a security partnership between Korea and the Qing dynasty. Over the years, Qing political and military influence had grown significantly. So strong was their political influence that one diplomat wrote in 1882 that the Qing "regarded [Korea] as part of the empire and dispatched troops" (Paine 2002, 55). Later, another Qing diplomat claimed to be effectively "the king" of the Korean region he managed (Paine 2002, 65). Military influence had also expanded. Korea had accepted Qing assistance to handle peasant rebellions as early as 1882, including aiding with training, military planning, financial aid, and constructing munitions factories (Larsen 2020, 95). The growing partnership between Korea and the Qing, coupled with Japan's corresponding desire to curb this influence, prompted Japan's intervention (Paine 2017, 16), as understood by academia (Buzo 2022, 32).[1]

This context aligns with our theory on preventive war, which emphasizes the provocative potential of impending alliances. In this chapter, we delve

[1] We credit George Boardman, an undergraduate researcher in our research lab, for discovering and conducting research on this case.

The Window Before. Brett V. Benson and Bradley C. Smith, Oxford University Press.
 DOI: 10.1093/9780197806760.003.0004

deeper into this theory, illustrating that the First Sino-Japanese War is not an isolated example. We examine several additional cases where countries initiated military actions to prevent the formation of rival alliances. The historical evidence from these cases supports our theory's core mechanism: The anticipation of being disadvantaged by a new alliance drives the target state to use military force to block the alliance's formation.

Despite a historical pattern of targeted states launching preemptive attacks, the cases examined vary in significant ways, leading to two key insights. First, there is variation in the scale of preventive attacks. In some instances, attacks were limited to small skirmishes, while in others, they escalated into full-scale wars. Second, the success of these military actions in preventing alliances varied. In two cases, the attacks successfully thwarted the formation of enemy alliances, but in a third case, the alliance formed despite the aggression. These variations raise the questions: What accounts for the difference in scale of attacks, and why do states undertake these risky and costly attacks when there is a substantial chance of failure? This chapter expands upon our theory to address these variations in the scale of attacks and their success in preventing alliances.

We analyze three illustrative cases: Russia's 2008 attack on Georgia, the People's Republic of China's (PRC) 1954–55 strikes on Chinese Nationalist-held islands in the Taiwan Strait, and Russia's 2014 and 2022 invasions of Ukraine. Each case involved attempts to halt the formation of an impending alliance but differed greatly in scale. In the Taiwan Strait Crisis, the PRC conducted limited attacks on small islands. In contrast, Russia's 2008 attack on Georgia, aimed at blocking Georgia's NATO ambitions, was a short conflict lasting five days with approximately 300 casualties. More recently, Russia's incursions into Ukraine—initially limited in 2014 with Crimea's annexation and the Donbas conflict—escalated into a full-scale invasion in February 2022, with devastating consequences. These cases highlight significant variation in the scale and effectiveness of attacks intended to prevent alliances.

In addition to variation in the scope of preventive actions, the historical record points to variation in their effectiveness. The 2008 Russo-Georgia War successfully blocked Georgian accession to NATO. To this day, Georgia is not counted among the NATO member states. However, armed conflict is not guaranteed to stop an alliance—it might fail. In spite of the knowledge that such wars are costly and risky, states targeted by alliances sometimes fight anyway. For example, in 1954, the PRC launched a limited war on several islands in the Taiwan Strait to discourage the United States from implementing an alliance with the Chinese Nationalists on Taiwan. But the attempt failed; within months, the US and the Chinese Nationalists had formed a mutual defense treaty. Many scholars have blamed the attack for *motivating* the alliance. Are such failed attacks a product of miscalculation? We expand our theory to account for the risk that conflict might not succeed in blocking an alliance. Instead of seeing this as a miscalculation, we show that targets may knowingly risk failure and yet choose to attack anyway. This extends the logic of rational gambles discussed in the previous chapter to the behavior and incentives of states targeted by alliances.

In what follows, we expand our theory to account for these two sources of variation. We analyze an extension of the model that allows targets of alliances to choose small-scale attacks rather than full-scale war. In our baseline model in the previous chapter, war has two features: It blocks an impending alliance, and, as in most formal models, it determines the winner of the disputed political issue. In this chapter's extension, full-scale war has the same attributes, but small-scale attacks are different. They are modeled as costly actions that may block an alliance with some probability, but that do not end the game with a resolution of the political issue. This setup captures realistic features of small-scale attacks in real-world preventive wars. Typically, aggressors launch such limited attacks with the purpose of discouraging an alliance, but the scale of war is not expansive enough to settle the larger underlying dispute between enemies.

How large-scale wars block alliances is straightforward. A successful full-scale war often results in victory by the aggressor over territory and/or sovereignty, which then automatically prevents that territory from being included in an enemy alliance. For example, if, hypothetically speaking, Russia in 2008 fought and won an all-out war with Georgia that resulted in a Russian takeover, then NATO membership for Georgia would have become a moot point. In the 1954–55 Taiwan Strait Crisis, if, rather than attacking the small offshore islands, Mao Zedong had launched a successful full-scale amphibious assault on Taiwan itself and put an end to Chiang Kai-shek's government, then the idea of a US–ROC alliance would have died with the demise of the Republic of China (ROC).

The mechanism of the effect of a small-scale attack on an alliance is more subtle, because in such cases the aggressor typically does not attack with the intention of eliminating the opponent and thereby enabling itself to unilaterally settle the underlying disputed issue. Rather, in these limited wars, the target's goal is to block the alliance and thus keep alive the possibility of bargaining over the disputed issue on favorable terms. As we will see, small-scale attacks such as those in the 2008 Russo-Georgia conflict, the initial 2014 attack of Ukraine, and the 1954–55 Taiwan Strait Crisis interfere with the implementation phase of the alliance by raising the specter of a larger war before the would-be allies are prepared to fight together, as allies. The target state must then decide whether to bargain or fight without an alliance, and either way, their payoffs do not include the benefits from an alliance. Or, they may accelerate implementation with the hope that the alliance might be put into force before conflict escalates. Our modeling extension captures this intuition by modeling the small-scale option as a probabilistic lottery, which affects the process of implementation but does not aim to eliminate the opponent as a large-scale war would. That is, these small-scale attacks aim to arrest the alliance directly, allowing the target and potential allies to continue bargaining.

This simple but intuitive extension yields both expected and novel results. Intuitively, we discover that targets of alliances will aim to minimize costs while blocking an impending alliance. Accordingly, they will opt for limited skirmishes if the cost of such an action is small relative to the probability that it blocks the alliance. We find that this cost–benefit trade-off depends crucially on the speed of implementation of an alliance, as well as how large a power shift the alliance will cause if it is successfully implemented. What makes preventive limited conflict attractive is that such attacks can be very inexpensive and, in return, the blocking strategy introduces a new lottery over the existing probability that an alliance is successfully implemented. This creates additional friction for the alliance implementation process, lowering the probability that it successfully comes into force in equilibrium. Simply put, if the cost of a small-scale attack is low enough, gambling on it may be preferable to choosing a costlier, full-scale war.

In addition to this intuitive cost–benefit trade-off, our results reveal a novel trade-off that arises when states may choose between small- and large-scale attacks. Interestingly, the availability of small-scale military action may increase or decrease the level of conflict prompted by an impending alliance in comparison to our baseline model, depending on the circumstances. On the one hand, if small-scale blocking is cheap enough, then targets might use this violent option even when, without the small-scale option, alliances *would be implemented peacefully*. Because the blocking strategy decreases the chances of successful implementation, targets may gamble on cheap blocking attacks instead of bargaining to allow alliances to form peacefully. The option of limited attacks expands the possibility that armed conflict might occur when standard bargaining models otherwise predict peace. This novel finding improves our theoretical understanding of states' incentives for fighting limited wars, and it greatly advances our interpretation of real-world contexts in which states seek to block alliances using violence at such a small scale that the attacks seem wasteful and without purpose.

On the other hand, we find that small-scale attacks might be used as an alternative to full-scale war. If the anticipated power shift is large enough and/or the speed of implementation is fast enough that a full-scale preventive war would be triggered, then the target can also use a small-scale blocking strategy instead. This result holds up to a point. The greater the expected power shift, the less willing a target will be to use a small conflict with limited scope and the more likely it is to opt for a bigger war that has a better chance of successfully blocking the alliance and locking in the pre-implementation distribution of power. When the power shift is large enough, then the target just prefers to launch a large-scale war to resolve the entire political issue once and for all.

In addition to these findings, our theoretical analysis offers insight about how we should interpret historical cases of failed attempts to block alliances. Importantly, these failed attempts are not necessarily the result of a miscalculation. Military action might only successfully block an alliance with some probability, and targets may knowingly take this risk anyway. Our model suggests that attacks to stop alliances are best understood as rational gambles. Thus, in real-world contexts, if the cost of a limited attack is low enough, then a target may try one even if it is far from guaranteed to stop the alliance. Indeed, prospective allies may very well respond to small-scale preventive attacks by trying to hasten the speed of implementation, rather than calling it off. Without the benefit of the analysis that we provide here, assessments of limited attacks in real-world situations may (understandably) mistakenly point to the target's attacks as causing the enemy alliance.

Our analysis provides an alternative explanation. The anticipation of an alliance portends an undesirable power shift for the target of the alliance. And the target has options for how to forestall this. It may launch a full-scale war to outright win the political dispute and block the alliance, or it may allow the alliance to form peacefully and then deal with the negative consequences of the power shift in future bargaining. A third option is that it may pay a significantly lower cost to try to make implementation of the alliance much harder. If the small-scale attempt is successful, then the target receives the enormous benefit of bargaining indefinitely with an unallied enemy. And if it fails, it might not have been very expensive, especially relative to the cost of living with a fully implemented enemy alliance or launching a full-scale war.

In this chapter, we lay out these results formally. We then provide an in-depth, nontechnical explanation of these theoretical results. Following the full description of the theoretical results, we provide some quantitative evidence in support of the main result of our theory: that alliances are most dangerous just before they are signed. We use data on historical alliances and militarized disputes to show that the probability that a member of an alliance is targeted by military force is highest in the year before the official signing date of the alliance compared to all other years in a 10-year window before and after signing.

After discussing the quantitative evidence, we lay out three detailed case studies: the 2008 Russo-Georgian War, the 1954–55 Taiwan Strait Crisis, and the 2014–22 Russian actions in Ukraine. In discussing these cases, we illustrate the core theoretical mechanism from our theory in the previous chapter, while also providing qualitative empirical evidence for the theoretical extensions examined in this chapter. In all three cases, we show that the instigators of violence have a common motivation for the use of military force. In each case, leaders of countries were motivated to pursue a new alliance targeting another country. The targets of those potential alliances worried enough about the disadvantages of a future power shift that they decided to use armed conflict to try to prevent it. We then go beyond this core result to account for the variation in size of each armed conflict and how effective they were in blocking the impending alliance. We examine the historical details of these cases to show that the theoretical conditions that predict this variation are at play in the historical narratives of each of these cases, and these factors affect the historical decision-makers' incentives as our theory predicts.

4.1 Theory: How States Block Enemy Alliances

We now extend our theory to account for variation in decisions to use limited versus full-scale wars to block the implementation of military alliances. Naturally, such conflicts are not guaranteed to prevent an alliance. The decision to use armed conflict as a preventive instrument involves a natural trade-off. One might invest more to increase the chance of successfully blocking an alliance, or one might choose to conserve costs and accept a greater risk of failing to block it. Leaders of states understand this trade-off and optimize when making decisions about how to interrupt an enemy alliance, sometimes choosing less expensive limited wars with a lower probability of success while at other times going all out with an expensive, large-scale conflict that has a higher chance of stopping the implementation of an alliance.

In this section, we extend Chapter 3's formal model by relaxing the assumption that fighting by State 2 always decisively blocks an alliance. This adjustment enables us to consider why a country might launch a preventive action even if it is not guaranteed to work. To evaluate the trade-off directly, we endogenize the decision to choose a less expensive but less effective preventive war. We analyze a model in which enemies of an impending alliance can choose a very costly war that guarantees failure of the alliance, or a less costly war that might not successfully block the alliance. These modeling extensions highlight an important theoretical insight: Wars to stop alliances are a rational gamble that enemies of the alliance might find to be worthwhile. That is, even knowing that the attempt might fail, enemies of alliances might still choose to try. Going further, enemies might choose limited wars that are less effective, and those wars might in fact fail to stop an alliance. In these situations, war occurs and the alliance materializes, not because the instigator stumbled into a conflict through miscalculation, but because the instigator knew the strategy could fail and still considered it a cost-effective gamble.

4.1.1 Formal Extension and Analysis

In the baseline model, the targeted state has only a very blunt tool with which to stop alliance implementation. With certainty, war prevents the alliance from coming into force, effectively ending the game. While this model was useful for illustrating the connection between alliance formation and commitment problems, it abstracts away from the broader set of tools available to states wishing to stop an alliance. States often take actions short of war to prevent the implementation of alliances forming against them. Readers who wish to skip the formal presentation in favor of a prose description of the results can advance to Section 4.2 without loss.

Throughout, we will refer to such actions as *small-scale attacks*. These are a wide set of actions that states might employ to try to prevent or forestall the implementation of an enemy alliance. One type is the limited military action, such as the 2014 Russian invasion of Crimea. From a theoretical standpoint, blocking actions have three important features that distinguish them from full-scale war, and are thus not present in the baseline model.

First, blocking actions are typically intended to slow or prevent an alliance's implementation without also settling the underlying bargaining issue through force. Indeed, states may take such actions *while still bargaining* with the prospective allies. (This stands in contrast to the baseline model, in which the only tool available to stop an alliance effectively ended the interaction, both preventing the alliance from coming into force and initiating a game-ending war to settle the policy dispute.)

Second, actions short of war are not guaranteed to prevent the alliance, but do so only probabilistically. To incorporate this feature, we model "blocking" as a costly action whose only effect is to prevent (with some probability) the implementation of an alliance. The action does not bring the game to an end, and it does not initiate a costly lottery over the disputed policy.

Third, small-scale attacks are less costly than full-scale wars. The tradeoff is that, unlike full-scale war, they don't always work. This is intuitive and foreshadows the main calculation states face when considering these actions: whether the reduced probability of blocking an alliance is justified by the smaller costs.

To formally incorporate these features into our theory, we extend the model from the previous chapter as follows. (All aspects of the model remain unchanged except for the following components.) In any period in which $s^t = N$ and an alliance has not been implemented in the current period, when State 2 is faced with an offer of x^t, it now has three rather than two choices. As in the baseline model, it may accept x^t or reject. Accept means State 2 accepts State 1's offer to resolve the dispute peacefully. Reject means State 2 refuses the bargaining attempt and full-scale war follows. The payoffs and state transitions following each of these decisions by State 2 are as in the baseline game. But now we allow State 2 a third choice: to take action in an attempt to block the alliance. If State 2 chooses to block in period t, then each player receives their respective policy payoff for x^t. State 2 also pays a cost of blocking, $c > 0$, in the current period. Finally, a decision to block affects the transition of the state. We add a third component, B, to the state space, making it $\Omega = \{A, N, B\}$. B represents State 2 successfully (and permanently) blocking the implementation of the alliance. In a period in which $s^t = B$, play proceeds directly to State 1 making an offer, with State 3 unable to offer an alliance and State 1 unable to join. Further, war payoffs in periods in which $s^t = B$ are w_i for each player i. In a period in which $s^t = N$ and an alliance was not implemented in the current period, if State 2 chooses to block, then $s^{t+1} = B$ with probability b and $s^{t+1} = N$ with probability $1 - b$. The B state is absorbing, such that in any period in which $s^t = B$, $s^{t+1} = b$ with probability 1.[2]

We now turn to the formal analysis of this extended model. Our first result characterizes when an attack of some kind must occur on the equilibrium path of play.

Proposition 4.1. *Consider an equilibrium in which State 3 extends an alliance and State 1 joins on the path of play in every period in which $s^t = N$. If $c < \frac{\delta br\Delta}{1-\delta}$, then State 2 does not accept an offer of x^t on the path of play in any such equilibrium.*

This result characterizes *when* the target will take an action to prevent implementation of an alliance in equilibrium. It paints the trade-off as a straightforward one: If the cost of blocking is low enough, then the target will never simply accept an offer without trying to block an alliance, perhaps through a small-scale attack, in equilibrium. This foreshadows a result that we will discuss in greater detail in the next section: These small-scale attacks may occur under conditions in which peaceful bargaining occurred in the previous chapter's model.

While Proposition 4.1 indicates when some level of fighting will occur, it does not say when a small-scale attack will occur. After all, our goal in this section is to outline the conditions under which states will choose to forgo full-scale, costly wars to pursue less costly means of preventing an alliance's formation. The following result shows that if the low-cost condition in the previous result holds, small-scale wars occur if the power shift is not too large. Otherwise, large-scale war occurs.

[2] The assumption that the B state is absorbing is not necessary for the results, but it does significantly simplify the presentation of the logic and so we opt for the simpler specification here. Qualitatively similar results hold in a model in which blocking does not permanently prevent an alliance from occurring.

Proposition 4.2. *If*

$$c \leq \frac{\delta br\Delta}{1-\delta} \tag{4.1}$$

and

$$\Delta \leq \frac{(1-\delta)(1-w_2-c)}{\delta r(1-b)} \equiv \overline{\Delta},$$

then there exists an equilibrium in which blocking occurs on the path of play. Strategies in this equilibrium are as follows:

- *State 1 joins an alliance after State 3 invites in every period in which* $s^t = N$. *State 1 offers* $x^t = 1 - w_2 - c - \frac{\delta r(1-b)\Delta}{1-\delta}$ *in every period in which* $s^t = N$ *and an alliance has not been implemented. In any period in which* $s^t = A$ *or an alliance has been implemented in the current period, State 1 offers* $x^t = 1 - w_2'$. *In any period in which* $s^t = B$, *State 1 offers* $x^t = 1 - w_2$.
- *If* $s^t = N$ *and an alliance was not implemented in the current period, State 2 blocks if and only if* $x^t \leq 1 - w_2 - c - \frac{\delta r(1-b)\Delta}{1-\delta}$, *and rejects otherwise. If* $s^t = A$ *or an alliance has been implemented in the current period, State 2 accepts if and only if* $x^t \leq 1 - w_2'$ *and rejects otherwise. If* $s^t = B$, *then State 2 accepts if and only if* $x^t \leq 1 - w_2$.
- *State 3 chooses to extend every period in which* $s^t = N$.

With these theoretical results established formally, in the next section, we provide a detailed prose description. In particular, we focus on inequalities 4.1 and 4.2 presented in the preceding proposition, describing each qualitatively and connecting them to equilibrium behavior in the model.

4.2 Discussion of Formal Results

The formal analysis in the previous section characterizes the trade-off between an expensive war that will certainly prevent an alliance versus a limited, less expensive military action that *might* prevent it. There are two main findings. The first, described by Proposition 4.1 and presented again in inequality 4.1, is the no-peace condition. This is a necessary condition for small-scale attacks to be adopted as a blocking tactic. When this condition is met, the target will not accept the peaceful implementation of an enemy alliance: There will be either a small-scale attack or a full-scale war.

The second finding is the war-size condition, inequality 4.2 as presented in Proposition 4.2. This tells us when the target chooses small- versus large-scale war. If the no-peace condition is met, then the target decides what level of violence to use to try to block the enemy alliance. The main intuition of the war-size condition is straightforward: as either the anticipated power shift from or the implementation speed of the impending alliance increases, then the attractiveness of full-scale war for blocking the alliance increases. There is another, less obvious insight from the war-size condition. Small-scale attacks might be used as an alternative to both peace and full-scale war. This suggests pessimism for the frequency of violence and optimism for the overall level of violence. The pessimistic side is that targets might use small-scale violence even when, without this option, alliances would be implemented peacefully. This implies that the availability of limited forms of violence expands the blocking toolkit and reduces the target's tolerance for allowing even relatively unprovocative alliances to occur peacefully. The optimistic side is that small-scale attacks may often substitute for full-scale wars. There are larger anticipated power shifts that will lead to small-scale attacks *if that is an option*, and war otherwise. And if small-scale attacks substitute for full-scale war at least some of the time, this option might reduce the overall level of violence.

We discuss the no-peace and war-size conditions in greater detail in the following two sections and the results are summarized in Table 4.1.

4.2.1 No-Peace Condition

The no-peace condition in Proposition 4.1 is a necessary condition for small-scale probabilistic blocking. If this condition is not met, then the logic of the analysis in Chapter 3 holds, with alliances either being implemented peacefully or, depending on the size of the anticipated power shift and speed of implementation, blocked by a full-scale war. If the no-peace condition is met, then small-scale blocking becomes a possibility. In fact, when prospective partners try to implement an alliance and this condition is met, then alliances will not be implemented peacefully. The target will always resort to some level of violence to try to stop the alliance.

Table 4.1 Summary of theoretical results

	Result	Description
Chapter 4		
Proposition 4.1	No-peace condition	A settlement allowing an alliance to be implemented without some violent resistance is not possible if small-scale attacks are relatively inexpensive relative to the probability of successfully blocking an alliance.
Proposition 4.2 (a)	War-level condition	If the no-peace condition is met, then moderate power shifts will result in small-scale attacks and large power shifts will result in full-scale attacks.
Proposition 4.2 (b)	More aggression, less war	If small-scale attacks are cheap enough, then small-scale attacks will occur when alliances would otherwise have been peacefully implemented; small-scale attacks will also occur when full-scale wars would otherwise break out.

What does the condition actually tell us? It says that if sufficiently inexpensive small-scale violent options exist (low c), then the prospective allies cannot make an offer that will entice the target not to use some type of violence to block the alliance. We saw in the previous chapter that such conciliatory offers exist when the target's only other option is to resort to full-scale violence both to block the alliance and to resolve the underlying political dispute. With only the coarse options of either peacefully conceding the alliance or launching full-scale wars, targets are open to being compensated for tolerating new alliances. When the no-peace condition is met, then targets have cost-efficient small-scale attack options that they prefer to such compensation, because they carry the possibility that an alliance will not be implemented. If small-scale attacks are cheap enough, then peace is not an option.

Another critical factor in the no-peace condition is the probability (b) that a small-scale attack successfully blocks an alliance. The higher this probability relative to the costs, the more attractive violence becomes and the less likely the target is to accept a bargain to allow the alliance to take place peacefully.

Why do bargaining concessions fail to satisfy the target when the no-peace condition is met? In the baseline model in the last chapter, we saw that when implementing alliances, the prospective partners compensate the target up to the point where the target is indifferent between fighting a full-scale war and getting the continuation value of bargaining under the risk that the alliance will eventually be implemented. A target that has no small-scale option has only a blunt choice between bargaining and full-scale war. The target's payoff for bargaining instead of fighting a war amounts to getting its pre-implementation bargaining payoff right away, plus its future (expected) post-implementation war payoff, which depends on the probability (r) that an alliance is implemented.

If the overall probability that an alliance gets successfully implemented can be reduced, then the target's continuation payoff increases. This is exactly what having the option of a small-scale attack accomplishes. With the small-scale option, no longer is the target's value of not fighting a simple lottery between a post-implementation war payoff with probability r and a pre-implementation continuation payoff of bargaining with probability $1 - r$. Instead, small-scale blocking introduces another lottery. With probability b, the target successfully blocks the alliance and can lock in its pre-implementation war payoff. With probability $1 - b$, the small-scale attack fails but the target gets the undesirable post-implementation war payoff only if the allies successfully implement, which occurs with probability $1 - r$. Thus, by using a small-scale attack, the target lowers the probability of getting its post-implementation payoff from r to $r(1 - b)$, which is the probability of implementation multiplied by the probability that a small-scale attack does not block the alliance. Similarly, the small-scale attack increases the probability that the target can lock in its more desirable pre-implementation war payoff at $1 - r(1 - b)$. With a lower probability of getting the undesirable post-implementation war payoff and a higher probability of getting the desirable pre-implementation war payoff, the target can in fact do better with a small-scale attack than it can with a peaceful bargaining offer.

Of course, the benefit of a small-scale probabilistic attack comes at a cost (c), and it depends crucially on the probability (b) that the attack is successful. If the cost is high and/or the probability of blocking is low, then the no-peace condition may not hold. Therefore, the target only rejects peace as an option if a small-scale attack is cheap enough and the chance of successfully blocking is high enough.

4.2.2 War-Level Condition

As we saw in the last section, if prospective partners try to implement an alliance and the no-peace condition is satisfied, then peace is not an option. The target will try to block the alliance by resorting to some level of violence.

In this section, we discuss when the target will opt for small-scale versus large-scale wars. Throughout the section, we assume that the no-peace condition is satisfied.

The main factors that determine this choice can be seen in the war-level condition in Equation 4.2 (in Proposition 4.2). They are the size of the anticipated power shift and the speed of implementation. For large power shifts and high implementation speeds, full-scale wars to block and to finalize settlement of the underlying political issue become more attractive. The intuition for this argument follows the logic presented in Chapter 3. The larger the anticipated power shift, the less the target expects it will get in future bargaining with the fully implemented alliance. Expecting greater future losses encourages the target to use the more expensive full-scale option to increase the chances of preventing the power shift.

If the anticipated power shift falls below the Δ^* (see Equation 3.1 in Chapter 3), then without a small-scale option, the target would accept a bargaining concession in exchange for allowing the enemy alliance to be implemented peacefully. But given this option, targets will use small-scale attacks instead of taking the concession.

Even though this option expands the scope of armed conflict to a greater range of possible circumstances, it also substitutes for large-scale war in some situations. Thus, small-scale violence may decrease both peace and the intensity of armed conflict. Table 4.1 summarizes these findings. Under what conditions does this substitution happen? In the baseline model, full-scale war occurs when the anticipated power shift is greater than Δ^*. For such sizable power shifts, targets may use small-scale attacks instead of full-scale war when the option is available. Formally, this occurs when $\Delta^* < \Delta < \overline{\Delta}$.

How might we interpret this formal argument? Two factors make small-scale conflict an attractive alternative to full-scale war. First, the anticipated power shift must be large enough that a mutually satisfactory bargaining settlement that can compensate the target for its future losses does not exist. However, if the power shift is too large, the target's future losses will be too great to accept and full-scale war is more likely. Second, the probability that a small-scale attack successfully blocks the shift must be high relative to the costs of small-scale attacks. The higher the probability of successful blocking and the lower the costs of a small-scale attack, the more the target is willing to use a small-scale attack instead of full-scale war to try to prevent larger power shifts.

An implication from the formal analysis is that, empirically speaking, small-scale attacks are likely to be commonly used to attempt to prevent impending alliances. The reason is that, in practice, small-scale attacks are often very inexpensive yet (in some circumstances) have a good chance of successfully blocking. For example, Russia's invasion of Georgia in 2008 cost Russia an estimated 12.5 billion rubles—far less than the likely cost of a full-scale invasion. Meanwhile, the probability that small-scale attacks might successfully block NATO expansion is high. Under NATO rules, prospective members cannot be involved in separatist or other ongoing civil conflicts. NATO membership confers the largest shift in military power on a new member of any existing alliance. Without a small-scale attack option, such a power shift might very well trigger a full-scale preventive war. Yet, given the high probability that small-scale attacks might successfully block new NATO membership, they are cost-efficient substitutes.

Even if the probability of successful blocking is not as high as in the NATO case, cheap small-scale attacks might still be common. We have explained that small-scale attacks substitute for peaceful bargaining as long as the no-peace condition is met. This means that as long as small-scale attacks are cheap enough, targets might use them even when they would never consider launching a full-scale war. For many reasons, full-scale war is often off the table: It is too expensive, the likelihood of winning the entire underlying issue is too low, the anticipated power shift from the impending alliance is not threatening enough for full-scale war to be worthwhile, and so on. Under each of these circumstances, the target might decide to gamble on small-scale attacks if their costs are sufficiently low. The PRC's campaign of shelling small offshore islands in 1954 can be understood through this lens. A full-scale war to settle the Taiwan issue once and for all was militarily infeasible in 1954. Thus, rather than thinking of this small-scale campaign as a substitute for a large-scale war, we should think of it as resulting from the no-peace condition. The shelling campaign was indeed inexpensive in terms of the direct costs of ordnance and battle deaths. Even if the PRC calculated that there was only a moderate probability of successful blocking, the no-peace condition tells us that the small-scale gamble is worthwhile if it is cheap enough.

4.3 Quantitative Evidence of Disputes

Beginning in this section, and throughout the remainder of this chapter, we turn to the empirical record to evaluate our theory. In this section, we examine some quantitative evidence to evaluate our prediction about the timing of conflict. The theory connects alliances to the logic of shifting-power commitment problems. When framed this way, attacks to block alliances are best understood as attempts to prevent unfavorable power shifts. Accordingly, the theoretical findings in this and the previous chapter predict that an attack is most attractive to a targeted state just before implementation of the alliance and when the expected power shift will occur rapidly. Is there evidence of this relation in the quantitative data on military alliances? In this section, we examine an interval of time around the signing of military alliances to check for spikes in militarized disputes targeting signatories of an impending alliance just before the alliance is signed.

To do this, we compare the annual frequency of disputes targeting any alliance member in the five years before and the five years after signing. We use Alliance Treaty Obligations and Provisions data (Leeds et al. 2002), which documents the date of signing for historical military alliances around the world from 1815 to 2018. We also use Correlates of War Militarized Interstate Disputes (MIDs) data (Sarkees and Wayman 1816), which records uses of force between countries in the years from 1816 to 2014. We construct an alliance-year level data set for each of the five years before the signing and the five years after. We use only alliances that include defensive and/or offensive provisions. Years are coded as 12-month intervals from the day of signing, not calendar years. This ensures that coding does not confuse the timing of signings and disputes that fall in the same calendar year. Years –5 through –1 are the five consecutive 12-month intervals before an alliance was signed; year 0 is the 12 months that started when it was signed; and years 1 through 5 are the five consecutive 12-month intervals after the signing day. We then create a "disputes" indicator variable that is coded 1 for a given year if there is at least one MID initiation targeting any alliance member in that year, and 0 otherwise. We restrict this variable to MIDs in which an actor uses force or initiates a war. These actions correspond to full-scale or small-scale war in our theoretical model.

We conduct a simple analysis to compare the mean frequency of disputes in each year before and after signing. Consistent with the theory, we see the most hostility in the year immediately before an alliance is implemented (Figure 4.1). By definition, year 0 begins with the signing of the alliance. The figure shows a clear spike in disputes directed at an alliance member in year –1, the 12-month window just before the signing. The probability of a dispute in year –1 is nearly 0.25, up by almost seven points from the year before. There is no jump of similar magnitude in any other year before or after. Another pattern that is consistent with our theory is that the probability of

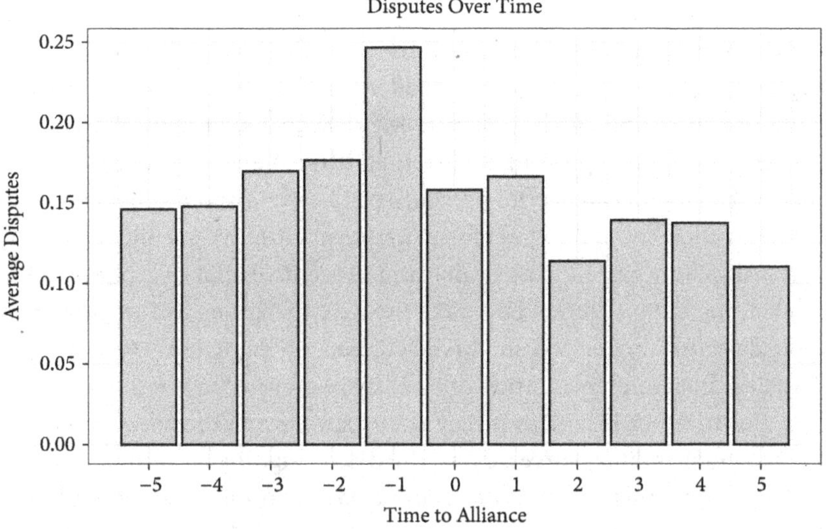

Figure 4.1 Militarized disputes in years around alliance signing

a dispute appears to be increasing in each year before an alliance is signed, but disputes drop off after that and continue (roughly) to decrease in the subsequent years. This suggests that, consistent with our theory, the most dangerous time in the life of an alliance is before it is implemented, and, consistent with much of the theoretical literature on military alliances, there appears to be some evidence of a deterrent effect after an alliance is signed.

It is important to point out that the evidence presented here is merely suggestive. Several caveats are in order. First, the analysis is not a regression, and inferences about causality cannot be drawn from these data. There may be many reasons outside our theory that account for an increase in disputes before an alliance is signed. Nevertheless, the observed trend is consistent with our theory, suggesting that the relations we have identified likely account for at least some of it. Indeed, one of the qualitative cases analyzed in greater detail below, the 1954 Taiwan Strait Crisis, is a clear-cut illustration of our theory and is also one of the instances in the quantitative data in which a recorded militarized dispute occurs before an alliance is formally signed.

Second, we hasten to point out that our theory predicts that at least some preventive armed attacks will successfully block alliances from being implemented. These successful attacks are not included in the data, because the alliances never came into effect, and our data only include alliances that were successfully implemented. This does not undermine the relevance of the patterns observed in Figure 4.1, because, as we discussed in this chapter, attacks may often be launched even if there is a chance that they will fail to block the alliance. Hence, the data included here only account for failed attempts to prevent alliances, and thus they may in fact underestimate the actual frequency of preventive attacks. Without reliable data on attempted alliances that did not form, a true quantitative examination of the relationship between alliance timing and preventive attacks is not possible.

Third, the data included here take the date of signing as the implementation date. As mentioned in the discussion of implementation delay in Chapter 2, final implementation of an alliance may occur at signing in many cases, but in other instances it may occur later, when the allies are able to integrate their military forces. Thus, the date of signing is a rough proxy for the date of implementation. With accurate data on implementation for every alliance, we might expect the frequency of disputes to be even lower in years 0 through 5.

In spite of these three shortcomings, which likely combine merely to weaken the frequency of disputes observed in the data relative to expectations, the predicted pattern nevertheless appears. Militarized disputes targeting prospective allies do in fact spike just before alliances are signed. This phenomenon persists if we do not restrict MIDs to higher levels of violence and instead admit lower-level MIDs in the data. The pattern is also robust to a different setup of the data that includes all dyads with or without an alliance, as opposed to the alliance–year structure we have adopted here. Using a directed dyad data set, the probabilities of MID initiation are, of course, significantly lower. Nevertheless, the probability of MID initiation increases dramatically in the year before the dyad target receives an alliance. We also find that this pattern is persistent if we look at just defensive alliances versus both defensive and offensive alliances.

We also ran a simple regression to estimate the effect of years before and after signing on the likelihood that a dispute targets an alliance member. This analysis helps show whether the probability of militarized disputes is overall increasing as an alliance signing becomes imminent, and also whether the threat of militarized dispute decreases after an alliance is signed. The effect is positive and significant for years before an alliance is signed and negative and significant for the post-signing years. Taken together, the quantitative data show that the time before signing is comparatively dangerous. This pattern of hostility is consistent with our theoretical results.

4.4 2008 Russo-Georgian War

We now shift gears to examine some qualitative evidence of our theoretical findings. Our theory argues that a country might use violence to block an alliance between other countries if that alliance would result in a sufficiently large and rapid shift in power. We find evidence of this logic in the attempt to hasten Georgian entry into NATO and the resulting 2008 Russo-Georgian conflict.

Our equilibrium analysis, as demonstrated in Proposition 3.3, suggests that alliances may provoke conflict if implementation is expected within a relatively short time horizon. The outcome of the April 2008 NATO summit is an example. Georgia had been on a steady but slow path to membership since the 2003 Rose Revolution, when its president, Mikheil Saakashvili, made accession to NATO a foreign policy priority. Georgia strengthened its ties with NATO through active steps such as contributing forces to the International Security Assistance Force in Afghanistan. Efforts continued in October 2004 with the initiation of an Individual Partnership Action Plan for Georgia. This plan required that the separatist claims over the Abkhazia and South Ossetia regions be resolved. While these actions all represented steps towards Georgian accession, membership was still a distant event on the horizon.

Accession efforts suddenly accelerated at the April 2008 NATO summit in Bucharest, where US president George W. Bush lobbied for the extension of a Membership Action Plan (MAP) for Georgia. His proposal was met with reluctance from German and French leaders because of the status of Georgia's internal politics, including the separatist movements. In spite of this, Secretary General Jaap de Hoop Scheffer confirmed for the first time the inevitability of Georgian membership, stating that the issue would be taken up again at a summit in December 2008.[3] This represented a significant change in NATO's orientation towards Georgia, effectively making an unprecedented promise of eventual membership, conditional on resolution of the separatist issue (Khan 2008, 7). NATO membership was nearly within Georgia's grasp.

Saakashvili refocused his efforts on resolving Georgia's internal conflicts in a bid to satisfy the requirement laid out at Bucharest (Smith 2008, 135–137). The stakes were clear: Georgia would not be able to defend itself

[3] http://news.bbc.co.uk/2/hi/europe/7328276.stm

alone, but it could not count on NATO until it had dealt with the separatists. Speaking to the press on May 8, 2008, in response to mounting Russian aggression, Saakashvili said, "We have few combat units and NATO will not help us."[4] Without formal NATO membership, Georgia (State 1 in our model) would not receive the defensive military support it needed to maintain its territorial integrity. Membership would change this calculus, allowing Georgia to invoke NATO's Article 5, effectively increasing its defensive military capability (Lanoszka 2018, 12). As in the model, Georgia could not realize the military benefits of a NATO commitment in the present, but it had a chance to do so in the future by successfully completing domestic reforms and thus winning membership. Crucially, that future NATO support might enable Georgia to resist Russian encroachment.

Georgia's actions made clear that it sought to complete the path to NATO membership as quickly as possible. Georgia's NATO quest is thus consistent with our discussion of Proposition 3.3. If an alliance will result in a sufficiently large power shift, the potential allies may willingly risk war in an effort to make it happen before an adversary can act. Following the Bucharest summit, Saakashvili's public statements indicated a clear sense of urgency (Illarionov 2015, 64; Smith 2008, 135–140). These statements included repeated references to his contacts with various NATO members, in particular those in the United States, as well as a confident public prediction: "I am sure that we will become a NATO member before my Presidential term expires" (Smith 2008, 138).

Consistent with our theory, this acceleration of Georgia's NATO membership bid provoked a preventive strike from Russia. Vladimir Putin warned on the final day of the Bucharest meeting that NATO's promise to Georgia did not contribute to trust and predictability in NATO–Russia relations and would be destabilizing.[5] Russian ambassador to NATO Dmitry Rogozin echoed this, saying that "The attempt to push Georgia into NATO is a provocation."[6] And a mere two days after the NATO summit, Russia established direct diplomatic relations with leadership in both separatist regions (Illarionov 2015, 68). For Russian decision-makers, time was running out. Delay risked allowing Georgia into NATO, which would block their goal of

[4] https://old.civil.ge/eng/article.php?id=17792

[5] https://www.thetimes.co.uk/article/vladimir-putin-tells-summit-he-wants-security-and-friendship-96655h3k9nf

[6] https://www.spiegel.de/international/world/interview-with-russia-s-ambassador-to-nato-the-attempt-to-push-georgia-into-nato-is-a-provocation-a-540426.html

bringing the separatists out of Georgia and back into the Russian sphere of influence. Russia's long-term position was likely to only worsen over time (Stent 2008, 1104), so it had an incentive to achieve a more favorable outcome before its relative position declined (Lanoszka 2018, 13). Recognizing that its window of opportunity was closing, Russia escalated.

In August 2008, within just a few months of the April Bucharest meeting, Russia invaded Georgia. Separatist tensions in Abkhazia and South Ossetia had long been a barrier to Georgia's NATO membership aspirations, so Russia chose to aggravate them, by provoking conflict (Illarionov 2015, 49). Mere weeks after the Bucharest summit, Russia lifted sanctions against Abkhazia, emboldening the separatists. When Georgia sent troops to South Ossetia in response to separatist attacks, Russia responded by sending troops into Georgia on a purported "peace mission." The fighting lasted for nine days; over 300 people were killed and more than 1,000 wounded. Russia then granted official recognition to Abkhazia and South Ossetia, creating an additional hurdle on Georgia's path to membership. Statements of Russian decision-makers after the war make it clear that, in their minds, Georgian accession to NATO was provocative. For example, in September 2008, just after the conflict had died down, Russian president Dmitry Medvedev said, "What did NATO secure, what did NATO ensure? NATO only provoked the conflict, and not more than that."[7] And in 2011, Medvedev told Russian troops that Georgia would have already been a NATO member if Russia had failed to act.[8]

Consistent with our model, subsequent analysis by both academics and policymakers reinforces the notion that Russia was provoked by the prospect of Georgian NATO membership. As (Lanoszka 2018, 10) notes, analysts drawing on diverse approaches have concluded that Georgia's growing NATO ties drove the outbreak of the 2008 war. For example, Mearsheimer (2014) argues that the prospect of NATO membership was directly responsible for the 2008 conflict, with Russia aiming to stoke internal divisions in Georgia in order to keep Georgia out of NATO. Similarly, Blank (2008) points to the crucial role of NATO, suggesting that the "short-circuit" in Georgia's membership bid provided an opportunity for Russia to attack. Delcour and Wolczuk (2015) also argue that the specter of Georgia's future integration into NATO and other Western institutions has been a

[7] https://www.reuters.com/article/us-russia-medvedev-west/russia-says-nato-provoked-georgia-conflict-idUSLJ45058520080919

[8] https://in.reuters.com/article/idINIndia-60645720111121

key driver of Russian hostility. These analyses from the secondary literature suggest that our theoretical model provides a useful lens for interpreting the conflict between Russia and Georgia.

4.5 1954–55 Taiwan Strait Crisis

Our theory is also supported by evidence from the 1954–55 Taiwan Strait Crisis between the PRC and the ROC. In this crisis, the PRC attacked Chinese Nationalist positions on several small islands in the Taiwan Strait, just off the coast of mainland China. This case illustrates the core theoretical results regarding preventive war from Chapter 3, as the acting leaders of the PRC explicitly communicated that the goal of the armed attacks was to prevent the United States from allying with the ROC.

In examining this crisis, we highlight historical facts that substantiate three results from our theory. First, we show that, consistent with the conditions of preventive war established in Chapter 3, the leaders of the PRC anticipated the inclusion of the ROC in an undesirable alliance and attempted to prevent this alliance through their attacks. Second, as demonstrated in the formal results of this chapter, PRC leaders were aware that the strategic use of force might very well fail to prevent an alliance, but nevertheless deemed the tactic worth trying. Third, as also displayed in the theoretical results of this chapter, PRC leaders opted for small-scale military aggression because a full-scale war was cost-prohibitive. A small-scale conflict promised a reasonable chance of preventing at least a multilateral alliance and the inclusion of the offshore islands in said alliance.

In the first subsection, we evaluate the relevance of our preventive war result to this case. To apply the logic of the theory, we highlight the evidence from the crisis that corresponds to the conditions laid out in Chapter 3. We show that PRC leaders became aware of a potential alliance in 1953 and believed its implementation to be imminent. Furthermore, they anticipated that the inevitable power shift resulting from this alliance would effectively put Taiwan out of reach in the future. We provide evidence that decision-makers in the PRC believed preventive attacks would forestall implementation and might altogether block the inclusion of ROC-held territories in alliances with the United States and other countries. Delays in implementation throughout 1954 reinforced confidence in these blocking tactics.

In the second subsection, we consider the PRC's decision to use force despite no guarantee that it would prevent an alliance. Our theoretical results in this chapter demonstrate that targets of alliances might attack preventively even if there is some chance that the attack might fail to block the alliance. Historical evidence shows that PRC leaders fully understood that using force was risky. Nevertheless, they concluded that attacking was worthwhile. To shore up the chances of success, the PRC supplemented its attack with diplomatic efforts to discourage other countries from joining the ROC in a multilateral alliance.

The third subsection examines the PRC's decision to use limited force rather than a large-scale attack. Even though the PRC was working to prepare its military for a large-scale attack on Taiwan, it faced limited ability to launch a successful amphibious attack across the Taiwan Strait before the ROC's successful admission into an enemy alliance. Mindful of the closing window of opportunity, the PRC determined that a limited attack still yielded a sufficient probability of success. Consequently, the PRC bet on a limited preventive war.

Although the United States and the ROC eventually implemented a mutual defense pact, historical evidence reveals the PRC strategy to be partially successful. This attack on the offshore islands prevented a future multilateral alliance that included the ROC. Save for the US, many countries, and particularly Great Britain, did not want to be allied with the Chinese Nationalists in light of the ongoing risk of war with the PRC. Consequently, the ROC was never included in a multilateral alliance, even though the Southeast Asia Treaty Organization (SEATO) formed among other member states at the same time. Furthermore, the United States altogether lost enthusiasm for a Northeast Asia Treaty Organization. The evidence also shows that the military crisis of 1954–55 successfully blocked an alliance that would have extended security coverage to the Nationalist-held offshore islands.

In fact, the ongoing conflict in the Taiwan Strait nearly foiled the plan to form a bilateral alliance between the United States and ROC altogether. Faced with the PRC's preventive aggression, the Eisenhower administration considered alternative pathways for a security partnership short of a bilateral mutual defense pact. We present historical details linking PRC military conflict to the decisions made to exclude the ROC from a multilateral alliance, omit the offshore islands from any alliance, and almost nix a bilateral alliance between the United States and ROC altogether.

Despite the gains for the PRC, the fact remains that the attack on the islands ultimately failed to prevent the ROC's inclusion in a new alliance with the United States. Our examination of this case shows that, despite the attack failing to achieve this primary goal, the PRC's decision to launch a limited attack was a rational response to the anticipation of an imminent power shift from an impending enemy alliance. Further, our theory explains why the ROC and the United States proceeded with their alliance despite armed opposition.

4.5.1 The PRC Attacks to Prevent an Alliance

Throughout 1953 and early 1954, the PRC government was aware of the possibility of a mutual defense treaty forming between the ROC and the United States (Fravel 2007, 59). The newly elected Eisenhower administration broached the subject to the ROC ambassador in March 1953.[9] On December 18, the ROC proposed a treaty draft to the US ambassador to China, Karl Rankin, and in February 1954 the State Department began working on their own draft (Stolper 1985, 22–23). Diplomatic interactions, many of which were known to the PRC, increased through the first half of 1954 and intensified in the fall of 1954 with the start of official treaty negotiations in October.

In total, the implementation window lasted just under two years, beginning when the United States and the ROC both began to consider the possibility of an alliance in March 1953 and ending in March 1955 when the mutual defense treaty came into force. Contemporaneous diplomatic interactions underscore this lengthy time period. On October 14, 1954, Douglas MacArthur made the American case for a US–ROC mutual defense treaty in an official meeting with British and New Zealand diplomats. He said: "We ourselves desire such a treaty, and have for some time been considering it ... we have for some time planned to replace [the President's authority derived from the Korean war] with the unquestioned authority which would reside in a security treaty ratification by the US Senate."[10] Similarly, on October 18,

[9] FRUS, 1952-1954, China and Japan, vol. XIV, part 1, No. 83, "Memorandum of Conversation, by the Assistant Secretary of State for Far Eastern Affairs (Allison)," [Washington, DC] March 19, 1953.

[10] FRUS, 1952-1954, China and Japan, Volume XIV, Part 1, Document 342, "Memorandum of Conversation, by the Deputy Director of the Office of United Nations Political and Security Affairs (Bond)," [Washington, DC] October 14, 1954.

Secretary of State Dulles stated that "the basic idea of a mutual defense treaty with Nationalist China had been embryonic for some time past."[11]

The PRC interpreted the many diplomatic exchanges and public statements throughout 1953–54 as evidence that plans were underway to include the ROC in an alliance and perhaps even a multilateral treaty. In Beijing, *Renmin Ribao* (*People's Daily*, the state newspaper) accused the United States of trying to form military blocs in the region and claimed that the PRC would work to prevent the United States from including Taiwan in such blocs (Stolper 1985, 35–36).

Our theory explains how larger anticipated power shifts result in an expectation of worse future outcomes for the target of a prospective alliance. The situation in the Taiwan Strait Crisis falls in line with this logic. The PRC's leadership expected that a US defensive alliance commitment would prevent the achievement of important political objectives in the future (Fravel 2007, 58–59). In particular, taking Taiwan, concluding the ongoing civil war, and uniting China would become significantly more difficult and perhaps altogether impossible for the PRC (Li 2001, 144–145).

In July 1954, the CCP's Central Committee voiced these concerns, declaring that if the United States and Chiang sign "a treaty, the relationship between us and the United States will be tense for a long period, and it will become more difficult [for the relationship] to turn around. Therefore, the central task of our struggle against the United States at present is to break up the US-Jiang treaty of defense" (Christensen 2011, 137). A British reporter who visited China in August 1954 reported that Beijing feared Taiwan's inclusion in an alliance "would soon be decided in a way which would put it permanently out of reach of the Peking Claim, except at the price of a world war with all the western Powers and not merely the United States. ... Therefore, it was necessary to forestall this result."[12] Most directly, Mao told the Politburo on July 7, 1954, that "the Taiwan issue is a long-term problem, [but] we must think of some measures to destroy the possibility of the US and Taiwan signing the [defense] treaty" (Fravel 2007, 60). These statement efforts make clear that Mao believed that a US commitment would significantly undermine his military position in the strait and, consequently, preclude a favorable resolution of the Taiwan issue in the future.

[11] FRUS, 1952-1954, China and Japan, Volume XIV, Part 1, Document 351, "Memorandum of Conversation, by the Assistant Secretary of State for International Organization Affairs (Key)," [Washington, DC] October 18, 1954.

[12] The Times (London), February 26, 1955, 6.

Figure 4.2 PRC propaganda about breaking up the US–ROC alliance. This PRC propaganda art depicts a PRC soldier striding towards the island of Taiwan, with caricatures representing the US and ROC leadership retreating in fear. Artist: Gu Bingxin 顧炳鑫

In addition, PRC also launched a propaganda campaign to build support for breaking up the US–ROC alliance as illustrated in Figures 4.2 and 4.3. Figure 4.2 features a poster with the slogan "Liberate Taiwan and Complete Unification," depicting the People's Liberation Army attacking Chiang Kai-shek and what appears to be Dwight Eisenhower on the island of Taiwan. Figure 4.3 presents the message "Oppose the US-Chiang Treaty and Resolutely Liberate Taiwan," showing a PLA soldier poised to strike Chiang and an American serviceman in Taiwan, while tearing up a treaty document.

Consistent with our theoretical analysis in Chapter 3, the PRC used violence to deter other countries from joining an alliance with the ROC. Mao's strategy focused on timing, with PRC attacks coinciding with key decision points in the process of alliance implementation. Historical evidence suggests Mao timed his actions to discourage alliances when the PRC perceived rising momentum.

The first attacks began in March 1954 with a shelling campaign against Quemoy and limited naval and aerial fighting around the Tachen Islands.

Figure 4.3 PRC propaganda about breaking up the US–ROC alliance: "Oppose the US-Chiang Treaty and Resolutely Liberate Taiwan." Artists: Yang Zhiguang 楊之光 and Wang Xuzhu

These coincided with the initial US–ROC treaty talks. As a result, Dulles told the ROC ambassador to the United States, Wellington Koo, that an alliance would have to be delayed due to the difficulty of signing a treaty with a country actively fighting with the target of the alliance (Stolper, 1985, 24). US–ROC negotiations were put on hold for a few months, and a brief quiet period ensued.

In late July, the prospect of a US–ROC alliance picked up steam as the Kuomintang, the Nationalist Party of the Republic of China (KMT) pointed to September as a possible date for concluding the agreement (Stolper 1985, 37). Without committing to the September timeline, US Secretary of State John Foster Dulles confirmed at a news conference in August that the US government was considering a mutual defense treaty with the ROC.[13] In early September, reports emerged that Dulles might also be planning to travel to Taipei to conclude an agreement with the KMT.

On September 3, as the US–ROC relationship accelerated, the PRC launched an intense shelling of Quemoy. Following these attacks, Dulles threw cold water on the treaty talks again, this time attempting to back out of the alliance altogether. He proposed to Chiang the idea of pivoting away from a mutual defense treaty and adopting a presidential directive instead. Chiang adamantly opposed the idea and continued to press for a formal defensive alliance. The United States acquiesced, and treaty talks continued. On October 27, Dulles publicly confirmed that the United States was ready to move forward on the treaty (Stolper 1985, 41–49). A new surge of violence done by the PRC answered this key step in the negotiations. On November 1, the PRC launched an intense wave of attacks on the Tachen Islands. Despite Mao's efforts, after three weeks of negotiations, the agreement was signed by the United States and the ROC on December 2, 1954, ratified by the US Senate on February 9, 1955, and approved by President Eisenhower on February 11.

Implementation of the treaty was not without costs. Our theory predicts that allies often make concessions to the target to facilitate the successful implementation of an alliance. In this case, the cost of the mutual defense treaty included relinquishing the Nationalists' control over some of the offshore islands. Moreover, the treaty itself was scaled back to include only Taiwan and the Pescadores, which deliberately excluded explicit defense

[13] Walter Waggoner, "New Asian Line-up Studied by Dulles: Treaty Linking South Korea, Japan, and Nationalist China with the US is Weighed," *New York Times*, August 4, 1954, 1.

coverage of the islands. These islands, already hot with armed conflict as a result of the PLA's shelling campaign, were the key sticking point of treaty negotiations. The United States believed that an unambiguous defense commitment to these territories would likely escalate the ongoing conflict to a broader war with the PRC and perhaps the USSR. The US negotiators wanted to exclude these islands from the formal treaty language altogether, while the ROC pressed for a broader commitment over all Nationalist-held territories. The resulting treaty explicitly commits to defending Taiwan and the Pescadores. As a concession to the ROC, the treaty mentioned the common defense of "other territories as may be determined by mutual agreement." To restrain the ROC from taking advantage of this language to inflame tensions on the offshore islands, the United States insisted on secret treaty notes that forbade the ROC from committing their military forces without US agreement. The final terms of the formal treaty, therefore, deliberately excluded Nationalist-held islands along China's coast, leaving open the future disposition of those islands to prevent the PRC from escalating the armed conflict there.

Beyond excluding the offshore islands in the formal treaty language, the ROC physically withdrew from and conceded control of some of the islands. On January 10, 1955, as the United States was constitutionally ratifying the mutual defense treaty, the People's Liberation Army bombed the Tachen Islands. This bombing was followed by an amphibious attack on Yijiangshan Island. The United States and ROC made no move to protect these islands, allowing the PLA to take control of Yijiangshan without allied resistance. The United States additionally asked the ROC to abandon the Tachen Islands altogether. Chiang Kai-shek strenuously objected, but the United States insisted, threatening to abandon the ROC forces in the Tachen Islands. The ROC finally acquiesced and evacuated, leaving them in the hands of the PRC. The PRC's use of force finally subsided, and President Eisenhower signed the US–ROC mutual defense treaty on February 11, 1955. Chiang Kai-shek received a US defense commitment, but this came with the concession of control over some Nationalist-held offshore islands and a formal treaty that excluded other offshore islands from US protection.

Although the PRC attacks ultimately failed to block the alliance, this evidence suggests that, consistent with our model, they were motivated by preventive considerations. This interpretation is consistent with a consensus among Cold War historians that the PRC's aggression during this period was a direct result of the deepening US–ROC relationship, which undermined the PRC's bargaining position in the dispute. For example, Li (2001) traces PRC insecurity about the US–ROC alliance, pointing to Washington and Taipei's signing of a 1953 Agreement on Mutual Military Understanding as a key starting point. Zhang (1993, 191) also points to the deepening relationship between Washington and Taipei, suggesting that the formalization of a US commitment threatened the PRC by foreclosing the possibility of unification. Fravel (2007) highlights the shifting-power considerations, arguing that the PRC aggression in territorial disputes was a direct result of insecurity driven by the anticipation of a US–ROC alliance.

4.5.2 Probabilistic Blocking

In the theoretical results presented in this chapter, we show that targets of alliances might launch attacks to prevent an alliance even if they believe those attacks might ultimately fail. If the future downsides of the enemy alliance are severe enough, the target may calculate that trying is worthwhile despite being costly and risky. This implies that a preventive attack may very well be a rational bet even if the attack prompts the implementation of an alliance. In fact, observing prospective allies respond to a target's aggression by accelerating the timeline for implementation is entirely consistent with our theoretical analysis. Retrospective interpretations of such an event may mistakenly point to the target's use of force as causing the formation of an enemy alliance. The fear of an enemy alliance might prompt targets to strike preemptively, even if they doubt the attack's success, due to the risk of the alliance forming sooner than expected.

PRC leaders were in such a position in 1954, with only limited confidence in an attack. They were encouraged by what they perceived as daylight between the United States and the ROC, as well as growing differences between the United States and other countries, such as Great Britain and India, on US sympathies towards the ROC. Mao said to Zhou, "It seems as if the US still has some worries about signing a US-Chiang treaty of defense, and it seems they had not made the final decision" (Wang 2021, 96). The perception that the United States was hesitant gave the PRC hope that a limited attack might stall the negotiations.

However, this hope was not assured. To shore up their strategy, the PRC also adopted diplomatic measures to pressure the United States. The PRC hoped that a charm offensive towards the UK would drive a wedge between the United States and the UK on the matter of an ROC alliance. In August 1954, the PRC hosted a British Labour Party delegation. A major goal of the PRC in this visit was to persuade the British to side with the PRC on the matter of the ROC–US alignment. This visit was indicative of a broader diplomatic strategy to curry favor with the British (Wang 2021, 99–101).

The PRC also attempted to isolate the United States by forging ties with India, Burma, and Indonesia against the United States and acting in opposition to the implementation of SEATO (Wang 2021, 105–106). Had the attack on the offshore islands been certain to prevent a ROC alliance, these extra diplomatic efforts would not have been necessary. As it was, the PRC determined that a comprehensive military and diplomatic approach was required to reduce the attractiveness of any alliance, bilateral or multilateral, that included the ROC.

4.5.3 Limited Armed Conflict in the Taiwan Strait

In the formal analysis, we showed that in using force to prevent military alliances, targets choose the scale of war. If the probability of successfully preventing alliances using limited-scale attacks is high relative to the cost of a full-scale war, a small-scale action will be chosen. In the Taiwan Strait case, a full-scale war to settle the Taiwan issue once and for all was militarily infeasible in 1954. The United States was concerned that the PLA was ramping up amphibious capabilities with the goal of eventually attacking Taiwan. However, there was a consensus that this capability was years down the road. Thus, instead of replacing a large-scale war, the small-scale attack likely replaced a peaceful settlement. Because the costs of the shelling campaign were so low, it was worth the gamble to try to stop the alliance even if the PRC estimated only a moderate probability of successful blocking. The no-peace condition holds that this small-scale gamble is worthwhile if it is cheap enough.

4.6 Ukraine, Russia, and the NATO Question

Finally, we use our theory as a lens to understand the Russian aggression towards Ukraine since 2014. Since Russia's initial invasion of Crimea in 2014, many scholars have attempted to understand the role of Ukraine's NATO aspirations in driving the conflict. Such debate only intensified with the 2022 invasion of Ukraine. The debate over the causes of these conflicts has been heated, in particular on the question of whether NATO played a role. In this section, we engage in these discussions, using our model as a lens through which to interpret the strategic dynamics at play.

We begin by tracing the relevant history, beginning with Ukraine's independence after the dissolution of the Soviet Union. We trace this history with particular attention to Ukrainian interest in NATO membership, and Russian reaction to it. We use this history as an illustration of our theory's predictions that tie the expected speed of an alliance's implementation to preventive conflict. In particular, we provide evidence that, consistent with our theoretical argument, Russia's increasingly aggressive behavior is related to increases in the expected speed of Ukrainian NATO membership.

With this history laid out, we conclude by engaging in the ongoing debate over NATO's role in the conflict. We advance two points. First, we refute the claim, advanced by prominent scholars such as Mearsheimer (2014) as well as Vladimir Putin himself, that NATO posed an existential threat to the Russian regime. We reject this argument on several grounds, most prominently that NATO is a defensive alliance, and that the historical record indicates that, if anything, NATO members have been extremely reluctant to do anything that might bring them into direct confrontation with Russia. Second, we argue that although NATO did not pose a threat to Russia, or "provoke" Putin into action, Ukraine's anticipated NATO membership did create an incentive for Putin to strike. However, contrary to arguments tying NATO expansion to the conflict, our analysis suggests that the potential of NATO membership represented a barrier to Putin's goal of eventually dominating Ukraine and bringing it back into the Russian sphere of influence. Understood this way, NATO membership did play a role, but only because the potential of membership for Ukraine stood as a possible barrier to Russia's aggressive and expansionist hopes.

4.6.1 Russian Attacks on Ukraine, 2014–Present

To understand the development of the Russia–Ukraine conflict, and the role of NATO in it, it is useful to begin by briefly tracing the history of Ukraine–NATO relations since the fall of the Soviet Union. Overall, this relationship has advanced in fits and starts. Ukrainian political elites have varied in their orientation towards NATO membership. This back-and-forth nature of support at the elite level broadly reflects trends in Ukrainian public opinion over the same time, with interest in NATO membership waxing and waning. These political dynamics in Ukraine shed light on both the timing and the character of the Russian attacks on Ukraine. This history also sheds light on why Russia acted quickly in 2008 to block Georgia's NATO membership bid, but then took a "wait-and-see" approach to Ukraine, gradually escalating to full-scale war over a period of eight years beginning in 2014.

After regaining its independence with the dissolution of the Soviet Union, Ukraine quickly established a relationship with NATO. In 1992, Ukraine formally joined the North Atlantic Cooperation Council (NACC). This organization, a precursor to today's Euro-Atlantic Partnership Council, provided an organized forum for states outside of the NATO umbrella to consult with the alliance. Ukraine's participation in this forum led it in 1994 to be the first of the former Soviet states to join NATO's Partnership for Peace (PfP) program. In contrast to the multilateral nature of the NACC, PfP membership focused on fostering bilateral relationships, allowing Ukraine to tailor its interaction with NATO along a variety of political and military dimensions.

This cooperation continued over the next decade, with Ukraine slowly growing closer to NATO. The relationship deteriorated briefly in 2002 due to a revelation that then-president Leonid Kuchma had approved a transfer of Ukrainian weapons to Saddam Hussein. After a relatively brief period of tension, Ukraine contributed troops to the 2003 US-led invasion of Iraq. This did not immediately mend the relationship, but it set Ukraine back on a path towards a favorable orientation to NATO and the West.

This path of positive relations accelerated in the wake of the 2004 Orange Revolution, which saw Viktor Yushchenko replace Kuchma as President. This development was notable in the course of Ukraine–NATO relations, as Yuschenko supported Ukrainian accession to NATO. This stood in contrast to both his successor, Kuchma, as well as his rival in the election that spurred the 2004 protests, Viktor Yanukovych. Although Yuschenko pushed for closer ties between Ukraine and NATO, his efforts were undercut by countervailing political forces within Ukraine. This can be clearly seen in the events surrounding Ukraine's involvement in the 2008 NATO summit held in Bucharest.

As discussed previously, the 2008 NATO summit saw consideration of both Georgia and Ukraine as potential future members. However, Russia responded quite differently to the two cases. As we saw, Russia launched an attack on Georgia, aiming to bolster the separatists in Abkhazia and South Ossetia and thus block Georgia's path to NATO membership. But Russia took no such action against Ukraine, though *both* Georgia and Ukraine submitted bids for a NATO MAP at this same meeting. Receipt of a MAP is an important step towards joining the alliance, as it sets out a series of explicit requirements that, if met, will result in formal consideration for membership. Although both states were denied MAP status at the 2008 meeting, then-NATO secretary general Jaap de Hoop Scheffer reinforced the positive direction of NATO–Ukraine relations, stating that the possibility would be taken up again at the December 2008 NATO summit.[14]

Our theory points to the speed of implementation as a key factor in whether a new alliance will provoke aggression from a target. Consistent with this, we see that the expected speed of accession to NATO was a crucial difference between Georgia and Ukraine in 2008. What factors would have led to this difference? Domestic politics represented a stark contrast. As mentioned, though Ukraine's president Yushchenko pushed for tighter relations with NATO, broader forces in Ukrainian politics pushed back. Ukrainian society was far from united on the NATO issue. In fact, anti-NATO sentiment was a driving force behind a shutdown of the Ukrainian parliament from early January to late March of 2008. This shutdown was reflective of broader patterns of public opinion in Ukraine. According to Gallup polling, the Ukrainian public was quite skeptical of NATO membership at this time, with 40% of citizens identifying NATO as a "threat" and a mere 17% perceiving NATO as a provider of protection for Ukraine. In a simultaneous Gallup poll conducted in Georgia, the numbers were almost reversed, with 56% of respondents saying that NATO would serve to protect Georgia and a mere 10% saying that NATO represented a threat.[15]

Considering Russia's reaction to the possibility of Georgia's NATO membership, which was taken up at the same meeting, it is striking that no action was taken against Ukraine. But it is entirely consistent with the equilibrium logic of our model. Recall that the expected speed of an alliance's implementation is an important factor in whether conflict occurs in anticipation of a new alliance. As we have seen, there was a stark difference in the expected speeds of Georgian and Ukrainian entry into NATO. Georgia's

[14] http://news.bbc.co.uk/2/hi/europe/7328276.stm
[15] https://news.gallup.com/poll/127094/ukrainians-likely-support-move-away-nato.aspx

path seemed relatively clear, with public support as well as enthusiasm from Georgian leadership, but this was not the case with Ukraine. Russia was opposed to the idea of Ukrainian NATO membership but could observe that Ukraine's domestic politics made that unlikely to happen in 2008. Accordingly, Russia's opposition amounted to little more than diplomatic statements, which warned Ukraine against taking further steps.

In 2010, Viktor Yanukovych won the Ukrainian presidential election, further reducing the possibility of NATO membership for Ukraine. Yushchenko and the party he belonged to, the Party of Regions, were an important force in the anti-NATO sentiments that had manifested in 2008 with the shutdown of the Ukrainian parliament. During his campaign and in his early days in office, Yanukovych made several statements indicating a lack of interest in NATO membership.[16] Though he continued to cooperate informally with NATO in various ways, his presidency saw a significant slowing of the growth in Ukraine–NATO ties.

Yanukovych continued on this course until February 2014, when the Euromaidan protests led him to flee the country, relinquishing his office and ushering in a new era of Ukrainian relations with NATO and the EU. These protests were driven by Yanukovych's refusal to sign a cooperation agreement with the EU, instead choosing closer ties with Russia. This decision came in the wake of political and economic pressure from Russia, and immediately sparked widespread protests. It was obviously contrary to Russian interests, as the nature of the protests meant that Yanukovych's replacement would almost certainly be more favorable to NATO membership. And indeed, despite some initial attempts to diffuse tension with Russia, the new president, Petro Poroshenko, set Ukraine back on a path to NATO membership, renouncing Ukraine's nonaligned status in December 2014.

Given this, it is no surprise that Russia took military action in the wake of Euromaidan. Consistent with our model, this action achieved the goal of blocking Ukraine's NATO hopes. Recall that an important component of NATO's membership requirements is that aspirant member states must resolve any ongoing territorial or separatist disputes. Anticipating this, in March 2014, Russia stoked tensions among separatist groups in the Donbas region of Eastern Ukraine. This action also came in the wake of Russia's

[16] https://www.telegraph.co.uk/news/worldnews/europe/ukraine/7774665/Ukraine-drops-Nato-membership-pursuit.html

annexation of Crimea. Although the war in the Donbas cooled after the 2015 Minsk agreements, fighting continued at a low level, with combat deaths occurring regularly all the way through 2021. Russia's decision to take this action in the wake of Euromaidan, which led to a moderate increase in the expected speed of Ukraine's NATO accession, is consistent with our model. The limited nature of Russia's military action is also consistent with the theoretical analysis of this chapter.[17] This analysis shows that when implementation is rapid—but not too rapid—states will prefer small-scale conflicts aimed solely at blocking an alliance over trying to eliminate the opponent and settle the underlying political issue. It is reasonable to interpret the results of the Euromaidan protests in this way; Ukrainian NATO membership was by no means imminent in the wake of these events, but the prospect of membership had ticked up. Anticipating this, Putin launched a limited military action designed to preclude Ukraine from meeting the requirements for NATO membership.

This low level of conflict continued until February 24, 2022, when, after a months-long buildup of troops on the Ukrainian border, Russia launched a full-scale invasion. What factors contributed to Russia's decision to invade, rather than continue with the small-scale actions it had taken in the eight years since the 2014 invasion of Crimea and war in the Donbas? Again, our theoretical model provides a useful lens. Under the logic of this model, states targeted by alliances will choose large-scale, costly wars when the speed of potential implementation is high relative to the power shift it will cause.

There is much evidence that even though Ukraine had much work to do before it could become a NATO member, its prospects for membership rapidly accelerated beginning in 2020, with President Zelensky including NATO membership as an explicit goal in Ukraine's national security strategy. This was the first time since the 2008 Bucharest summit that a Ukrainian official had clearly set NATO membership as a priority. Indeed, mere months into his tenure as president, Zelensky raised the possibility of a MAP for Ukraine. Clearly, and as Russia understood, Ukraine would only grow closer to NATO, the European Union, and the West at large as time went on. Thus, given Putin's goal of preventing Ukraine from choosing its own destiny, it is no surprise that Russia chose to mount an all-out invasion in February 2022.

[17] For more on limited military strikes and their relationship to power shifts, see Schram (2021).

At each point in the history of Ukraine's relationship with NATO, our model provides useful insights into the strategic dynamics that shaped Russian responses. Importantly, these responses track with changes in the expected speed of Ukrainian NATO accession in a way that is consistent with our theoretical findings. The relationship was characterized by peace until 2014, when a modest change in Ukraine's membership prospects in the wake of Euromaidan-led Russia to launch a limited military action to block further progress towards NATO membership. These tensions culminated in the 2022 Russian invasion of Ukraine, which came in the wake of accelerations in Ukraine's path to membership. Thus, our model provides a useful lens through which to understand the strategic contours of this ongoing conflict.

4.6.2 Did NATO Provoke Putin?

What does our theory have to say about the connection between Ukraine's NATO aspirations and Russian aggression? The role of NATO in this conflict has been a topic of fierce and ongoing debate among academics and policymakers alike. To preview our answer, we reject the premise that NATO represents a threat to Russia, and we strongly disagree with the notion that NATO is responsible for the conflict in Ukraine. But this does not mean that the NATO question is irrelevant to Putin's motivations for both the 2014 annexation of Crimea and the 2022 invasion of Ukraine.

In the remainder of this section, we first point out the deep flaws in arguments that paint NATO as responsible for the conflict in Ukraine. We then apply our theory to the situation to elucidate the actual role of NATO. Our main argument is that NATO's role in the conflict is nuanced. On the one hand, we believe that it is wholly unreasonable to blame NATO for the conflict. On the other hand, the anticipation of possible Ukrainian membership in NATO undoubtedly shaped actors' incentives and behavior leading up to the crisis. In particular, NATO membership would have foreclosed future opportunities for Russia to meddle in Ukraine's domestic affairs. Anticipating this, Putin took action to prevent Russia's hold on Ukraine from slipping.

Perhaps the most prominent voice arguing for a role of NATO in inciting Russian hostility towards Ukraine is John Mearsheimer. Though others have made similar arguments, we will focus on Mearsheimer's version as it has received the most attention from scholars, policymakers, and commentators alike. Writing about the 2014 Russian invasion of Crimea, Mearsheimer (2014, 1) advances the bold claim that "the United States and its European allies share most of the responsibility for the crisis." He goes on to single out Ukraine's aspirations to join the Atlantic alliance, stating that "the taproot of the trouble is NATO enlargement." Mearsheimer argues that NATO's expansion to include former Soviet states has threatened Russia's core interests, leaving Putin no option but to use force to block further eastward expansion of the alliance.

However, this argument is flawed for a few reasons. First and perhaps most importantly, Mearsheimer's conception of the constellation of interests, and his blaming of the United States, NATO, and the West, writ large, are inconsistent with both the historical record and the widely accepted findings of empirical research in international relations. A core tenet of Mearsheimer's argument is that it is not Russia but the West that has revisionist aims. He writes, for example, that "when Russian leaders look at Western social engineering in Ukraine, they worry that their country might be next" (Mearsheimer 2014, 4)—suggesting that Putin perceives NATO as an *existential threat* to the Russian regime. Under this framing, if NATO were allowed to expand to include Ukraine, then Russia would be directly under threat, with Ukraine and the West potentially moving in to threaten the sovereignty and, ultimately, the existence of Russia as a state.

In this story, NATO is the aggressor, and Putin's action represents a last-ditch attempt at self-preservation, with Russia's survival at stake. However, there is little concrete evidence to support this bold claim. In framing the problem this way, Mearsheimer puts the cart before the horse. What the bulk of the evidence shows is that Russia is the aggressor in this situation, aiming to assert its will on a neighboring state, through force if necessary. Putin cares about NATO expansion not because NATO is a threat to Russia but because NATO might prevent him from acting as the aggressor in the future, effectively closing the door on his imperialist ambitions. NATO is not a threat to Putin's regime, but it is a threat to Putin's plans to meddle in Ukraine.

An important reason that it is implausible that NATO truly represents an existential threat to Putin is that NATO is a purely defensive alliance. Throughout its 74-year existence, NATO has never engaged in an offensive military action. Rather, NATO was carefully designed at its inception to limit the obligation of members to purely defensive military action. This is most famously embodied in the principle of collective defense, formalized in Article 5 of the North Atlantic Treaty. This article explicitly states that an attack on one of the members is to be considered an attack on all members. Thus, NATO's main obligation is *purely defensive* in nature and therefore cannot pose a threat to Russia. This idea is supported by an important line of empirical scholarship in international relations, which finds that defensive alliances are associated with peace rather than war (Leeds 2003). Furthermore, Ukraine's hypothetical membership in NATO belongs to the subset of alliances *most* associated with peace: a relatively minor military power joining a powerful defensive alliance (Benson 2011).

It is also clear that no current member of NATO wishes to engage in aggression towards Russia. We have mentioned, for example, the reluctance of France and Germany to speed Ukraine's accession for fear of antagonizing Russia. Clearly, NATO is not looking for a fight, and to interpret NATO expansion to include Ukraine as consistent with anything other than a Ukrainian desire for a defensive bulwark against Russian action strains credibility. Given this, it is reasonable to interpret Putin's public statements that NATO is an existential threat as disingenuous.

Given these considerations, it is quite implausible that NATO was genuinely perceived as an existential threat to Russia. What does this imply about the role of NATO in the ongoing conflict? It is tempting to conclude that the specter of potential NATO membership is entirely irrelevant to an understanding of Russian motivations for war with Ukraine. We believe that such a view is too strong. But if Russia was not threatened directly by NATO, then how could NATO membership for Ukraine have been a driving factor in Putin's decision to invade Crimea in 2014 and escalate to a full-scale invasion in 2022?

The answer lies in Putin's long-term goals. Clearly, Putin wants to bring Ukraine back into the Russian sphere of influence. However, he knows that NATO membership for Ukraine would effectively shut the door on this aspiration. As long as Ukraine remains outside the NATO security umbrella, Putin is free to throw Russia's military weight around, intimidating Ukraine and even using force to prevent it from growing closer to the West. However, just as the NATO member states are loath to enter directly into a confrontation with Russia, Putin is loath to do anything that might be perceived as an attack on a NATO member state. This logic matches that of our theoretical argument, drawing a connection between alliances, shifting-power commitment problems, and war. NATO's role in the conflict was not in threatening Russia's existence but in threatening the Russian regime's future ability to impose its will on weaker, less militarily capable states. Anticipating that NATO cannot commit to leaving Ukraine on the outside forever, Putin calculated that costly action to foreclose the possibility was preferable to bargaining from a weakened position in the future, and permanently losing Ukraine to the West in the process.

Mearsheimer, and those who argue similarly, fail to understand that there is a commitment problem at play here. The failure to recognize the deep commitment problem that drives this dispute is illustrated by Mearsheimer's key policy recommendation. Writing in 2014, Mearsheimer recommended that the United States and its allies "abandon their plan to westernize Ukraine and instead aim to make it a neutral buffer between NATO and Russia." He added that "to achieve this end, the United States and its allies should publicly rule out NATO's expansion to both Georgia and Ukraine."

But what action could the US or its NATO allies take to render such a commitment credible? In the anarchic world of international relations, there can be no guarantor of such a commitment. This is a striking oversight, as the fundamentally anarchic nature of international politics is a core tenet of the approach of Mearsheimer and other "realist" scholars.

Under anarchy, credible commitment to not pursue a valuable alliance is difficult, if not impossible. If a potential alliance partner is unable to take some action to prevent itself from joining an alliance, then enemies know that if, given the opportunity, an alliance will form. This subtle commitment problem is present in the Ukraine–Russia relationship. This commitment problem is clearly present in the context of Ukraine's political development since 2005, when President Viktor Yuschenko made NATO membership a policy priority. In tracing this history, we focus on the incentives and behavior of both Ukraine and NATO. In particular, we make two points. First, we provide evidence that Ukraine took concrete steps that undermined the credibility of any subsequent commitment to forgo the pursuit of NATO membership. Second, we provide evidence that although NATO placed some barriers on Ukraine's ability to join in the short term, its long-standing "open-door" policy also rendered any long-term commitment to keep Ukraine out of the alliance null.

As discussed in the previous section, Ukrainian domestic politics has trended westward over the last decade. Though there have been some setbacks, Ukrainian public opinion on NATO has trended positively over time, with a majority of Ukrainians identifying NATO membership as an important priority in the lead up to the 2022 Russian invasion. Responding to these trends, Ukrainian leaders have sought to make NATO membership an explicit policy goal. Following the backlash against then-president Viktor Yanukovych's rejection of the EU–Ukraine Association agreement and the subsequent Euromaidan protests, the Ukrainian parliament voted with an overwhelming majority to abandon Ukraine's previous "non-bloc" status. Importantly, the referendum emphasized the importance of ". . . achieving the criteria required to attain (NATO) membership."[18] The passing of this referendum clearly illustrates that Ukraine's sights were set on NATO membership. On February 19, 2019, President Poroshenko signed into law a constitutional amendment that enshrined pursuit of NATO membership as an explicit responsibility of the Ukrainian government. The text of the amendment is clear, requiring that: *"The President of Ukraine is a guarantor of the implementation of the strategic course of the state for gaining full-fledged membership of Ukraine in the European Union and the North Atlantic Treaty Organization*" (Article 102).

This constitutional amendment exacerbated well-known commitment problems stemming from leader turnover. As Wolford (2012, 2018) argues, elections may undermine the long-term credibility of promises made by leaders of democratic states. Though an incumbent may be able to credibly commit to a course of action in the short term, they are typically unable to constrain the actions of future officeholders. Consequently, an adversary may wish to fight in the present against an incumbent rather than face a more obstinate leader in the future. Given Ukraine's domestic political trends towards a more westward orientation since 2014, commitment to neutrality is unlikely to be viewed by Russia as credible. As an example of this, in a last-ditch attempt to end the 2022 war through a negotiated settlement during its first month, President Zelensky proposed the idea of Ukrainian neutrality.[19] Ultimately, this proposal was not taken seriously by Putin. The logic of commitment outlined above provides a compelling explanation for this. Anticipating that such a commitment lacked credibility in light of Ukraine's ongoing westward turn, Putin rejected this proposal and launched his attack.

[18] Quoted in "Ukraine Votes to Abandon Neutrality, Set Sights on NATO," *Radio Free Europe*, December 13, 2014, https://www.rferl.org/a/ukraine-parliament-abandons-neutrality/26758725.html

[19] "Ukraine offers neutrality in exchange for NATO-style security guarantees at Russia talks," *Reuters*, March 29, 2022, https://www.reuters.com/world/europe/ukraine-offers-neutrality-exchange-nato-style-security-guarantees-russia-talks-2022-03-29/

Ukrainian domestic political trends are only one source of commitment difficulty. Another major obstacle to Ukraine's ability to establish a credible commitment to remain neutral is NATO's "open-door policy." The importance of the open-door policy in the context of Ukraine predates the 2022 Russian invasion, as well as the 2014 annexation of Crimea by a significant margin. NATO made this policy explicit in 1992, following the breakup of the Soviet Union, with then-Secretary General Manfred Worner stating that "the doors to NATO are open" to former Soviet states that wished to join the alliance.[20] The open-door policy is also relevant for the Ukraine–NATO relationship. In particular, following the April 2008 NATO summit in Bucharest, the open-door policy was explicitly invoked in the context of potential Ukrainian membership.[21] In the days leading up to the invasion, reversing NATO's open-door policy was a key demand of Putin's. Clearly, NATO's unwillingness to revise its open-door policy undercuts the credibility of any promise by Ukraine to remain outside the alliance. Ukraine's inability to commit to remain outside NATO is a key factor, and this commitment problem sheds light on the strategic dynamics that led to the ongoing war.

Thus, our theory illustrates the issue with Mearsheimer's approach. Recall that one of our first theoretical results, formalized in Lemma 3.1, was that allies would *always* attempt to form an alliance in equilibrium if its expected benefits outweigh its expected costs. The logic of this result is straightforward and maps onto the case of Ukraine well. In the model, it is possible that the allies would be better off if they were able to commit *not* to form an alliance. This is because forming an alliance risks inviting conflict from the target of the alliance. However, given the military value of forming an alliance, if the prospective partners can form an alliance, they will.

4.7 Conclusion

In this chapter, we used our baseline theory of alliances, power shifts, and war as a jumping-off point to understand some important historical cases. In each case, an adversary of an impending alliance lashed out, using military

[20] "20 years of the Czech Republic, Hungary and Poland in NATO: Yesterday, Today and Tomorrow," *International Centre for Defense and Security*, April 22, 2019, https://icds.ee/en/20-years-of-the-czech-republic-hungary-and-poland-in-nato-yesterday-today-and-tomorrow/

[21] "NATO Decisions on Open-Door Policy," *NATO.org*, November 4, 2009, https://www.nato.int/cps/en/natolive/news_7218.htm

force in an attempt to prevent the alliance from being implemented. But the cases varied in terms of the scale of conflict. Accordingly, we extended our model to incorporate this variation. We saw that small-scale attacks to prevent alliances are sometimes preferable, but carry a significant drawback: They may fail, allowing the alliance to come into force anyway. Further, small-scale attacks enhance peace in some cases by replacing otherwise destructive wars, but increase conflict in other cases by replacing otherwise peaceful bargains. Applying the theoretical results, we gained insight into Russian aggression towards Georgia and Ukraine, as well as the 1954 Taiwan Strait Crisis.

While we studied cases in which war occurred in anticipation of an alliance, our theory also predicts that such wars can be avoided under some conditions. In the chapters that follow, we develop this argument further, extending our arguments both theoretically and empirically. We focus on two ways in which allies and their adversaries can take steps to avoid the provocative effect of new alliances. In Chapter 5, we study actions that allies themselves might pursue. Recall that in Chapter 3 we saw that potential partners might make concessions in advance of an alliance's implementation, effectively "buying off" a shared enemy by compensating them for the losses that would be expected once the alliance is implemented. However, we also saw that such deals were only possible if the anticipated alliance was not too powerful and was not expected to arrive too quickly. We consider these features in Chapter 5, studying how allies specifically alter the institutional design of alliances to make room for bargains that allow the alliance to come into force peacefully. We do this by first extending our theory to endogenize these features, allowing allies to select the terms of cooperation in a way that will limit the alliance's provocative nature. With this, we turn to the historical record, illustrating the theory's predictions by studying the inclusion of a reunified Germany in NATO, US security cooperation with Israel, and the recent NATO membership processes of Finland and Sweden.

Following this, we study another way that the provocative effect of alliances can be avoided. While Chapter 5 focuses on situations in which alliances come into force peacefully, Chapter 6 studies the phenomenon of negotiating away alliances entirely. We demonstrate that war and aggression are not the only tools targeted states can use to prevent alliances. Targets may themselves offer concessions to potential allies, in exchange for their dropping the alliance. We refer to these *quid pro quo* arrangements as anti-alliance "deals." We extend our theory once more to formalize the logic of these deals, outlining the conditions under which they are possible, as well as the conditions under which they are preferred to preventive war. We find that deals are preferable in some situations, but are unfortunately not always possible. To illustrate the logic of deals, we turn to the historical record, providing case evidence from the Louisiana Purchase, nineteenth-century neutrality pacts, and the United States' attempts to establish a network of alliances in East Asia in the 1950s.

5

Designing Alliances to Avoid War

The previous chapter highlighted the challenges of security cooperation, demonstrating how alliances often provoke preventive actions, including war, from rival states. Yet, history shows that many alliances are formed without conflict. This chapter extends our dynamic theory of alliance implementation to explore how allies can circumvent the provocative effects previously discussed. Building on our theory of dynamic commitment problems, we argue that war can be reliably avoided if allies carefully design their alliances to prevent triggering these effects. Specifically, by adjusting the size and speed of impending power shifts from new alliances, allies can prevent the emergence of commitment problems. We develop this argument in detail, presenting a theory of alliance design that addresses the core commitment issues in alliance formation.

Our argument on alliance design builds on a significant body of work in international relations. Over the past two decades, scholars have examined how the design of alliances shapes various important outcomes. The central insight from this research is that alliances, like other international institutions, are crafted with specific objectives in mind. This means that alliances are not uniform; there is considerable variation in the content of their treaties. Leeds et al. (2002) quantitatively document this variation, presenting data that highlight the diversity of military alliances over the past two centuries. According to the data, alliances may be established for defensive purposes or may involve commitments to offensive actions, among other dimensions of variation explored in the literature.

A substantial body of literature demonstrates that variation in alliance design significantly affects alliance performance. For instance, analyzing the content of alliance treaties is crucial for understanding their reliability—whether the partners will fulfill their obligations during conflict. Leeds (2000) shows that when specific treaty obligations are considered, alliances are reliable 74.5% of the time. Examining alliance content has also shed light on the relationship between alliances and war. Leeds (2003) argues that the question "Do alliances lead to peace or war?" is misguided, as alliances are

The Window Before. Brett V. Benson and Bradley C. Smith, Oxford University Press.
 DOI: 10.1093/9780197806760.003.0005

not uniform entities. Instead, they encompass a diverse range of treaties. Thus, defensive alliances, which require intervention in case of attack, tend to promote peace by deterring aggression. But offensive alliances, which involve joint offensive actions against adversaries, are linked to a higher likelihood of war because they raise the probability of success and distribute the costs of conflict. Thus, the specific design of alliances is crucial for understanding their impact on international stability.

As previous work shows, variation in alliance treaty content has significant implications for international outcomes. Morrow encapsulates this idea by saying that alliances are "explicit records of the allies' expectations of action in the case of war, and they specify the conditions under which the obligations are activated" (2000, 63). This emphasizes that alliances are not uniform; like all international institutions, they are deliberately designed with specific objectives in mind (Koremenos, Lipson, and Snidal 2001).

In this chapter, we build on these insights by studying how the design of alliances determines whether commitment problems arise in the process of their formation. This focus distinguishes our work from much of the previous work on the design and content of alliance treaties, which has focused on alliance *performance*—how alliance commitments influence outcomes once they are in place. In contrast, we focus on how the design of the alliance implementation process influences outcomes during and after implementation. In doing so, we highlight how the intentional design of alliances has consequences for alliance performance *but also* for adversary reactions to an anticipated alliance. In particular, we argue that an adversary's *expectations* about the design of an impending alliance determine whether it will be implemented peacefully in the first place.

Also, in contrast to earlier work that focuses on alliance treaty terms and provisions, we consider questions of design in broad terms, considering not only the design of treaty content but also how the implementation process is structured. From this perspective, our theory of alliance design applies generally to military cooperation relationships, even if the result is not an alliance treaty. Whenever prospective partners work together to implement a military cooperation agreement that portends a power shift, there is a possibility that they can modify the agreement or the implementation process to avoid preventive war that the power shift might otherwise trigger.

How can such modifications preserve peace? To preview our argument, consider that our theory links alliances to war through the classic dynamic commitment problem. Because alliances can significantly alter the distribution of power, potential adversaries will anticipate having a reduced ability to coerce the newly allied states. As demonstrated in the previous chapter, a sufficiently large and rapid power shift can lead to a commitment problem that sparks war. However, our theory also offers a solution: By adjusting the alliance's design to mitigate the size and pace of the power shift, it is possible to prevent the emergence of commitment problems and thereby avoid war.

Central to this solution is the concept of *expected strength*. This term encapsulates how the anticipated changes in power distribution due to an alliance impact perceptions of security and stability. In essence, an alliance's potential to trigger conflict is linked to states' expectations about the magnitude and speed of the power shift it will create. Both the size of the shift and the speed at which it unfolds contribute to this expected strength. Consequently, understanding how these factors influence expectations connects alliance design to the presence or absence of commitment problems. This chapter will focus on how allies can shape their cooperative relationships to adjust their alliance's expected strength, and thus (hopefully) balance the power dynamics in a way that fosters peace.

As we have seen in previous chapters, the likelihood of war is influenced by two factors that determine expected strength: the magnitude and speed of the anticipated power shift. A sufficiently high expected strength can provoke preventive war; however, if it becomes too high, the risk of war may actually decrease. This is because a very high expected strength can compel quicker implementation of the alliance, reducing the time available for the target to react.

Consequently, alliance designers can strategically adjust various elements to balance the provocative effects and raise the chances of peaceful implementation. Reducing expected strength sufficiently can ensure a peaceful outcome, while increasing it makes the alliance more provocative but also improves the likelihood of its implementation before the target has an opportunity to launch preventive actions.

What does this look like in practice? Alliance designers can shape both the content of alliance agreements and the implementation process to alter the size of the power shift and the speed of implementation. Practically speaking, the size only has one direction it can go: down. Unqualified alliance between states aggregates the total capabilities of those states. So, to adjust the shift size, states may limit the capabilities that each member state will commit to a common cause. This will typically reduce the expected strength of an alliance.

Speed, on the other hand, may be adjusted up or down, manipulating the process of implementation itself by, for instance, ratcheting up the speed of negotiations or fixing the institutional rules of implementation to slow the process. An example of speeding up negotiations is the accession of Finland to NATO. Worried about provoking Russian aggression, NATO leadership deliberately sped up the membership path, permitting Finland to join in record time. On the flip side, institutional rules for alliance formation may slow implementation. Constitutional rules requiring deliberative ratification are just one example. As another illustration, NATO rules for membership generally make the pathway to membership slow and arduous. For example, Georgia has been working to join the alliance for well over a decade, but has not yet met the standards required to receive a NATO Membership Action Plan, which is the first step to membership.

Another way to speed up implementation is to conceal the factors that slow implementation from an enemy. This effectively speeds up implementation by giving the targeted enemy a shorter time window to respond. Alliances are often negotiated in secret to avoid roadblocks *and* to limit the target's ability to respond with force. Secrecy may also play a role in alliance treaty content. Not only might designers wish to keep the implementation process secret, they may also choose to conceal the terms of the treaty to give the target the impression that the expected strength of the alliance is smaller or larger than it really is.

Speed may also be directly manipulated through the content of the alliance itself. As we noted in Chapter 2, some alliances, such as the 1894 Franco–Russian alliance, are capability dividers rather than capability aggregators. Such alliances eliminate the need for the time-consuming process of integrating disparate militaries. Choosing to design alliances for this purpose can speed up implementation significantly.

In sum, the expected strength of an alliance is a nuanced concept, and is driven by *both* the speed of implementation and the size of the resulting power shift. Allies have a wide range of policy tools to manipulate these factors. Thus, our theory offers alliance designers multiple options to mitigate the risks of war. They may adjust the expected strength down to guarantee peace, or up to reduce the probability of war. In this chapter, we consider these trade-offs in detail, extending our theory to understand why allies limit expected strength in some cases but increase it in others.

Adjusting expected strength down raises another question. In principle, prospective allies can restrict aspects of their cooperative relationship to mitigate the threat it poses and preserve peace by avoiding a commitment problem. But should we expect allies to actually do this? As we argue in this chapter, the answer is not straightforward. Limiting an alliance's expected strength presents a trade-off. On the one hand, it can help produce commitments that avoid provoking a preventive war, which is beneficial given the high costs of conflict. On the other hand, this restriction may weaken the alliance's effectiveness. Alliances offer significant peacetime advantages, such as bolstering members' resistance to aggression, improving bargaining outcomes, and deterring attempts to alter the status quo. Thus, allies must weigh the benefits of peace against the potential drawbacks of a diminished alliance.

Studying when restricting expected strength occurs in practice reveals a key novel insight of our theory: Designing alliances to avoid commitment problems involves a *deterrence–provocation trade-off*. Strengthening an alliance can enhance deterrence and improve bargaining outcomes during peacetime. However, if an alliance becomes too robust, it may provoke aggression from adversaries who seek to disrupt the emerging security relationship before it solidifies.

Adjusting expected strength upward also carries risks. It does not carry the same deterrence trade-off, but it also does not completely alleviate the risks of preventive war. If allies peacefully implement the alliance, they do not weaken the alliance or give up the post-implementation deterrence benefits. However, increasing expected strength makes the alliance even more provocative to the target *during the implementation window*. Because an increase in expected strength typically comes through an increase in implementation speed, the alliance has a better chance of being implemented peacefully because the target has less time to respond. However, as we discussed in Chapter 3, the risk of war is not eliminated.

In this chapter, we formally develop these arguments. Though the logic is a natural extension of the theory we have articulated in the previous two chapters, tracing it in detail delivers specific insights that can be compared to the historical record. We begin by describing how the size and speed of an alliance-induced power shift interact to drive commitment problems. In doing so, we build on the analysis of the previous chapters, highlighting exactly how these factors lead to peace. More precisely, we argue that limiting these factors opens the way for negotiations that can pacify the target of an alliance, compensating them for the expected future losses that will occur after alliance implementation.

With this framework established, we outline the conditions under which allies will pursue such an alliance design in practice. We extend the model to treat the institutional characteristics of an alliance as an endogenous choice and analyze equilibrium outcomes under this extension. We find that the decision to modify the design of an alliance depends crucially on its expected strength. If an alliance cannot be implemented quickly enough, or if the potential power shift is not big enough, the risk of provoking war outweighs the benefits of a faster or more powerful alliance. In such cases, allies will deliberately opt for a less powerful and more slowly implemented alliance to avoid inciting aggression. Conversely, if an alliance can be implemented swiftly or if a sufficiently large power shift is achievable, allies may choose to risk war, proceeding in the hope that this more provocative alliance will be fully realized before preventive conflict arises.

These arguments offer a novel perspective on the alliance formation process, suggesting that forming an alliance can sometimes be a rational gamble. The previous chapter provided examples where this gamble led to war or small-scale conflict, highlighting key empirical indicators of alliance-driven commitment problems and how these conflicts were fueled by the anticipation of an impending alliance. However, identifying alliances that successfully avoided conflict is harder. Specifically, how can we differentiate between cases where the gamble was successful and the alliance was swiftly implemented, and cases where content modifications enabled a potentially provocative alliance to proceed without conflict?

Fortunately, the theory developed in this chapter provides a framework for distinguishing these scenarios in the historical record. Our theory highlights two crucial factors. First, evidence of attempts to modify an alliance's content is essential. As we argue below, alliances are intentionally designed often to mitigate the threat they pose to an adversary's future goals. Given the risk–reward trade-off we identify, our theory suggests that allies will not adopt a middle-ground strategy between a risky alliance and a safe one (one without war risks). Instead, if they opt to risk war and pursue a rapid alliance implementation, they will aim to maximize both the alliance's strength and speed to justify the risk. Conversely, if they limit the scope of their cooperation, they will do so to completely eliminate the risk of war. Thus, our theory predicts that modifications to an alliance's content will occur only when the primary goal is to avoid war altogether.

Second, our theory identifies negotiations between prospective allies and a shared enemy as a critical distinguishing factor. As we saw in the previous chapter, if an alliance is provocative, pre-alliance bargaining with an enemy is often futile. This stems from the core commitment problem identified in our theory. Alliances are deemed provocative when prospective allies cannot offer sufficient concessions to offset the anticipated future losses due to the power shift induced by the alliance. Consequently, our theory implies that concessions are made and accepted only if they effectively appease the enemy of the new alliance. Therefore, observing successful pre-alliance negotiations between prospective allies and an enemy state indicates that the allies have chosen a strategy that avoids risk, opting instead to limit their commitments to facilitate negotiations and guarantee peace.

We apply these implications to illustrate the logic of our model using historical cases. The first is the addition of the territory of the former East Germany to NATO after the collapse of the Soviet Union. We illustrate that both factors indicated by our model are present in the historical record. NATO intentionally placed limits on factors such as troop placements during the process of bringing the unified Germany into the alliance. It also committed to a drawn-out timetable for the withdrawal of Soviet troops from East Germany. We argue that NATO's careful modifications were designed to reduce the expected power shift, creating space for negotiations with Russia to allow the alliance to come into force. We also show that Germany gave Russia large financial incentives, which served to compensate Russia for the future loss of influence over territory that had been under its control. Ultimately, the unified German state was folded into NATO's security apparatus peacefully. We show that our interpretation of the case is broadly consistent with that of Cold War historians, who have argued that NATO's careful negotiating prevented hostility and allowed Germany to join the alliance without conflict. Our theory enriches these explanations by pointing to reductions in the alliance's expected strength as a necessary condition for the success of these negotiations.

East Germany is an example where design choices were made to lower the expected strength of the alliance. We also examine cases where secrecy was used to accelerate the implementation process: In the 1894 Franco–Russian alliance and the 1904 Serbian–Bulgarian alliance, secrecy around the treaty negotiations was deliberately used to limit the reaction time of the alliance target. We also continue our examination of the 1955 US–ROC mutual defense treaty, which we began in the previous chapter. In this case, US and ROC leaders agreed to negotiate in secret specifically to circumvent obstacles that might otherwise have slowed implementation.

The rest of this chapter proceeds as follows. First, we develop the theory of peaceful alliances, showing how reducing an alliance's expected strength can pave the way for peace. Second, we extend our theoretical model to endogenize the design of alliances, allowing the allies to modify the strength of their commitments. Third, we apply these theoretical insights to the historical record, also highlighting the important role that secrecy plays in preserving peace. A final section sums up the argument.

5.1 Designing Alliances to Avoid Commitment Problems

To connect the design of alliance content to the presence or absence of commitment problems, we begin by illustrating the basic mechanics of our theoretical model, with an eye towards understanding the forces that create a commitment problem. In this section, we illustrate these forces in two steps.

First, we provide a detailed illustration of the model's equilibrium dynamics to show precisely *why* careful alliance design can preserve peace. We show that reducing an alliance's expected strength plays a key role in opening space for negotiations with states targeted by an alliance. In our model, war occurs because targeted states know that they will lose ground in future negotiations. And whether war occurs turns on whether targeted states can be compensated with concessions to offset these future losses. Tracing this logic, we argue that limiting the expected strength of an alliance reduces these future losses, making compensation possible.

Second, though our theory implies that it is possible in principle for allies to limit their commitments to one another to avoid provoking a shared enemy, it raises another question: Should we expect these limits to be imposed in practice? Limiting expected strength has the benefit of avoiding war, but also has a significant cost. It can make space for peaceful negotiation, but it also reduces the long-term security benefits the allies will enjoy once the alliance is successfully implemented. To analyze how this trade-off operates in practice, we extend our model to make alliance design choices endogenous. We find that allies will modify their commitments to avoid war in some cases, but not others.

5.1.1 How Alliance Design Creates Space for Negotiation

To understand how allies can avoid war by manipulating an alliance's expected strength, it is first necessary to connect expected strength to war under our theory. Recalling the analysis of Chapters 3 and 4, two factors determine whether an impending alliance will trigger preventive war: the size of the power shift (Δ) and the speed of alliance implementation (r).

We can get a first foothold towards understanding these dynamics by analyzing the conditions for war outlined in Chapter 3. In particular, recall Proposition 3.3, which says that a commitment problem, and war, will occur if a key condition is met. We can write this condition equivalently as

$$\Delta r > \frac{(1-\delta)(1-w_2)}{\delta}. \tag{5.1}$$

Writing the condition in this way is useful for understanding how the size and speed of a power shift jointly act to determine whether a commitment problem is present. In particular, we see that the left-hand side of the inequality is the interactive effect of the power shift's size and speed. If Δ increases, corresponding to an increase in the size of the power shift, the condition becomes more likely to hold. Similarly, if r increases, corresponding to an increase in the speed of alliance implementation, the condition becomes more likely to hold.

Thus, it is necessary to consider the size *and* speed of an alliance-induced power shift to understand how modifications to an alliance can preserve peace. Thus, we will refer to Δr as the *expected strength* of the alliance. This expression points to a key lesson of our theory: An alliance may trigger war because of a state's *expectations* of how the alliance will alter the distribution of military power in the international system. Thus, an increase in either the speed or size of a shift increases an alliance's expected strength. Some factors contribute to the size of a power shift, and others contribute to expectations about how quickly it will arrive. Our argument points to the importance of both of these factors, so we focus throughout this chapter on how allies can shape their cooperative relationships to modify an alliance's expected strength.

What is the specific mechanism connecting the expected strength of an alliance to commitment problems and war? As discussed in detail in the preceding chapters, bargaining between prospective allies and a shared enemy is key. An enemy state anticipates that it will be in a weaker position if an opposing alliance comes into force. Alliances aggregate military capabilities, so once an alliance has been implemented, the allies can more effectively resist aggression from enemy states. Recognizing this, enemy states know that once an alliance comes into force, they will no longer be able to effectively use force—either directly on the battlefield or through coercion in peaceful bargaining—to achieve their objectives. This creates an incentive for enemies to reject proposals in bargaining before alliance implementation, so they can fight from a position of strength rather than negotiate in the future from a position of weakness.

This dynamic consideration opens the way for peace, but only if conditions are right. Anticipating an enemy's concerns about the future, prospective allies have an important tool at their disposal: concessions in the present. By offering concessions, allies reduce an enemy's incentive to fight, as fighting threatens peaceful concessions that can be won in the present without shouldering the cost of war. However, concessions are not a panacea. Allies must be able to offer an enemy sufficient compensation for their anticipated future losses. What determines whether such a deal is feasible?

We can draw on the analysis of the previous chapters to illustrate when such deals are possible. We discuss the mechanics of equilibrium play informally here, and refer the reader back to the exposition in Chapters 4 and 5 for the technical details. Recall the decision calculus of the enemy of an alliance (State 2 in our model) in a period in which the alliance has not yet been successfully implemented.[1] Facing a peaceful offer in such a period, State 2 has two options. One is war, which yields their pre-alliance payoff in all future periods. The other option is to accept a peaceful settlement. From State 2's perspective, accepting such an offer involves a dynamic trade-off. On the one hand, if the allies offer a generous settlement, then the short-term payoff is quite advantageous. On the other hand, accepting a settlement in the present risks having the alliance come into force in the future, which implies less advantageous settlements in the long run. It is clear that for concessions to be attractive to State 2, the short-term gains they offer must compensate for long-term losses.

This is why the expected strength of an alliance is important: It determines the scope of the long-term losses State 2 risks by forgoing war in the present. In turn, this determines the size of the concessions necessary to compensate

[1] This logic carries over to nonstationary equilibria as well, though the presentation is more cumbersome. We discuss history-dependent strategies and nonstationary equilibria in the following chapter.

State 2 for these future losses. As the strength of an alliance grows, more and more concessions are necessary. If the alliance's anticipated strength is too high, the allies may not have sufficient resources to compensate State 2. In this case, even though the allies may desire negotiations that would placate State 2, such a deal is simply not feasible. This is exactly what drives Inequality 5.1. If the expected strength of the alliance (Δr) is too high, then negotiations are doomed to fail.

Fortunately for the allies, expectations about an alliance's strength are not determined exogenously. Rather, the strength of an alliance is a direct product of its institutional design. In our model, intentional design is the key mechanism that connects the design and management of alliance content to war. Modifications to a planned alliance can change the value of Δr, lowering the expected strength of an alliance enough to create space for negotiations.

While this implies that allies may avoid war by modifying an alliance to reduce its expected strength, it raises an important question: Will such modifications be made in practice? The answer is not obvious, as watering down an alliance to allow space for bargaining has costs and benefits. The benefits are clear: If war can be avoided, then the allies avoid its costs, and they will also have the benefits of an alliance once implementation is complete. However, reducing the expected strength of an alliance to preserve peace means that the allies will have less ability to resist future aggression or to benefit from their aggregated force at the bargaining table in the future.

How do allies navigate this trade-off? So far our theoretical framework treats Δ and r as exogenous factors, so we cannot yet make claims about how allies might endogenously manipulate these factors in equilibrium to avoid war. In the following section we rectify this, extending the model to allow these factors to be endogenously chosen by the allies.

5.1.2 When Will Allies Manipulate Expected Strength?

When will allies limit the expected strength of their alliance commitments to avoid war? If the point of an alliance is to deter aggression, it seems puzzling that allies would intentionally limit the scope of their mutual commitments just to *reduce* the power-aggregating effect of a security partnership. However, as we have argued above, deterrence is only one goal of the alliance formation process. Prospective allies must also be mindful of how their enemies will react in anticipation of new commitments that would alter the distribution of military power. If the alliance-induced power shift looks to be sufficiently large and rapid, the enemy state may launch a war to stop the alliance before it gets off the ground. This implies that allies do not unambiguously benefit from increases in the anticipated strength of an alliance.

Thus, allies might want to weaken their alliance because a stronger alliance is more likely to provoke preventive war, and war is costly and risky. In many cases, to avoid provoking a shared enemy, allies may wish to limit some aspects of their alliance even if increasing them would have clear benefits. If an alliance comes into force quickly, the allies benefit more by quickly enjoying the benefits of military cooperation in bargaining with a shared enemy. And if the power shift from such cooperation grows, the bargaining benefits also grow. But so does the likelihood of war.

This trade-off is why alliance design is not a straightforward choice. In designing their cooperative agreements, allies must strike a careful balance between enhancing deterrence and risking provocation. Though war is costly and risky and therefore worth avoiding, doing so may itself cost too much, by weakening the alliance so that it carries essentially no benefits in the peaceful period following alliance formation. This makes clear why it is necessary to consider not only *why* allies might intentionally limit the military benefits of their agreements but also *when* they will choose to do this in practice.

As a first cut, it is useful to think about how the equilibrium welfare of the allies changes as a result of changes in the expected strength of the alliance. This helps illustrate why considering alliance design as an endogenous choice is worthwhile. If either strengthening or weakening an alliance always made the allies better off, then the choice would not be particularly interesting. However, as we will show, there is a real trade-off here; the equilibrium welfare of the allies is not monotonic in the expected strength of the alliance. We formally demonstrate this trade-off in the following proposition.

Proposition 5.1. *The equilibrium utilities of States 1 and 3 are*

1. *nonmonotonic in Δ, and*
2. *nonmonotonic in r.*

This proposition shows that designing alliance content is not trivial. Rather, there is a real trade-off between the benefits of strengthening an alliance and the risk of provoking an enemy. But the mere fact that the utilities are not monotonic in the expected strength of an alliance (measured through Δ and/or r) does not paint the whole picture. The nature of this nonmonotonicity is important. To see why, consider two possibilities for what a nonmonotonic relationship between an alliance's power and equilibrium payoffs might look like.[2] One possibility is that the relationship has a U shape. In this case, we should expect, all else equal, to see allies bias the design of their alliances towards the extremes, either emphasizing deterrence or avoiding provocation. Another possibility is that the relationship has an inverted-U shape. In this case we should expect allies to pursue a balanced approach, finding an optimal middle ground that pursues the highest level of deterrence that does not lead to provocation.

Interestingly, the function has neither of these shapes. Rather, the nonmonotonicity arises from a *discontinuity* in the payoffs of the players. Before we move on to extend the model to incorporate an endogenous choice of anticipated alliance strength, it is useful to explain the nature of this discontinuity in equilibrium welfare to clarify the allies' incentives.

We show a diagram of equilibrium welfare as a function of the size of the power shift, Δ, in Figure 5.1.[3] The first thing to note about the figure is the point at which the discontinuity occurs, Δ^*. Recall from Chapter 3 that Δ^* is the point at which an alliance becomes provocative. Why does the discontinuity occur at this point? For values of $\Delta < \Delta^*$, the alliance comes into force peacefully because State 1 is willing to offer concessions to State 2 to compensate it for future losses due to the alliance-induced power shift. As Δ increases, but remains below Δ^*, the allies' equilibrium welfare increases. Bargaining dynamics drive this increase. In this region, equilibrium play is peaceful, with State 1 calibrating its offer to render State 2 indifferent between accepting and starting a war. Therefore, the bargaining gains for State 1 are constant in such periods, but as the size of the power shift increases, State 1's expected future gains are increasing. The combination of these two forces leads to marginal increases in equilibrium welfare in this region.

Once Δ exceeds Δ^*, however, State 2 chooses to reject *all* offers in equilibrium. This means that if the alliance is not implemented immediately,

[2] There are many possibilities here. For presentational purposes, we consider just two to illustrate the stakes of understanding this relationship for our theory.

[3] The relevant figure for the speed of the power shift (r) is analogous, so for ease of presentation we focus on implementation speed here.

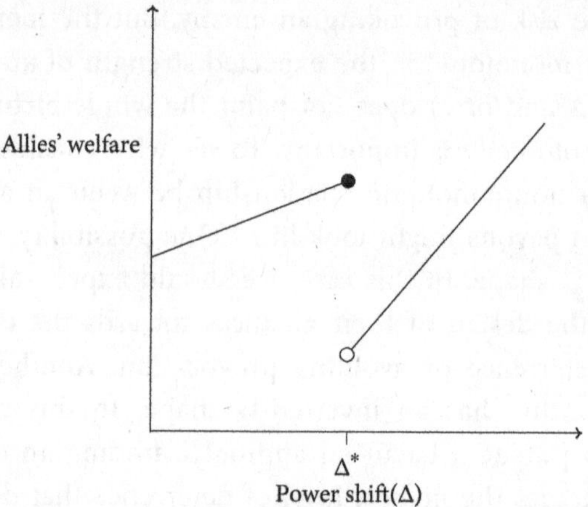

Figure 5.1 Effect of power shift on equilibrium welfare.
Note: This figure plots the discontinuity in equilibrium welfare as a function of Δ, the size of the alliance-induced power shift. The relevant figure for the speed of the power shift, *r*, is analogous. The horizontal axis includes only power shifts for which alliances form with positive probability on the path of play in equilibrium.

which occurs with probability *r*, a preventive attack will occur. Because this preventive attack occurs prior to implementation of the alliance, the allies receive their pre-implementation war payoffs, losing out on the surplus that otherwise comes from peaceful bargaining. This accounts for the step downward in the allies' equilibrium welfare at Δ*. For values of Δ that are barely above Δ*, the equilibrium probability of war jumps discontinuously from 0 to 1 – *r*, driving the step down in equilibrium utility. Interestingly, however, as Δ increases further above Δ*, the allies begin to view the trade-off differently. This is because higher values of Δ may compensate for the risk of war, which is constant, as it is a function of *r*. For very high values of Δ, the benefits of an alliance, if the allies are able to implement it quickly, are very large. In this case, the allies may prefer to pursue an alliance that they know carries a risk of war. As the graph indicates, for high enough values of Δ, the allies may prefer to attempt implementation of a provocative alliance, knowingly engaging in a risk–reward trade-off that balances the risk of war against the rewards of a powerful and quickly implemented alliance.

This foreshadows the trade-offs that emerge when the allies endogenously manipulate the expected strength of their alliance commitments. In Figure 5.1, it is clear that values of Δ to the far right of the figure will maximize the allies' utility, even though this would risk war. But in practice this may not always be possible. Though power shifts from alliances are often substantial, they are not unlimited. States have finite resources and capabilities to commit to the battlefield. Consequently, the feasible strength of an alliance is constrained by the resources and capabilities available to the potential allies. As we will show, these constraints are key to understanding when allies will seek to limit their commitments to avoid war, and when they will pursue risky alliances that provoke aggression from enemies.

Ultimately, whether allies limit expected strength comes down to the maximum feasible strength of the alliance. If it is high enough, they will choose to pursue a risky alliance, justifying the risk of war by implementing the alliance before their adversary can react. But if it is not high enough, allies will intentionally water down their commitments to open space for negotiations, guaranteeing peace in the process.

With this understanding of the trade-offs, we extend the model to make the size and speed of the power shift resulting from alliance an endogenous choice. To ease the presentation, we extend the baseline model presented in Chapter 3, abstracting away from the small-scale conflicts considered in the previous chapter. We consider two simple extensions of the baseline model that endogenize w_2' and r, respectively. Endogenizing these two factors allows us to consider whether allies will intentionally limit the expected strength of an alliance.

In the first extension, suppose that before $t = 1$, State 3 selects the extent of the power shift from the alliance by choosing some $w_2' \in [\overline{w}, w_2]$, where $\overline{w}$ represents the maximum feasible power shift resulting from an alliance with State 1. In the second extension, State 3 selects a value $r \in [0, \overline{r}]$, where $\overline{r}$ is the greatest speed with which State 3 is able to provide State 1 with the military benefit of an alliance. In each extension, after either w_2' or r is selected, play proceeds as in the baseline model. To focus on the most interesting case in which it is feasible for State 3 to select values of w_2' or r that produce a risk of war, suppose that $\overline{w} < w_2 - \frac{(1-\delta)(1-w_2)}{\delta r}$ and that $\overline{r} > \frac{(1-\delta)(1-w_2)}{\delta(w_2-w_2')}$. Then there always exist conditions under which the allies will choose to limit the expected strength.

Proposition 5.2. *The conditions under which State 3 endogenously limits the size or speed of the shift in power from alliance are as follows:*

1. *In the extension with endogenous w_2', there exists a unique $\hat{w}_2 < w_2 - \frac{(1-\delta)(1-w_2)}{\delta r}$ such that if $\overline{w}_2 > \hat{w}_2$, State 3 sets $w_2' = w_2 - \frac{(1-\delta)(1-w_2)}{\delta r}$, and war does not occur in equilibrium. Otherwise, the allies set $w_2' = \overline{w}_2$, and war occurs with positive probability.*

2. *In the extension with endogenous r, there exists a unique* $\hat{r} > \frac{(1-\delta)(1-w_2)}{\delta(w_2-w_2')}$ *such that if* $\bar{r} < \hat{r}$*, State 3 sets* $r = \frac{(1-\delta)(1-w_2)}{\delta(w_2-w_2')}$*, and war does not occur in equilibrium. Otherwise, the allies set* $r=\bar{r}$*, and war occurs with positive probability.*

Thus, maintaining peace by avoiding provocation is often in the allies' best interests. To trace the logic, we focus on the extension in which w_2' is chosen endogenously.[4] On the one hand, if a large enough power shift is feasible, the allies may still choose to risk war, balancing the risk of attack against the benefit of a very strong alliance. On the other hand, if the largest possible power shift achievable is not very large, then State 3 chooses to limit the extent of the power shift resulting from its alliance commitment to State 1. Recall that this value of w_2' produces the largest possible shift in power that does not provoke aggression from State 2. In choosing this value, State 3 balances the trade-offs highlighted in the preceding discussion; the power-enhancing benefits of the alliance are maximized, while the risk of enemy provocation is minimized.

This result shows that the deterrence–provocation trade-off discussed above can break either way. The allies' choice depends on the maximum feasible strength of the alliance. If this strength is high enough, it justifies the risk of war, and the allies choose to push their cooperation to the brink, engaging in a race to implement the alliance before an enemy can strike. Otherwise, the allies limit their commitments to make way for negotiations that pacify an enemy, removing the alliance's provocative effects altogether.

5.1.3 Discussion of Formal Results

Before we turn to the case analysis, we provide a summary of this chapter's key theoretical points. For convenience, Table 5.1 gathers the key theoretical insights from this chapter.

First, we showed that the allies' equilibrium utility is nonmonotonic in the *expected strength* of an alliance. This is because increases in expected strength have offsetting effects. On the one hand, expected strength increases the allies' long-term payoffs once implementation occurs. On the other hand, if expected strength is sufficiently high, war occurs. Therefore, the

[4] The logic in the extension with endogenous *r* is analogous.

Table 5.1 Summary of theoretical results

	Result	Description
Chapter 5		
Proposition 5.1	Nonmonotonic utility	Allies' utility does not uniformly increase or decrease in the expected strength of the alliance
Proposition 5.2 (a)	Endogenous power shift size	Increases in the size of an alliance-induced power shift increase allies' equilibrium welfare up to a point, then lead to a discontinuous decrease in utility
Proposition 5.2 (b)	Endogenous implementation speed	Increases in the speed of alliance implementation increase allies' equilibrium welfare up to a point, then lead to a discontinuous decrease in utility

allies' utility increases in expected strength until a critical threshold is met and the alliance becomes provocative. At this point, war occurs in equilibrium and the allies' utility jumps downward.

Second, we build on this insight to study how allies might endogenously choose the expected strength of an alliance. We show that their choice depends on whether they can push the expected strength sufficiently high or not. If a sufficiently high expected strength is feasible, then it is worth it for the allies to risk war to push through a provocative alliance before an enemy can react. Otherwise, allies will limit expected strength, maximizing their payoff by implementing an alliance that does not provoke war.

5.2 Manipulating Alliance Content in Practice

Two important points emerge from this chapter's theoretical analysis. First, adjustments to the expected strength of an alliance can allow otherwise provocative alliances to be implemented peacefully. Second, these modifications are sometimes in the best interests of the allies, as a weakened peaceful alliance may be preferable to a stronger one that carries a risk of provoking preventive war. In this section, we compare these theoretical insights to the historical record to demonstrate that these arguments help to explain observed patterns of alliance behavior. We illustrate the mechanism with two cases. First, we show that the peaceful inclusion of the unified Germany in NATO was driven by an intentional reduction of the alliance's expected strength. Second, we show that the United States sought to quickly push through a defense pact with the ROC before the PRC could react.

The rest of this section proceeds as follows. First, we consider NATO's inclusion of the unified Germany after the fall of the Soviet Union. We argue that both factors indicated by our theory are present in this case, and that the logic of reducing an alliance's expected power provides a useful lens to understand this historic event. This case also illustrates how content modification works in practice, detailing the tools NATO used to carefully design the unified Germany's entry into the alliance in a way that created space for peaceful negotiation with Russia.

Next we consider the US–ROC mutual defense pact. In this case, the allies raced to implement their commitment quickly, using a crucial tool of statecraft: secrecy. Secrecy is a common feature of military alliances. Studies have shown that allies often use secrecy to avoid signaling their common interests to enemy states (Bils and Smith 2023) or to conceal contradictory alliance commitments from other allies (Kuo 2020). We argue that the US–ROC pact highlights a third, complementary explanation for secrecy: It can speed the implementation of an alliance, shrinking an adversary's window of opportunity to engage in preventive war.

5.2.1 Reducing Expected Strength: The Case of German Unification

Our theory implies that the mere fact that an alliance comes into force peacefully does not entail that the alliance was not provocative. Rather, as we have argued above, provocative alliances induce a risk–reward tradeoff, with allies racing to implement the alliance before an enemy can react. This means that some provocative alliances will come into force peacefully—when implementation happens before an enemy can successfully mount a preventive attack. Simply put, under our theory, two distinct logics can generate the same outcome of peaceful alliance implementation. For this reason, care is required to differentiate cases in which provocative alliances were implemented swiftly and peacefully from alliances that were implemented peacefully because of intentional design that reduced their expected strength.

Fortunately, our theoretical framework provides observable implications that can guide us in distinguishing the two categories of alliances that come into force peacefully. In particular, it points to two factors that differentiate peaceful alliances that are governed by the logic of this chapter from those governed by the logic of the previous chapters. First, we should expect to observe allies taking action to reduce the expected strength of an alliance only in cases where the logic of this chapter applies. As we have seen, allies have two options when trying to implement an alliance. On the one hand, they can modify it to open space for negotiations, which guarantees peace but comes at the cost of a weakened alliance and concessions to an enemy state. On the other hand, they can knowingly forge ahead with a provocative alliance, hoping that implementation succeeds before the enemy can react. In the second case, because an enemy will attack if afforded a window of opportunity to do so, there is no incentive for the allies to limit the expected strength of the alliance. This stands in contrast to the approach described in this chapter, where allies limit the expected strength of an alliance to guarantee peace. This implies that we should observe allies taking actions to limit expected strength if and only if the logic of this chapter applies.

Second, we should expect to observe serious negotiations only in cases where allies intentionally limit the expected strength of an alliance, ensuring peace by the logic laid out in the previous section. Recall that reductions to an alliance's expected strength work precisely because they open space for negotiations that compensate the enemy of the alliance for expected future losses. This stands in stark contrast to the equilibrium behavior considered in Chapter 4, in which the enemy of an alliance will reject any proposal. In that case, equilibrium offers are not taken seriously by the enemy of an alliance. This implies that we should observe meaningful negotiations between potential allies and a shared enemy if and only if the logic of content modification described in this chapter applies.

The 1990 reunification of Germany and the subsequent inclusion of the newly unified German state in NATO fundamentally upended the Cold War security order. Though West Germany had been a NATO member since 1955, unification posed a provocative new question. Would the East German territory, formerly covered under the Soviet-led Warsaw Pact, come under the security umbrella of NATO? In February 1990, Gorbachev expressed opposition to the prospect of NATO expansion to include a unified Germany (Newnham 1999, 428–429). Yet Germany reunified and peacefully joined NATO without provoking Soviet action.

The case bears a striking resemblance to the structure of the formal model. NATO allies, led by the United States,[5] sought the inclusion of the unified Germany in NATO. As a result, German diplomats worked to find solutions that would allow this. These roles are analogous to those of States 3 (the United States) and 1 (Germany), respectively, in our model. The Soviets played a role akin to that of State 2, bargaining with the prospective allies while maintaining the threat to use military action to block the alliance from coming into force.

Consistent with our theoretical analysis, concerns over what the Soviets might do in anticipation of unification and NATO expansion figured prominently in the 1990 negotiations. At the outset of negotiations, Gorbachev's approval of a unification deal was far from guaranteed. A key complicating factor was the roughly 400,000 Soviet troops stationed in East Germany. This gave Gorbachev significant leverage (Sarotte 2014*a*, 31). The possibility of military resistance to an unfavorable reunification arrangement was real, and in the period leading up to reunification, Gorbachev repeatedly resisted pushes from Soviet military officials for action (Newnham 1999, 428). A simple refusal to remove Soviet troops from the East could have had disastrous consequences. Consequently, the United States planned for a worst-case scenario involving Soviet military action in the GDR (Sayle 2019, 221–222). Hoping to avoid such a confrontation, US diplomats prioritized learning how to win Gorbachev's assent to Germany's unification and inclusion in NATO (Shifrinson 2016, 22).

How was this approval gained and provocation avoided? The logic of our equilibrium analysis highlights some important factors, which are clear in the historical record. Proposition 3.2 describes the conditions under which an alliance may come into force peacefully without provoking a shared enemy. For an alliance to come into force peacefully in equilibrium, the resulting shift in power cannot be too large or too fast. In other words, the alliance's expected strength must not be too high.

Consistent with this logic, provisions such as troop limits and withdrawal timelines were key to winning Soviet assent for the unified Germany's membership. In particular, the United States pushed for "nine assurances" that

[5] It is widely acknowledged that the United States led the way in reunification talks, with NATO allies largely following the agenda set by US negotiators (Moens 1991; Sarotte 2010, 130; Sayle 2019, 228).

were designed to make the transition less threatening. Key among these provisions were limits on NATO troops in previous Soviet territory, as well as a relaxed withdrawal timeline and limits on the placement of nuclear weapons in German territory. A particularly important concession was Helmut Kohl's agreement to limit the number of troops in the Bundeswehr to 370,000 (Sarotte, 2010, 125–130). These provisions served to moderate the size and speed of the power shift resulting from membership, rendering the change less provocative. Gorbachev, in his memoir, indicates that these limits to the power and timeline of the transition to unification and full NATO membership were key in opening up the possibility of a negotiated settlement (Gorbachev, 1996, 527–529).

With an opening for peaceful bargaining over unification and NATO expansion, a final agreement could be constructed to win Gorbachev's approval. Consistent with the logic of our Proposition 3.2, Germany made concessions to pacify the Soviets. In a meeting early in the negotiation process, US president George H.W. Bush suggested that West German chancellor Helmut Kohl's "deep pockets" might help facilitate a deal (Rice and Zelikow 1995, 215). Germany then followed through with substantial loans to the Soviets. Even public observers noted the importance of these loans in securing Soviet agreement on the NATO issue. For example, the July 1990 issue of the *Economist* featured a political cartoon depicting Gorbachev holding open a door for Helmut Kohl labeled "NATO," while Gorbachev's other hand clutched a bag of Deutsche Marks. Years later, the then deputy national security advisor Robert Gates recalled the importance of these concessions, writing that US and German diplomats aimed "to bribe the Soviets out of Germany" (Gates 2011, 492).

There is much agreement among Cold War historians that the factors highlighted in our theory played a pivotal role. For example, Sarotte's historical analysis paints the US–German strategy of positive incentives as central to the eventual outcome: "The carrots they decided on were large sums of money and the reform of NATO" (2014*a*, 171). Many scholars have focused on the role of financial incentives, and in particular the importance of German loans and financial support for Soviet troop relocation (Wettig 1993; Newnham 1999, 2002; Sarotte 2010). Others point to actions that limited NATO's military threat, pointing to the role of concrete reforms as well as diplomatic negotiations and concessions (Asmus 2004, 6; Goldgeier 2010, 14–17; Shifrinson 2016; Sarotte 2014*b*).

5.2.2 Risky Implementation: The Case of US–Taiwan Relations

Though allies sometimes wish to avoid war altogether by tempering the expected strength of their commitments, in other cases they may wish to rush implementation. Though this strategy carries a risk of war, this risk can be mitigated if allies are able to increase the speed of implementation sufficiently high. Increasing implementation speed has offsetting effects. On the one hand, it increases the provocative potential of the alliance, possibly triggering a preventive war. On the other hand, if the alliance is quickly implemented without intervention, its deterrent benefits will take effect before an adversary can respond. In this section, we consider the case of US–Taiwan relations to illustrate how speedy implementation works in practice. Our analysis points to secrecy as a critical factor that enables provocative alliances to be implemented quickly, reducing the risk of preventive war.

Many historical military alliances were established in secret (Bils and Smith 2023; Kuo 2020). Various motivations underpin this secrecy. According to Bils and Smith (2023), secret alliances maintain ambiguity regarding states' alignments in uncertain environments. Kuo (2020) suggests that secrecy helps states hide commitments that might conflict with other treaty obligations. Ritter (2004) argues that secrecy prevents potential adversaries from countering the alliance. A key insight from the literature is that, unlike transparent alliances which deter conflict by signaling commitment (Morrow 2000), secret alliances are believed to increase the likelihood of armed conflict by adding uncertainty to decision-making (Bils and Smith 2023; Bas and Schub 2016).

We offer an additional explanation for secret alliances with different implications for war. Our theory of dynamic alliance implementation posits that leaders are motivated to conceal the implementation process when the window for implementation is long enough to invite preventive attacks from potential targets. By keeping negotiations and military integration covert, allies can reduce the time targets have to detect and counteract the shifting power dynamics. Concealing the implementation process effectively accelerates its pace by cutting the target's reaction time.

Our analysis, as outlined in Chapter 3, shows that increasing implementation speed, r, can have offsetting effects, ultimately resulting in a lower probability of war once the implementation speed exceeds a certain threshold. While very high speeds may increase the provocative nature of the alliance, they also reduce the target's opportunity to launch a preemptive attack. Consequently, many of the most provocative alliances are formed peacefully because targets are unable to counteract the alliance before it has been implemented in practice. Prospective allies have an incentive to push up implementation speed if *r* is high enough that the attempt to form an alliance is provocative but not so fast that the target has enough time to launch an attack before the allies can bring the power shift into force. Secret implementation may be used as a tool to accelerate *r*.

How can secrecy accelerate the implementation of an alliance? As discussed in Chapter 2, the speed of implementation, denoted as *r*, is influenced by numerous factors, both political and military. Additionally, accelerating alliance implementation is not solely dependent on the allies; it also depends on the readiness of the targeted adversary. If allies can quickly implement an alliance but the enemy can match pace with swift preventive attacks, the relative speed of *r* remains slow.

Given the various factors that can impede implementation from both the ally and adversary sides, allies possess several strategies to influence *r* and avoid preventive attacks. They might expedite their own treaty negotiations and military integration efforts. Alternatively, they could introduce obstacles to hinder the target's ability to conduct preventive strikes. Both approaches can speed up *r*, making the alliance both more provocative and more likely to be successfully implemented without conflict.

Secrecy can improve the chances of a peaceful alliance implementation. By concealing various political and military factors detailed in Chapter 2, allies can reduce the target's response time, thus accelerating the implementation process and enhancing the likelihood of achieving the alliance without conflict. If the target is unaware of ongoing treaty negotiations, their opportunity to respond is limited by the duration they remain uninformed. Additionally, secrecy can protect the negotiation process from interference by hostile domestic actors, preventing potential delays and disruptions.

Secrecy can also speed the military dimension of implementation. For example, the Cuban Missile Crisis began with the Soviet attempt to secretly house nuclear missiles in Cuba, a case of attempted alliance which we examine in detail in the next chapter. US intelligence discovered Soviet–Cuban attempts to implement this military commitment, and the crisis that followed illustrates how *r* captures the relative speed between allies' efforts to implement an alliance versus the target's ability to respond in time to block it. Once the aim to implement the Soviet–Cuban alliance was no longer a secret, a race ensued between the United States and the opposing Soviet Union and Cuba. Could the United States stop the implementation of the alliance before the power shift came fully into force? The motivation for secrecy in this case was, effectively, to shorten the US reaction time.

Importantly, perfect secrecy is not necessary for this strategy to be effective. Covert implementation can lower the likelihood of an attack if it allows allies to complete the power shift before the target can respond. Even late-stage revelations or persistent uncertainty during implementation may hinder a target's ability to act promptly.

Many European military alliances signed in the nineteenth century were conducted in secret. Evidence suggests that our theory accounts for at least some of these secret arrangements and can also explain the use of secrecy in certain twentieth-century alliances.

The mutual defense pact between the United States and the Republic of China, which came into force on March 3, 1955, took over a year and a half to implement. As we discussed in Chapter 4, the PRC government frequently made its displeasure known regarding the US–ROC talks on a military alliance. How, then, did secrecy play a role if the PRC was already aware of this initiative?

As we discussed in Chapter 4, as an attempt to block a US–ROC mutual defense pact to defend Chinese Nationalist-held territories, including the island of Taiwan, the Pescadores, and other offshore islands, the PRC launched a series of attacks lasting from September 1954 through the treaty's ratification in March 1955. After the PRC aggression began, the United States plotted a two-pronged strategy to accelerate implementation. First, they negotiated the treaty terms in secret to bypass domestic political obstacles that might stall implementation. Second, they tried to build a secret coalition that, once formed, would pressure the PRC to stop using aggression.

The United States and ROC launched formal but secret negotiations at the beginning of October. Secretary of State Dulles asked Karl Rankin, US Ambassador to the Republic of China, to impress on Chiang Kai-shek the absolute necessity for secrecy: "please stress necessity for absolute secrecy. You should tell him that due to absence of key Congressional leaders from Washington we cannot complete our consultations re mutual defense security treaty for at least three weeks, when Congressional elections will be over and Senate reconvened."[6] With the mid-term congressional elections only three weeks away, the Eisenhower administration worried that certain members of Congress might throw up roadblocks to negotiations before the United States and ROC finalized the language and had a chance to explain the treaty plan to individual members of Congress in person. Dulles further conveyed the following to Chiang Kai-shek: "If .... the matter were to become public before our private explanations, then we fear that some Senators would publicly commit themselves to opposition, and once they are publicly committed then their conversion to support becomes extremely difficult. Also, the precise procedure we should adopt will depend to some extent upon the outcome of the November Congressional elections which will determine whether the Republicans or Democrats will organize the next Senate which would have to consider this treaty."[7]

In addition to concerns about domestic opposition, the Eisenhower administration was also building an international coalition to oppose PRC aggression in the Taiwan Strait. The plan was for New Zealand to introduce a resolution to the UN Security Council condemning PRC aggression against Nationalist-held offshore islands. The United States hoped that international pressure might induce the PRC to cease their attacks, thereby creating an open pathway for treaty implementation to move forward. However, to put the plan in place, the United States needed to build a coalition and make more progress on treaty negotiations. Chiang Kai-shek would not agree to a UN ceasefire resolution unless treaty negotiations had first been completed and announced to the Senate. Meeting these objectives, then, became a matter of timing. According to the ambassador from New Zealand, the representative who would be responsible for proposing the resolution to the Security Council, "his Government would like to see the shortest possible time elapse between the announcement by the U.S. Government regarding the proposed treaty and the announcement of the New Zealand initiative."[8]

Announcing the treaty and then moving quickly to the UN action, if successful, would accelerate the pace of implementation and avoid increased hostilities from the PRC. Secrecy would shield treaty talks from disruptions

[6] FRUS, 1952–54, China and Japan, vol. XIV, part 1, No. 343, "The Acting Secretary of State to the Embassy in the Republic of China," [Washington, DC] October 14, 1954.

[7] FRUS, 1952–54, China and Japan, vol. XIV, part 1, No. 344, "The Acting Secretary of State to the Embassy in the Republic of China," [Washington, DC] October 14, 1954.

[8] FRUS, 1952–54, China and Japan, vol. XIV, part 1, No. 361, "Memorandum of Conversation, by the Deputy Director of the Office of United Nations Political and Security Affairs (Bond)," [Washington, DC] October 26, 1954.

caused by members of Congress who intended to slow treaty negotiations, as well as slow preventive aggression by the PRC. However, in order to accomplish this strategy, treaty negotiations would need to be kept secret as would the diplomatic efforts to build the UN coalition.

The plan took much longer than both sides had hoped. Negotiations over treaty language between the United States and ROC dragged on for a month and a half with multiple lengthy meetings, extending well beyond the US mid-term elections. Walter Robertson, Assistant Secretary for Far Eastern Affairs and chief treaty negotiator for the United States, began to get impatient. In one round of negotiations, he told ROC negotiators that "Secretary (Dulles) wanted to conclude the negotiations immediately," and then he proceeded to stress the need for secrecy, urging that "the situation would be full of dynamite if a leak occurred."[9]

In addition, the UN plan failed to achieve a ceasefire. New Zealand submitted its motion to the UN as planned, and the UN invited the PRC to participate in a ceasefire discussion. The PRC rejected the invitation and the UN effort lost steam from there.

Meanwhile, in early November, the PRC stepped up its aggression by expanding its attacks from Quemoy to the Tachen Islands. The timing of the new attacks lined up with suspicion by US officials that there had been a leak of treaty negotiations and the New Zealand plan.[10] A *Washington Post* article alongside requests for clarity on the US plan from Australian diplomats confirmed suspicions that information had been leaked.[11] Robertson faulted these leaks for disruptions in negotiations.[12]

The solution to the resulting wave of PRC aggression was to move faster. When asked by British diplomats how increased tensions impacted US thinking about the Taiwan Strait, Livingston Merchant, the US Assistant

[9] FRUS, 1952–54, China and Japan, vol. XIV, part 1, No. 382, "Memorandum of Conversation, by the Director of the Office of Chinese Affairs (McConaughy)," [Washington, DC] November 4, 1954.

[10] FRUS, 1952–54, China and Japan, vol. XIV, part 1, No. 377, "Memorandum of Conversation, by the Director of the Office of Chinese Affairs (McConaughy)" [Washington, DC] November 2, 1954.

[11] FRUS, 1952–54, China and Japan, vol. XIV, part 1, No. 384, "Memorandum of Conversation, by the Counselor (MacArthur)" [Washington, DC] November 5, 1954; FRUS, 1952–1954, China and Japan, vol. XIV, part 1, No. 387, "Memorandum of Conversation, by the Director of the Office of Chinese Affairs (McConaughy)" [Washington, DC] November 9, 1954; Chalmers M. Roberts, "Authority to Attack China Vetoed by Ike: U.S. Plane Attack in China was Vetoed," *Washington Post*, November 8, 1954, pp. 1–2.

[12] FRUS, 1952–54, China and Japan, vol. XIV, part 1, No. 392, "Memorandum of Conversation, by the Director of the Office of Chinese Affairs (McConaughy)" [Washington, DC] November 12, 1954.

Secretary of State for European Affairs, replied that the uptick in tensions, "argued for speed."[13] The ambassador from New Zealand conveyed to US diplomats the nervousness of his foreign minister, who was anxious to initiate the New Zealand ceasefire in the UN. He relayed that his government feared the "continued absence of diplomatic activity on the subject of the offshore islands increased the chances that the Chinese Communists would persist in their probing activities, with the danger that these activities might at any moment be expanded into large-scale hostilities."[14] Robertson continued to put pressure on ROC negotiators, both pressing them to move faster and informing them, despite the leaks, that the text of the treaty needed to be kept secret: "the longer the delay in completing the treaty negotiations the more irresponsible speculation there would be. He stressed the importance of reaching full agreement, or else discontinuing the negotiations. ... we were holding the Treaty text very close. It went from person to person only by safe hand. No extra copies were made. The people who are handling it will not talk. The whole thing is being carried forward on an intimate basis."[15]

The treaty was finally signed on December 2, 1954, but had yet to be ratified by the US Senate. The PRC responded to the new treaty by saying, "The treaty had been described as provocative and, indeed, as an act of war. 'Grave consequences' would almost certainly follow."[16] The PRC made good on their threat, launching the largest attack yet on the Tachen Islands on January 10, 1955. The ROC noted to Robertson that the "scale of the January 10 attack was larger than any Communist air action in the Korean War."[17] As the PRC intended, the attacks were posing problems for ratification of the treaty. The Democratic National Committee circulated a memo to members of Congress questioning the mutual defense treaty. The delays to implementation along with the preventive aggression from the PRC were taking their toll.

[13] FRUS, 1952–54, China and Japan, vol. XIV, part 1, No. 379, "Memorandum of Conversation, by the Assistant Secretary of State for European Affairs (Merchant)," [Washington, DC] November 3, 1954.

[14] FRUS, 1952–54, China and Japan, vol. XIV, part 1, No. 388, "Memorandum of Conversation, by the Deputy of the Office of United Nations Political and Security Affairs (Bond)" [Washington, DC] November 9, 1954.

[15] FRUS, 1952–54, China and Japan, vol. XIV, part 1, No. 388, "Memorandum of Conversation, by the Director of the Office of Chinese Affairs (McConaughy)" [Washington, DC] November 22, 1954.

[16] FRUS, 1952–54, China and Japan, vol. XIV, part 1, No. 388, "Memorandum of Discussion at the 228th Meeting of the National Security Council," [Washington, DC] December 9, 1954.

[17] FRUS, 1955–57, China, vol. II, No. 8, "Memorandum of Conversation, Department of State," [Washington, DC] January 12, 1954.

Dulles recognized that the lengthy implementation time was making the United States susceptible to PRC aggression. He pointed out "that he thought one of the factors back of the communist activity at this time was in the hope that they would scare us out of ratifying the treaty. With ratification an accepted fact, it might take some of the heat out of the situation. If they think they can frighten us out of the treaty, they will continue their activity, and the Secretary considered it very desirable that we act on the treaty as soon as possible." He went on to emphasize this point: "one of the factors in this flare-up of activity is the feeling of the communist Chinese that they can frighten the United States from going through with this treaty. Once we nail this treaty down, there is some chance that the Chinese communists may tend to abate their efforts."[18]

Both the ROC and the Eisenhower administration felt the pressing urgency of ratification. To console anxious leaders in Taipei, Eisenhower pushed the Senate to expedite the ratification hearings from February 7 to February 2, though this small shift was of little comfort to either government. The crisis on the offshore islands remained at a constant state of alert until the treaty was finally ratified on March 3.

The 1954–55 Taiwan Strait Crisis underscores the role of secrecy in minimizing enemy provocations. Keeping the treaty secret was intended not only to prevent the PRC from learning about its implementation but also to avoid pre-election disruptions from Congress. While treaty talks and the international coalition plan were kept quiet, the PRC did little to escalate attacks. However, in cases when it was no longer possible to conceal these maneuvers, the PRC escalated hostilities. The leaders of both countries were clearly aware that the treaty implementation process was vulnerable to the PRC attacks. No longer able to operate under secrecy, the allies made every effort to speed up implementation before the crisis escalated further.

5.2.3 Secrecy in European Alliances

The case of US–Taiwan relations is not unique. Secrecy is a tool commonly used by allies to speed up implementation. We illustrate the generality of this

[18] FRUS, 1955–57, China, vol. II, No. 22, "Memorandum of Conversation, Department of State," [Washington, DC] January 20, 1954.

feature of alliance politics with two examples from European history: the 1894 Franco–Russian Alliance and the 1904 Serbian–Bulgarian Alliance.

1894 Franco–Russian Alliance

The implementation of the Franco–Russian alliance took four years due to several delays in negotiations. The partnership was developed in stages, with discussions kept strictly secret to avoid provoking a preventive attack from Germany (Snyder 1984, 118–121). In 1891, France and Russia established an informal entente, which at the insistence of the French was advanced to a military convention in 1892.

The Russians, aiming primarily to deter German aggression, were wary of provoking Germany through public knowledge of their alliance. Consequently, they were hesitant to formalize the agreement, fearing that ratification in the French parliament might expose the alliance.

The French, having lost Alsace-Lorraine to Germany in the Franco–Prussian War, had less concern for the status quo. They were eager to secure a formal commitment from Russia and less concerned about provoking Germany. To expedite the process, the French threatened to reveal the negotiations to the French parliament, making the pursuit of a military pact public and pressuring the slow-moving Russians to commit more firmly in private.

After various domestic and international distractions in 1892–93, formal negotiations resumed with greater urgency due to heightened tensions between Russia and Germany. The alliance was finally formalized and came into effect in January 1894.

1904 Serbian–Bulgarian Secret alliance

Serbia and Bulgaria concluded two secret treaties in 1904: the Treaty of Friendship, which among other things proposed a customs union between the partners; and the Treaty of Alliance, which called for mutual military assistance against third-party attack. The Treaty of Friendship stipulated that allies could disclose its terms only after preliminary agreement. The Treaty of Alliance was intended to remain secret (Merjanski 2007, 30–31).

At the time the alliance was being negotiated, Russia was expanding its influence into the Balkans, and anti-Austrian resistance in Serbia, Bulgaria, and other Balkan states was on the rise. Bulgaria and Serbia both feared that disclosure of the treaties would spark fierce countermeasures from the Austria–Hungarian monarchy and perhaps the Ottoman Empire (Merjanski 2007). These fears were born out when, on learning about the Treaty of Friendship, the Hapsburgs launched the Pig War, a trade war targeting Serbian pork, from 1906 to 1908.

5.3 Conclusion

In this chapter, we have argued that alliance design determines whether alliances cause commitment problems and war. By manipulating the design of their security commitments, allies can alter the expected strength of an impending alliance. Increasing an alliance's expected strength enhances the benefits of an alliance once implemented, but also makes preventive war by an enemy more likely. By reducing an alliance's expected strength, allies can reduce its provocative effects, though this will also reduce the benefits of the alliance once implementation occurs. These forces generate a crucial deterrence–provocation trade-off, and we have argued that understanding this trade-off is key to understanding the connection between alliances and preventive war.

Our theoretical analysis showed that the deterrence–provocation trade-off can break in either way. In some cases, allies will accept a risk of war to try to implement a provocative alliance. In other cases, allies will intentionally limit their commitments to ensure peace. Our theory offers an explanation of how this choice is made. The choice depends on how much the allies can feasibly increase the expected strength of an alliance. At a high enough expected strength, it makes sense to risk war to enjoy the benefits of a strong alliance. In this case, the allies will try to implement the alliance as quickly as possible, reducing the window of time in which an enemy could react to forestall it. But if the highest expected strength of an alliance is not strong enough, then the risk of war cannot be justified. In this case the allies will try to *reduce* the alliance's expected strength to a level that is not provocative. This will eliminate the risk of war, guaranteeing that the alliance is peacefully implemented. In this case, the long-term surplus captured by avoiding war outweighs the losses from reducing the alliance's expected strength.

Our theory also provides some important empirical implications that help untangle the complicated relationship between alliances and war. In particular, it helps disentangle two distinct mechanisms through which alliances might come into force peacefully. On the one hand, provocative alliances can be implemented peacefully if they are implemented quickly. Rapid implementation brings about an alliance's deterrent benefits before an adversary can react. On the other hand, some alliances come into force peacefully because they were not provocative to begin with. In this case, when the expected strength of the alliance is not too high, concessions offered to an enemy are pacifying, eliminating the incentive for preventive war altogether. In our case analysis we drew on our theory to identify observable markers that distinguish between these two cases. Thus, even though the outcome is the same, our theory can distinguish between two distinct logics of peaceful implementation.

This chapter's arguments also have lessons for future empirical work on the relationship between alliances and war. In particular, our work highlights that alliance design is an evolving process, and its importance manifests well before the date of an alliance treaty's signing. As we have argued in this chapter, understanding the politics of alliance implementation, and how they lead to war or peace, requires understanding the strategy allies use in designing their commitments. This requires data on specific factors indicated as important by our theory. An important task for future work is to quantitatively measure these factors, including exogenous constraints on the strength and speed of an alliance, efforts to manipulate an alliance's expected strength, and efforts to keep the military and political dimensions of implementation secret from enemies of an alliance.

Our work also has important policy implications. For example, it suggests that long-standing alliances like NATO face constraints that other alliances do not. NATO has stringent membership requirements, which put severe limits on the speed with which new members can be brought into the alliance. Our theory suggests that this prevents alliances like NATO from quickly bringing in allies, with the exception of cases like the recent accession of Finland, a state that conveniently already met membership standards. This constrains NATO's flexibility, effectively forcing it to pursue the strategy of peaceful negotiation when adding a new member, so it is unable to quickly add new members, such as Georgia and Ukraine, that need to reform to meet its membership standards.

Our theory also has implications for contemporary US relations with Taiwan. In particular, the United States must act with caution if it chooses to engage in deeper cooperation with Taiwan. Any increase in US support for Taiwan will clearly be met with hostility from China. To avoid preventive war, the United States must carefully navigate the deterrence–provocation trade-off discussed in this chapter. A careful assessment of the factors that determine which strategy towards a deeper alliance relationship is warranted, this should be the first step for policymakers considering deeper US–Taiwan security cooperation.

6
Deals to Prevent Cooperation

In the Warring States period (453–221 BCE), China was divided into multiple kingdoms that competed for political and territorial control. Some formed alliances for common defense and competitive advantage. During this period, the kingdom of Qin, which would ultimately prevail over the other kingdoms and unite China, became increasingly powerful and began to use its strength to expand its territory. Other states grew nervous and formed alliances for self-defense. These threatened to block Qin's eastward expansion. In response, Qin used various tactics to prevent alliances or break them up. In one instance, Qin bribed the kingdom of Chu to prevent the revival of a previous alliance between Chu and Qi. A Qin diplomat traveled to Chu and offered territorial concessions in exchange for Chu's breaking off its relationship with Qi. The concessions were accepted, and Chu turned away from Qi, enabling Qin to deal with each kingdom separately as opposed to a united bloc (Chao 2016).

This example from ancient China illustrates the reach of the underlying logic of the provocative characteristics of alliances. States facing opposing alliances are disadvantaged in future bargaining interactions and thus often have incentives to break up those alliances. But there are means other than war for doing this.

In the preceding chapters, we began by illustrating the connection between anticipated alliance formation and war. Though our initial findings painted a bleak picture, we moved on to consider the tools states use to avoid this. As the previous chapter detailed, one important approach relies on altering the content of an alliance—limiting either the speed with which it arrives or the shift in power it causes—to render it less threatening to an adversary. When this path is taken, alliances are observed coming into force peacefully, after being carefully modified to limit the threat they pose to adversaries.

When these content moderations work, they facilitate peace through deals in which the prospective allies make concessions to an adversary ahead of the alliance's implementation. These concessions provide the target of the

The Window Before. Brett V. Benson and Bradley C. Smith, Oxford University Press.
 DOI: 10.1093/9780197806760.003.0006

alliance with more than it could realistically expect to obtain through threats of war in the present, compensating it for future losses due to the eventual implementation of the alliance. Under this approach to peacebuilding, benefits flow from the prospective allies to the targeted state.

However, this is not the only strategy that states might use to avoid the commitment problem inherent in alliance formation. There is another approach, as illustrated by the kingdom of Qin in the Warring States period. The target of the alliance may use concessions to entice allies away from each other. If this works, peace prevails, because the alliance never happens.

That alternative is the subject of this chapter. We proceed as follows. First, we formalize the logic of anti-alliance deals in the context of our dynamic model of alliance formation. Formalizing this logic allows us to study the conditions under which such deals are feasible. We find that concessions are only part of the story. Successful deals also require a credible threat of punishment. Without that, potential allies have an incentive to renege on the terms of a deal designed to keep them out of alliance, reaping the benefits of concessions while also forging ahead with the implementation of a beneficial security partnership. Second, we leverage our formal analysis to detail the logic of anti-alliance deals further, with an eye towards understanding when deals will occur rather than war. Ultimately, our analysis suggests that this question is one of equilibrium selection, as deal equilibria always coexist with the bellicose equilibria described in Chapters 3 and 4. Finally, we discuss a number of prominent cases in which deals occurred. We use these cases to illustrate the logic of deal equilibria and to test the empirical plausibility of our theoretical framework. We find evidence consistent with the logic of anti-alliance deals in some important cases, including the Louisiana Purchase and the Cuban Missile Crisis. We also discuss how the logic of anti-alliance deals explains the prevalence of neutrality pacts throughout history.

6.1 The Logic of Anti-Alliance Deals

In this section, we extend our analysis to incorporate deals designed to stop alliances. This analysis reveals how targeted states can use carrots and sticks to induce prospective partners to forego alliance altogether. Thus, in the logic of this chapter, peace is maintained not through alterations to an alliance itself but through deals that cause the alliance to never come into force in the first place.

The key theoretical difference between the logic of alliance deals and the logic of previous chapters is that alliance deals emerge from expectations about *contingent punishment strategies*. This type of logic features prominently in the international relations literature. A familiar example is cooperation in the iterated prisoners' dilemma. As is well known, cooperation cannot be sustained as an equilibrium of the finite-horizon prisoners' dilemma. However, in an infinitely repeated version of the game, if players are sufficiently patient, then mutual cooperation can be sustained through the use of "punishment strategies." These strategies condition on past behavior, ensuring that players who defect will be punished for some number of rounds. The expectation of such punishment in the future induces states to cooperate today, tipping the scale in favor of the long-term gains from cooperation against the short-term benefit of defection.

Our explication of alliance deals rests on this logic. In these equilibria, alliances do not occur on the path of play even though the alliance is quite powerful and thus the commitment problem inherent in alliance formation detailed in previous chapters applies. Rather, in these equilibria prospective allies enter into an implicit deal with the targeted state of a potential alliance. How are these deals sustained? As a preview to the logic of such "deal" equilibria, consider the following. On the path of play in such an equilibrium, the prospective partners choose not to try and implement an alliance. In exchange, they extract relatively large concessions from the targeted state. Such a concession serves as a "carrot" that convinces the allies to forego an otherwise attractive alliance.

However, these carrots are only part of the story: such deal equilibria involve the "stick" of punishment as well. The second crucial component of a deal equilibrium involves expectations of punishment off the equilibrium path. In particular, if either of the prospective partners deviates in an attempt to implement an alliance, play reverts to a "punishment" strategy profile wherein war occurs on the path of play. This serves as a disincentive that, when combined with the positive inducement of concessions, prevents the prospective partners from implementing an alliance. In the analysis that follows, we detail this logic formally, tracing the conditions under which such equilibria can be sustained.

From a technical perspective, investigating such deals does not require any extension to the core ingredients of our model. Thus we maintain the simplest version of the model, as presented in Chapter 3, to present these equilibria. Presenting these equilibria simply entails a relaxation of our equilibrium selection criteria. In previous chapters, we focused on stationary, Markov perfect equilibria. This was appropriate for studying empirical situations in which alliances *do* occur on the path of play. In the equilibria studied in previous chapters, we focused on situations in which the players use simple, behavioral rules. In each period, the prospective partners either sought to implement an alliance or not. If so, the targeted state chose to accept the offered bargains or go to war in an attempt to stop the alliance. As we detailed, these equilibria delivered important insights about the connection between alliances, commitment problems, and war, in spite of the relatively simple behavior they entail. However, these equilibria did not involve players conditioning on components of the history of play that are not payoff-relevant. Thus, we have not yet considered equilibria in which players implement conditional punishment strategies, which necessarily require them to condition on payoff-irrelevant features of the history of play.

In this chapter, we simply focus on subgame perfect equilibria of the baseline model presented in Chapter 3. Of course, the equilibria we studied in previous chapters were themselves subgame perfect, but they also satisfied the additional Markov restriction, which requires players to avoid conditioning on payoff-irrelevant features of the history of play. The relaxation to subgame perfection allows us to study settings where players implement conditional punishment strategies.

More specifically, we are interested in studying equilibria that satisfy three conditions: an alliance does not occur on the path of play; war does not occur on the path of play; and such an equilibrium exists under parameter values in which war occurs under the baseline analysis in Chapter 3. In particular, that third condition entails that

$$a < r(w_2 - w_2')/(1 - \delta) \tag{6.1}$$

and

$$w_2' \leq w_2 - \frac{(1 - \delta)(1 - w_2)}{\delta r}. \tag{6.2}$$

The first two of these conditions are straightforward. As discussed in the introductory paragraphs of this chapter, our goal is to understand the logic of "deals" that are designed to maintain peace by preventing an alliance. Accordingly, to explain this phenomenon we need to find peaceful equilibria in which alliances do not occur on the path of play. This accounts for our first two requirements—that an alliance does not occur on the path of play, and that the path of play is peaceful. The third condition is more subtle. The reason we make these parameter restrictions is that we want to focus on situations where a deal meaningfully maintains peace by preventing an otherwise provocative alliance.

Recall that the analysis of Chapters 3 and 5 showed that alliances may come into being without causing war. If we find that deal equilibria exist only under these conditions, they will be weak tools for preventing the commitment problem inherent in alliance formation. That is, if such equilibria exist only under conditions in which alliances are not provocative, then they may serve to stop alliances, but not the dangerous alliances that are the focus of our analysis. Recall that Proposition 3.3 establishes that the implementation of an impending alliance becomes especially provocative when it threatens to produce a rapid and substantial shift in the balance of power. By focusing on these conditions, we are able to gain insight into meaningful deals that prevent otherwise dangerous alliances from occurring.

We refer to a subgame perfect equilibrium satisfying these three conditions as a "deal equilibrium," because they involve a deal between prospective allies and an enemy. On the path of play in a deal equilibrium, an alliance does not occur because targeted states offer concessions that, when combined with the expectation of punishment for reneging, induce the prospective partners to forego the process of alliance implementation altogether. The following proposition formally presents the conditions under which such equilibria exist.

Proposition 6.1. *If $a < r(w_2 - w_2')/(1 - \delta)$ and w_2' lies in an intermediate range, then a deal equilibrium exists in which an alliance does not occur on the path of play.*

More precisely, if

$$\frac{w_2 - [(1 - r)(1 - w_1) + (1 - \delta)a]}{r} \leq w_2' \leq w_2 - \frac{(1 - \delta)(1 - w_2)}{\delta r}, \tag{6.3}$$

then the following strategy profile constitutes an equilibrium:

1. *In any period in which $s_t = N$, State 3 does not offer an alliance and State 3 does not accept if an offer is made. State 1 offers $x^t = 1 - w_2$. State 2 accepts an offer if and only if two conditions are met: $x^t \leq 1 - w_2$ and no attempt to offer or form an alliance was made in the current period. In a period in which $s_t = N$, following an (off-path) deviation*

to form an alliance, if implementation fails, then State 2 rejects all offers.

2. *In any period in which $s_t = A$ or an alliance was implemented in the current period, the players use the strategies described in Proposition 3.3.*

To begin, we unpack the equilibrium strategies detailed in Proposition 6.1 to formally illustrate what such a deal entails. Let us focus on the behavior of States 1 and 2. The first important feature of deal equilibria to note is that States 1 and 3 never attempt to implement an alliance on the path of play. As discussed above, this contrasts with the equilibria studied in previous chapters, in which the allies would always try to implement an alliance if it was sufficiently attractive.

What sustains State 1's willingness to forego an attempt to form an alliance? The key is the expectation of punishment from State 2 if such an attempt is made. Looking at the equilibrium strategies above, we can see that State 2's reaction to a proposed settlement of x^t is conditional on what happened in the past. If States 1 and 3 have *never* attempted to form an alliance in the past, then State 2 is willing to accept an offer that yields the same payoff as its no-alliance war payoff, w_2. However, if States 1 and 3 have ever attempted and failed to implement an alliance, then State 2 will reject *any* offer of x^t.

This conditional response is precisely what keeps State 1 from reneging—attempting to implement an alliance with State 3 before State 2 can do anything about it. To illustrate this logic, consider the strategic situation from State 1's point of view. Anticipating State 2's behavior, State 1 faces a trade-off when it considers whether to attempt an alliance. On the one hand, if implementation can be pulled off quickly, in the present period, then State 2 is left with no choice but to accept the new reality that an alliance has formed against it, accepting an offer of $1 - w_2'$ in every future period.

This clearly benefits State 1, tempting it to attempt alliance implementation. However, failed implementation carries a significant drawback, as State 2 rejects all offers following a failed attempt to implement an alliance. This, of course, entails State 1 facing a war that yields its pre-alliance war payoff of w_1. An attempt to implement an alliance carries this trade-off, minus the cost of attempted implementation. State 1's other option is to stick to its equilibrium strategy as prescribed in the proposition, forgoing an attempted implementation of a new alliance and rather offering $1 - w_2$, which it knows State 2 will accept in every period. Comparing these approaches, we see that State 1 prefers to forego an alliance if the payoff from no alliance is at least as great as the expected utility of risking alliance implementation. Formally, comparing these payoffs requires

$$1 - w_2 \geq r(1 - w_2') + (1 - r)w_1 - (1 - \delta)a. \tag{6.4}$$

Algebraic manipulation of this expression yields

$$\frac{w_2 - [(1 - r)(1 - w_1) + (1 - \delta)a]}{r} \leq w_2', \tag{6.5}$$

as required by Proposition 6.1. In particular, this is the left-hand part of inequality 6.3, which is a necessary condition for the strategies outlined in Proposition 6.1 to constitute a subgame perfect equilibrium. Interpreting this condition, we can see that as long as the power shift resulting from an alliance is not too large, State 1 cannot profitably attempt to implement an alliance, reneging on its deal with State 2. However, if the power shift exceeds this threshold,[1] then the risk of attack is justified by the benefits, and it is not possible to prevent State 1 from making an alliance with State 2 through a combination of rewards and threatened punishments.

With the logic of State 1's behavior pinned down, we now need to understand why State 2's threat of punishment is credible. Without a credible threat to attack following a failed implementation attempt, the logic that holds this deal equilibrium together falls apart. Fortunately, understanding State 2's incentives is straightforward. Looking to State 2's equilibrium strategies, we see that as long as State 1 does not attempt to form an alliance, State 2 is willing to accept any offer that gives it at least its no-alliance war payoff, w_2. On the path of play, State 1 never attempts to implement, so State 2 knows that the distribution of power is stable. For this reason, the standard logic of equilibria in bargaining games dictates that State 2 be willing to accept such offers.

However, if State 1 ever attempts to renege on this implicit deal, the calculus changes for State 2. After such an event, State 2 rejects any offer made by State 1. This "punishment strategy" is sustainable for precisely the same

[1] Recall that lower values of w_2' indicate larger power shifts.

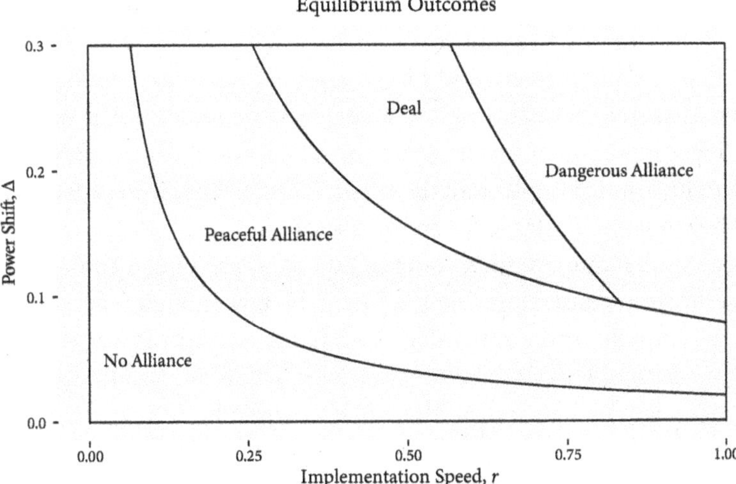

Figure 6.1 Equilibrium outcomes of the model in which we allow for deals to stop alliances. The parameter values used to generate this plot are $w_1 = 0.35$, $w_2 = 0.3$, $\delta = 0.9$, and $a = 0.2$. This figure demonstrates how deals to stop alliances create new space for peace. Compared to Figure 3.2, a new range of outcomes appears where alliances may come into force peacefully through the use of the deals described in this chapter.

reason that the equilibria described in Chapter 3 were possible. As long as the power shift from alliance is large enough that

$$w_2' \leq w_2 - \frac{(1-\delta)(1-w_2)}{\delta r}, \tag{6.6}$$

State 2 and all other players simply revert to the strategies described in Proposition 3.3. This condition dictates the right-hand part of inequality 6.3. Thus, as long as the power shift is large enough, State 2 can credibly threaten to revert to this punishment strategy, which ultimately deters State 1 from reneging on the implicit deal involved in the equilibrium strategies described above. On the path of play an alliance never occurs, and peace prevails

With a basic understanding of the equilibrium behavior that sustains such deals, we can now consider the conditions under which they exist. To further illustrate the logic of these equilibria, we describe each of these conditions and trace the incentives that generate them. Alliance deal equilibria exist when two conditions are satisfied: the cost of alliance implementation, a, is sufficiently low; and the power shift resulting from alliance implementation, w_2', lies in an intermediate range.

The first condition must hold for a straightforward reason: The alliance must be attractive enough that the allies wish to implement it in the first place. This requirement ensures that the allies would, in the absence of a deal, actually want to implement the alliance. Otherwise, such deal equilibria would be trivial in the sense described above.

The second requirement is more subtle. It arises out of the tension of two equilibrium constraints. First, w_2' must be low enough (corresponding to a large enough power shift) that the alliance represents a real threat to the targeted state. This requirement, as discussed above, guarantees that in the absence of an alliance deal, the alliance would be sufficiently provocative to generate a positive probability of war, as discussed in Chapter 3. On the other hand, w_2' cannot be too low (corresponding to an extremely large power shift with implementation). This constraint arises because if the alliance is too attractive, then there is no deal the target can afford that will dissuade the prospective partners from attempting to implement the alliance. In other words, the concessions needed from the targeted state to prevent the alliance are so large that the targeted state would prefer fighting.

In sum, deals based on history-contingent punishment strategies offer an alternative path to avoid the war-provoking effects of alliances. In this case, the provocative alliance does not come into force at all. Rather, concessions from the target of an alliance induce prospective allies to forgo implementation altogether. Table 6.1 summarizes this chapter's key insight. In the following section, we evaluate this theoretical implication against the historical record.

6.2 Cuban Missile Crisis

The theoretical analysis in this chapter demonstrates that targets of alliances may resort to negotiations to try to stop the implementation of an enemy alliance. This finding holds for a range of military cooperation agreements, even if the enemy partnership is not a formal military alliance *per se*. In this section, we show that the Cuban Missile Crisis happened because the United States discovered that Cuba and the Soviet Union were working together to implement a new military partnership that included a Soviet guarantee to defend Cuba with nuclear weapons placed in Cuba. The United States

Table 6.1 Summary of theoretical results

	Result	Description
Chapter 6		
Proposition 6.1	Deals to stop alliances	If an alliance-induced power shift's size is intermediate, then the target of an alliance may offer a deal that stops implementation and guarantees peace

perceived that this partnership, once implemented, would profoundly alter its position with respect to both Cuba and the Soviet Union.

Consistent with our theory, the Soviet Union recognized that the time required to deploy the missiles in Cuba made the emerging partnership vulnerable to US intervention. To mitigate this risk, the Soviet Union and Cuba deliberately kept their agreement secret and attempted to covertly install the missiles before the United States could respond. This effort to manipulate the transparency of the partnership during implementation is consistent with our analysis of secret alliances in Chapter 5. However, the United States discovered the plan and considered the options that we analyze in the other chapters of this book. The Kennedy administration discussed launching preventive attacks, which we analyzed in Chapter 3. They considered a military blockade of Cuba, which is consistent with a probabilistic blocking strategy analyzed in Chapter 4. The administration also discussed offering a preventive deal, which is the strategy we examine in this chapter.

The Kennedy administration ultimately decided against preventive strikes due to the high anticipated costs of war with the Soviet Union compared to other options. Instead, they opted for a limited blockade to halt the transportation of Soviet military equipment. However, the blockade alone proved ineffective, as much of the military equipment had already arrived in Cuba before its implementation. Consequently, the United States sought to negotiate a deal, offering to guarantee Cuban security and to remove American nuclear missiles from Turkey in exchange for the Soviet Union dismantling its missiles in Cuba. This offer, coupled with the threat of preventive war if it were rejected, eventually led to a resolution. The Soviet Union accepted the proposal, withdrew its missiles from Cuba, and ended its partnership with Cuba.

In this section, we demonstrate that the Cuban Missile Crisis and the subsequent deal between the USSR and the United States follow the logic of our theoretical framework. We start by showing that the Soviet Union and Cuba agreed to form a military cooperation partnership to secure Cuba and gain a strategic advantage over the United States. We then explain why the Soviets insisted on secrecy, given the vulnerability of the alliance to US interference before its full implementation. Next, we illustrate that if the Soviet–Cuban partnership had been implemented, it would have shifted the balance of power in a way that the United States anticipated would threaten its interests. We then discuss the Kennedy administration's deliberation over various options to prevent the Soviet–Cuban partnership before the implementation window closed. The administration's consideration of these options mirrors the logic outlined in our theoretical analysis. We show that the administration ruled out a preventive war as too costly, pursued a probabilistic blocking strategy, and ultimately offered a deal that successfully blocked the imminent Soviet–Cuban alliance. The deal was effective largely due to the credible threat of costly war if the agreement was rejected.

In 1960, the Soviet Union and Cuba embarked on a new relationship, beginning with economic cooperation to alleviate stress in Cuba caused by US sanctions. This partnership brought Cuba into the Soviet sphere of influence. The partnership extended to military cooperation when the Soviet Union began to supply arms to Cuba (Crankshaw 1970, 544). After the Bay of Pigs and the Berlin Crisis, Castro requested greater military assistance from the Soviet Union, including the provision of Soviet surface-to-air missiles (Fursenko and Naftali 1997, 139). In May 1962, Khrushchev ordered Soviet officials to prepare an agreement to defend Cuba with Soviet military capabilities, including nuclear missiles. This order was spelled out in a meeting of the Central Committee: "Come to an agreement with F[idel] Castro, conclude a military treaty regarding joint defense. Station nuclear missiles [there]. Carry this out secretly. Then declare it. Missiles under our command. This will be an offensive policy."[2]

Khrushchev believed an effective agreement to defend Cuba required the deployment of new military capabilities. In a letter to Castro, after the crisis ended, he explained the Soviet motivations for sending missiles:

> The imperialists of course wanted to bring the Cuban nation to death, not to victory. And the US imperialists have great forces for coming down upon

[2] "Central Committee of the Communist Party of the Soviet Union Presidium Protocol 32," Wilson Center, Digital Archive, URL: https://digitalarchive.wilsoncenter.org/document/central-committee-communist-party-soviet-union-presidium-protocol-32

> tiny Cuba; and Cuba of course will not be able alone to withstand their war machine for long. ... In the name of Cuba's defense we proposed placing missiles in Cuba. If American imperialism had initiated their invasion, then no protests of ours, no demonstrations lasting for three shifts, three weeks, or even three months would have stopped American imperialism. Only one fear could hold them back, the understanding that if they started an invasion, then the missiles would do their business, and the cities of America would fall to ruin. We understood that the placement of that sort of weaponry in Cuba was the most effective means for defending Cuba available at that point in time. We believed that Cuba needed arms for holding back the USA from another invasion of Cuba.[3]

In his statement, Khrushchev underscored the importance of having robust military capabilities to support a deterrent threat. He argued that mere verbal assurances—protests and declarations—are insufficient on their own. According to Khrushchev, the credibility of a defense commitment hinged on the tangible presence of military power. This necessity for a tangible show of force often involves complex coordination with allies, which cannot always be achieved immediately. Khrushchev was, therefore, defending the time-consuming process involved in placing missiles in Cuba.

By the spring of 1962, the Soviets had delivered over $250 million worth of military equipment to Cuba. This arsenal included 394 tanks and self-propelled artillery, 888 automatic and anti-aircraft guns, 41 military aircraft, 13 ships, 13 radar systems, 308 radio sets, and 3,619 automobiles, in addition to tractors and other technologies. Soviet personnel were also sent to train Cubans in operating these equipment (Fursenko and Naftali 1997, 166). As Khrushchev stated, "The main thing was that the installation of our missiles in Cuba would, I thought, restrain the United States from precipitous military action against Castro's government. In addition to protecting Cuba, our missiles would have equalized what the West likes to call 'the balance of power'" (Crankshaw 1970, 546).

The Soviets decided to install 24 R-12 missiles with a range of 1,020 miles and 16 R-14 missiles with a range twice as long. This deployment of 40 missiles was intended to double Soviet capacity to strike the US mainland. Additionally, the Soviets planned to position 80 nuclear cruise missiles

[3] "Letter from Khrushchev to Fidel Castro. Re: Point 3, Protocol No. 80," January 31, 1963, Wilson Center, Digital Archives, URL: https://digitalarchive.wilsoncenter.org/document/letter-khrushchev-fidel-castro-0

to protect the Cuban coastline (Fursenko and Naftali 1997, 188). By late September 1962, the Soviet Union had sent 114 shipments to Cuba, of which 94 had already arrived and 35 were still en route (Fursenko and Naftali 1997, 213).

Soviet leadership understood that the United States would have an incentive to strike preventively if they discovered the Soviet–Cuban military cooperation before the partnership could be fully implemented. As an illustration of this awareness, in March 1962, Khrushchev declined a Cuban offer to allow the Soviet Union to install an intelligence center in Cuba to provide active support to revolutionary movements in Latin American countries. The Soviets feared that the United States would use such an installation as a pretext to launch a second invasion of Cuba (Fursenko and Naftali 1997, 168). Yet, Khrushchev was willing to risk placing Soviet nuclear missiles on the doorstep of the United States. To reduce the risk of preventive attacks by the United States, Khrushchev tried to keep the project secret until the materials had been delivered and installed. The Kremlin believed that the United States would "swallow the missile" once they were installed (Fursenko and Naftali 1997, 196). To maintain secrecy, Khrushchev asked that, to provide a signal of US intentions to improve relations, Kennedy stop aerial surveillance of Cuba. The Soviet aspiration to achieve the benefits of an alliance without exposing itself before the alliance could be fully implemented supports our theory's emphasis on the vulnerability of the implementation window.

In October 1962, the United States resumed regular reconnaissance flights after detecting a significant buildup of Soviet military personnel in Cuba. Military intelligence uncovered three missile sites, each equipped with four launchers. This discovery prompted immediate concern within the Kennedy administration about a potential shift in the balance of power. A nuclear-armed alliance between the Soviet Union and Cuba threatened to significantly alter US–Cuba and US–Soviet relations.

Debate within the administration focused on the implications of this shift. General Taylor of the Joint Chiefs of Staff warned that "Cuba could become a powerful military problem in any contest we would have with the Soviet Union and a threat in any other part of the world" (May 1997, 127). Secretary of State Dean Rusk analyzed the potential impact on future negotiations between the United States and the Soviet Union, suggesting that the Soviet Union might be "critically encouraged to go ahead and eventually feel like they've got it made as far as intimidating the United States" (May 1997, 127).

Secretary of Defense Robert McNamara highlighted the broader implications, noting that the Soviet missiles in Cuba posed a "political problem" that could affect the cohesion of US alliances and influence future interactions with Khrushchev (May 1997, 84). President Kennedy, for his part, feared that increased Soviet strength in Cuba could weaken the US position in Berlin relative to the Soviet Union (Crankshaw 1970, 555).

In addition to anticipating the future downsides of the Soviet–Cuban military partnership, the Kennedy administration recognized it had a limited amount of time to act. Surveillance imagery revealed that the existing missile installations were not yet operational and that more missiles were in the process of being transported and installed. Records of ExComm (the Executive Committee of the National Security Council) deliberations reveal the administration's awareness of an impending deadline after which the Soviet missile force would be fully operational, bringing the United States under Soviet nuclear threat and fundamentally altering US bargaining strength. Under pressure to act before the implementation window closed, Kennedy said: "I don't think we've got much time on these missiles. ... We can't wait 2 weeks while we're getting ready to roll" (May 1997, 71).

Motivated by this urgency, ExComm's discussion turned to devising a strategy to prevent such a power shift before it was too late. CIA director John McCone presented three obvious options: do nothing, launch preventive strikes, or impose a military blockade of Cuba. Doing nothing was a nonstarter. Preventive war gained traction early in the deliberations. Kennedy said:

> Maybe we just have to take them [the missiles] out and continue our other preparations if we decide to do that. ... We're certainly going to do number one [surgical strike]. We're going to take out those missiles. The questions will be whether, what I would describe as number two, which would be a general air strike. That we're not ready to say, but we should be in preparation for it. The third is the general invasion. At least we're going to do number one. So it seems to me that we don't have to wait very long. We ought to be making those preparations. (May 1997, 71)

The Joint Chiefs pressed for a comprehensive attack on Cuba, including a surprise air strike together with a general invasion (May 1997, 127). After more consideration, however, Kennedy was convinced that such an attack, which would likely kill thousands or tens of thousands of Russian troops, would trigger Soviet retaliation and thus escalate to a large-scale conflict, including a Soviet attack on Berlin and perhaps nuclear war.

In spite of the persistence of several ExComm advocates of preventive war to stop the implementation of the alliance, this option lost steam as the first option. Instead, the case for a blockade gained traction. The purpose of the blockade was consistent with the strategy of probabilistic blocking analyzed in our theory in Chapter 4. The hope was that a blockade might reduce the risk of large-scale war (compared to a direct attack) while still increasing the probability that the Soviets might withdraw their missiles. After hearing Kennedy's October 22 speech to the American people, in which he revealed his intention to impose a blockade, Khrushchev was relieved that the United States was not planning an attack and initially decided to continue installing the missiles (Fursenko and Naftali 1997, 241). By the time the blockade came into full effect, almost all of the missiles had arrived in Cuba. Khrushchev admitted as much in a letter to Kennedy: "I assure you that on those ships, which are bound for Cuba, there are no weapons at all. The weapons which were necessary for the defense of Cuba are already there. I do not want to say that there were no shipments of any weapons at all. No, there were such shipments. But now Cuba has already received the necessary means of defense" (May 1997, 488).

Khrushchev ordered four ships carrying missile materiel to turn around, but the installation of already-delivered materiel continued. Realizing the futility of the blockade, Kennedy remarked: "Well, our quarantine itself won't remove the weapons. So we've only got two ways of removing the weapons. One is to negotiate them out, or we trade them out. And the other is to go over and just take them out. I don't see any other way we're going to get the weapons out" (May 1997, 464).

The question of whether to "trade them out" or "take them out" guided all ExComm deliberations going forward. McNamara floated the possibility that a blockade might give way to a negotiated solution. He described a hypothetical resolution as follows: "You have agreed to take your missiles out of Turkey and Italy, and the Soviets have agreed either to take them out of Cuba or impose some kind of control comparable to your control over the missiles in Turkey and Italy. Now, that's the best possible solution" (May 1997, 165).

The president agreed that the Jupiter missiles would be on the negotiation table (May 1997, 199–200). The first offer of a deal came from Khrushchev. In his memoirs he recalled how this came about: "We could see that we had to reorient our position swiftly. 'Comrades,' I said, 'we have to look for a dignified way out of this conflict. At the same time, of course, we must make sure that we do not compromise Cuba.' We sent the Americans a note saying that we agreed to remove our missiles and bombers on the condition that the President give us his assurance that there would be no invasion of Cuba by the forces of the United States or anybody else" (Crankshaw 1970, 533).

Khrushchev offered the following opening proposal: "Let us therefore show statesmanlike wisdom. I propose: we, for our part, will declare that our ships, bound for Cuba, will not carry any kind of armaments. You would declare that the United States will not invade Cuba with its forces and will not support any sort of forces which might intend to carry out an invasion of Cuba. Then the necessity for the presence of our military specialists in Cuba would disappear" (May 1997, 490).

A few days later, Khrushchev added the demand for the removal of the Jupiter missiles from Turkey: "I make this proposal: We agree to remove those weapons from Cuba which you regard as offensive weapons. We agree to do this and to state this commitment to the United Nations. Your representatives will make a statement to the effect that the United States, will evacuate its analogous weapons from Turkey" (May 1997, 506).

Kennedy sent his brother, Robert Kennedy (RFK), to meet in secret with Soviet Ambassador Dobrynin to discuss the deal that would eventually successfully bring an end to the crisis and block the impending Soviet–Cuban military partnership. RFK demanded immediate termination of work on the Cuban missile sites:

> The most important thing for us, is to get as soon as possible the agreement of the Soviet government to halt further work on the construction of the missile bases in Cuba and take measures under international control that would make it impossible to use these weapons. In exchange the government of the USA is ready, in addition to repealing all measures on the "quarantine," to give the assurances that there will not be any invasion of Cuba and that other countries of the Western Hemisphere are ready to give the same assurances—the US government is certain of this. (Russian Foreign Ministry archives, translation quoted in. (Lebow and Stein 1994, 523–526)

When asked about the Turkish missiles, RFK offered: "If that is the only obstacle to achieving the regulation I mentioned earlier, then the president doesn't see any insurmountable difficulties in resolving this issue" (Fursenko and Naftali 1997, 282). The United States insisted that the removal of the Jupiters be kept secret so as not to damage relations with US allies in NATO. The United States and Soviet thus made a deal to end the crisis and to end the military partnership between the Soviet Union and Cuba. The United States agreed to lift the blockade, to give public assurances of nonaggression towards Cuba, and to remove the Jupiter missiles from Turkey (Fursenko and Naftali 1997, 284). Khrushchev agreed to remove the Cuban missiles immediately, under UN supervision, and to halt further cooperation with Cuba, which included transferring Soviet weapons to the island. In November 1962, the Soviet Union did not sign the agreement of general military cooperation and mutual assistance with Cuba, as had been planned.

The threat of a preventive war made a negotiated solution increasingly plausible. Once it became evident that the blockade would not prevent the missiles already in Cuba from becoming operational, President Kennedy faced a stark choice: either negotiate their removal or initiate direct action to eliminate them (Copeland 2000, 202). The Executive Committee of the National Security Council (ExComm) sensed that time was running short and that the Soviets might soon gain a strategic advantage. Consequently, the administration determined that the options were clear: either negotiate the removal of the Turkish missiles or proceed with an invasion of Cuba (Copeland 2000, 203).

In negotiations with Dobrynin, RFK was careful not to issue an ultimatum. However, the US position was a de facto ultimatum. Dobrynin pointed out in his dispatch that Kennedy requested a response within one day and emphasized that "time is of the essence" (Russian Foreign Ministry archives, translation quoted in (Lebow and Stein 1994, 523–526). In his memoirs, Khrushchev said that RFK told Dobrynin that the military might take over. In Khrushchev's words: "Even though the President himself is very much against starting a war over Cuba, an irreversible chain of events could occur against his will. That is why the President is appealing directly to Chairman Khrushchev for his help in liquidating this conflict. If the situation continues much longer, the President is not sure that the military will not overthrow him and seize power. The American army could get out of control" (Crankshaw 1970, 551–552).

In his memoirs, RFK made it clear that the president was under a great deal of pressure to attack. RFK's account is consistent on the point that it was made clear that force was the alternative to a deal. He recalled: "We had to have a commitment by tomorrow that those bases would be removed. I was not giving them an ultimatum but a statement of fact. He should understand that if they did not remove those bases, we would remove them. ... Time was running out. We had only a few more hours—we needed an answer immediately from the Soviet Union. I said we must have it the next day" (Kennedy 2015, 107–109).

A letter Khrushchev later sent to Castro, to justify the deal to withdraw the missiles, also said that the alternative was war.

> If, succumbing to popular feelings, we would have allowed ourselves to be swept along by the most aroused sectors of the populace and we would have not achieved a reasonable agreement with the US government, war would have broken out, and it would have resulted in millions of dead. The survivors would have blamed the leaders for not having taken measures to prevent this war of extermination. ... We have lived through some very serious moments; a global thermonuclear war could have broken out. Of course, the United States would have suffered enormous losses, but the Soviet Union and the entire socialist bloc would have also suffered greatly. It is difficult to say how it would have turned out for the Cuban people. First of all, Cuba would have been burned in the bonfires of war. Without a doubt the Cuban people would have fought bravely but, also without a doubt, the Cuban people would have heroically perished. We are fighting against imperialism, not to die, but to use all our potential, to lose as little as possible and to win more later on, to overcome and to see communism triumph.[4]

Cubans felt betrayed by the Kennedy–Khrushchev deal. Upon learning about the deal, Cuban President Dorticós expressed deep disappointment in the Soviet agreement to remove weapons from Cuba. Soviet leaders tried repeatedly to explain that the deal benefited Cubans by extracting a concession from Kennedy to guarantee the security of Cuba. However, Castro expressed distrust in US security assurances.[5] He believed the deal would

[4] Premier Khrushchev's Letter to Prime Minister Castro, October 30, 1962, Wilson Center, Digital Archives, URL: https://digitalarchive.wilsoncenter.org/document/letter-khrushchev-fidel-castro-0

[5] "Cable from USSR Ambassador to Cuba Alekseev to Soviet Ministry of Foreign Affairs, October 28, 1962, Wilson Center, Digital Archives, in URL: https://digitalarchive.wilsoncenter.org/document/cable-ussr-ambassador-cuba-alekseev-soviet-ministry-foreign-affairs-0

embolden Americans and likely result in a less-secure Cuba.[6] Without the missiles, there was little military capability left from the Soviet–Cuban partnership that might deter the United States. Even Khrushchev admitted the emptiness of Kennedy's promise not to attack Cuba in the future. While touting US nonaggression pledges as a major victory of the crisis outcome, he admitted that "one cannot rely on them as an absolute guarantee."[7] A year later, Secretary of State Dean Rusk noted that Soviet–Cuban relations had become "tense" as Soviet forces continued to draw down in Cuba.[8] The Cubans rightly felt betrayed because the Soviets took the only meaningful carrot in the deal, which was the concession to withdraw the Jupiter missiles in Turkey. The Soviets broke off the meaningful commitments that might have enhanced Cuba's security once the partnership was implemented, because the United States discovered the partnership before it was implemented and credibly threatened to launch a war unless Khrushchev accepted the concession and terminated the partnership.

6.3 Louisiana Purchase

The theoretical analysis in this chapter demonstrates that targets of alliances may resort to negotiations to try to stop an impending enemy alliance. France's historic agreement to sell the Louisiana Territory to the United States illustrates this motivation. The deal between France and the United States, which resulted in the United States purchasing the Louisiana Territory and nearly doubling the size of the United States, was motivated by Napoleon's desire to prevent an alliance between the United States and the UK.

In 1800, Spain secretly ceded Louisiana to France. To solidify this transfer, France needed to establish a military presence in Louisiana and secure control over the Mississippi River's west bank. By 1801, France had begun implementing this plan by dispatching military forces to secure New Orleans.

[6] "Prime Minister Castro's Letter to Premier Khrushchev, October 31, 1962, Wilson Center, Digital Archives, URL: https://digitalarchive.wilsoncenter.org/document/cable-ussr-ambassador-cuba-alekseev-soviet-ministry-foreign-affairs-0

[7] "Letter from Khrushchev to Fidel Castro, January 31, 1963, Wilson Center, Digital Archives, URL: https://digitalarchive.wilsoncenter.org/document/letter-khrushchev-fidel-castro-0

[8] Cable from Dutch Embassy, Washington (Van Roijen), 1 November 1963, Wilson Center, Digital Archive, URL: https://digitalarchive.wilsoncenter.org/document/cable-dutch-embassy-washington-van-roijen-1-november-1963

Once news of the France–Spain deal emerged, the United States threatened to ally with Great Britain to block French control of New Orleans. This potential UK–US alliance posed a significant threat to France's broader ambitions, both in North America and Europe. To counter this threat, Napoleon decided to sell the entire Louisiana Territory to the United States.

In this section, we illustrate that upon learning of Spain's secret cession of Louisiana to France, President Jefferson actively sought an alliance with the UK and prepared to consider war with France if necessary to prevent French expansion. We then demonstrate how Napoleon's decision to sell the Louisiana Territory was a strategic move to avoid the formation of a UK–US alliance.

When Thomas Jefferson assumed the presidency on March 4, 1801, the Third Treaty of San Ildefonso, which secretly transferred Louisiana from Spain to France, had already been agreed upon. Gradually, Jefferson's administration became aware of this land transfer and France's plans to fortify its presence in the West. France intended to establish a stronghold along the Mississippi River, which would not only support French colonies in the West Indies but also obstruct American westward expansion.

Although the transfer of territory was not scheduled to be finalized until 1802, France needed to first secure its Caribbean colonies and establish control over New Orleans. This provided the United States and Great Britain with a window to counteract France's plans. Jefferson initiated unofficial diplomatic communications with Napoleon through Pierre Samuel du Pont de Nemours, a French official residing in the United States. Through du Pont, Jefferson issued a veiled threat: "The inevitable consequences of their taking possession of Louisiana will cost France, and perhaps not very long hence, a war which will annihilate her on the ocean. ... That [war] may yet be avoided is my sincere prayer, and if you can be the means of informing the wisdom of Buonaparte of all its consequences, you will have deserved well of both countries."

Jefferson also sent Robert Livingston, the US ambassador in Paris, instructions for dealing with Napoleon on the matter of Louisiana. Jefferson said that a French-occupied Louisiana would become "a point of eternal friction with us." He continued by raising the prospect of an alliance with Great Britain:

> The day that France takes possession of N. Orleans fixes her sentence which is to restrain her forever within her low water mark. ... From that moment

> we must marry ourselves to the British fleet and nation ... and having formed and connected together a power which may render reinforcement of her settlements here impossible to France, make the first cannon which shall be fired in Europe the signal for the tearing up any settlement she may have made, and for holding the two continents of America in sequestration for the common purposes of the United British and American nations.[9]

Jefferson's threat was clear. If Napoleon took possession of Louisiana, the United States was willing to ally with Great Britain to wage war against France *both* in the western United States and in Europe.

By the summer of 1802, Jefferson openly threatened to ally with Great Britain. Edward Thornton, the British ambassador to the United States, reported Jefferson's intentions to the British foreign minister. According to Thornton, Jefferson "makes no scruple to say that if ... the United States should be unable to expel the French ... they must have recourse to the assistance of other powers, meaning unquestionably Great Britain."[10]

On the British side, there was increasing support for an alliance with the United States to counteract France's control over Louisiana. Ambassador Thornton, recognizing France as a common threat, advocated for the alliance to oppose France (Perkins 1955, 285). Thornton noted that any country that incurred the enmity of France "acquires by that act alone the friendship of Great Britain; and that, where the relations are so intimate as they are between her and the United States, this must be speedily followed by her active co-operation."[11] To advance the alliance, Jefferson sent James Monroe as a special emissary to join Robert Livingston in Paris to press the US case on Louisiana with the French government. Monroe was instructed to proceed to London to negotiate the alliance if Napoleon could not be persuaded to abandon his plans for Louisiana. French Ambassador Pichon informed the French foreign minister, Talleyrand, that Mr. Monroe "has *carte blanche* and that he will go to London if he is badly received in Paris."[12] In April 1803, Madison authorized Monroe and Livingston to pursue the British alliance, stating: "if France should avow or evince a determination to

[9] Jefferson to Livingston, April 18, 1802, Paul L. Ford, ed., The Writings of Thomas Jefferson, VIII (New York, 1897), 145. Madison had already expressed the same idea in less striking language; Madison to Livingston, Sep 28, 1801, quoted in Irving Brant, James Madison, Secretary of State (Indianapolis, 1953), p. 71.

[10] Thornton to Foreign Secretary, July 3, 1802, FO 5/35.

[11] Thornton to Foreign Secretary, March 9, 1803, FO 5/38.

[12] Pichon to Talleyrand, February 18, 1803, Lyon, *Louisiana in French Diplomacy*, 202–3.

deny the US the free navigation of the Mississippi, your consultations with Great Britain may be held on the ground that war is inevitable."[13]

By the spring of 1803, Napoleon knew that a war with Great Britain was inevitable and that pressing expansion into Louisiana would result in expanded conflict with the British and the United States. The threat of an alliance and war opened up the possibility of a deal. Du Pont set forth the calculation for such a deal in a correspondence with Jefferson: "Consider what the most fortunate war with France and Spain would cost you. And contract for a part—a half, let us say. The two countries will have made a good bargain. You will have Louisiana ... for the least possible expense; and this conquest will be neither [animated] by hatred nor sullied by human blood."[14] The Jefferson administration made it known that the United States was open to considering halting its plans for a US–British alliance as part of a deal that would include a halt to France's plans in Louisiana. In May 1802, Secretary of State James Madison instructed Ambassador Livingston to let Napoleon know that the alliance and the war could be prevented if France left Louisiana in Spanish possession or sold Louisiana and Florida to the United States.[15]

In late 1802 and early 1803, Livingston laid the groundwork for the Louisiana Purchase through his diplomatic talks in Paris. At the same time, Napoleon's military expedition to secure Saint-Domingue in the Caribbean, which was designed as a prelude to the occupation of New Orleans, was suffering catastrophic losses. This increased the risk of confronting joint US–British opposition to French possession of Louisiana. When James Monroe arrived in Paris in April 1803, Napoleon was already resolved to sell Louisiana. He was convinced that he would indeed face the British navy if he tried to take and hold Louisiana, and he calculated that it would be better to sell instead. He instructed his negotiator, François Barbe-Marbois, to make the deal, noting that the main motivation for making the deal was to avoid confronting the United States together with England:

> I renounce Louisiana. It is not only New Orleans that I will cede, it is the whole colony without any reservation. I know the price of what I abandon, and I have sufficiently proved the importance that I attach to this

[13] Madison to Monroe and Livingston, Apr 18, 1803, Department of State, Instructions to Ministers, VI.

[14] Du Pont to Jefferson, April 30, May 12, 1802, *Correspondence*, 60, 63.

[15] Madison to Livingston, May 1, 1802, Department of State, Instructions to Ministers, VI.

> province. ... I renounce it with the greatest regret. To attempt obstinately to retain it would be folly. ... I direct you to negotiate this affair with the envoys of the United States. ... It is to prevent the danger, to which the colossal power of England exposes us, that I would provide a remedy. (Kukla 2009, 257)

In May 1803, Monroe and Livingston signed the Louisiana Purchase Treaty on behalf of the United States, effectively ending Napoleon's ambitions for French expansion in the Americas and eliminating the need for a US alliance with Great Britain. George Cabot, a Federalist who opposed the Louisiana Purchase, summarized the rationale behind France's decision as follows:

> The cession of Louisiana is an excellent thing for France. It is like selling us a ship after she is surrounded by the British fleet. It puts into safe keeping what [France] could not keep herself, for England could take Louisiana in the first moment of war, without the loss of a man. France could neither settle it nor protect it: she is therefore rid of an incumbrance that wounded her pride, [while France] receives money and regains the friendship of our populace.[16]

For France, the alternative to ceding the territory to the United States would have been a challenging scenario involving the need to defend and maintain Louisiana against a potential US–British alliance. By selling the territory to the United States, France removed the incentive for the United States to seek British military support, thus avoiding a future confrontation. This decision aligns with the equilibrium analysis of alliance deals discussed earlier: By agreeing not to enter into a military partnership with the UK, the French effectively secured a favorable outcome and avoided potential conflict.

6.4 Neutrality Pacts

The strategic dynamics at play in both the Cuban Missile Crisis and the Louisiana Purchase are examples of broader patterns of diplomacy. As we have seen, broader conflict was avoided in each of these cases through

[16] George Cabot to Rufus King, July 1, 1803; Henry Cabot Lodge, ed., *Life and Letters of George Cabot* (Boston, 1878), 331. Quoted in Kukla, Jon. A Wilderness So Immense (p. 235).

careful negotiations; parties headed for conflict were able to locate a mutually preferable deal, in which concessions were granted in exchange for the abandonment of a budding alliance. Below we argue that this logic provides insight on alliance treaties more generally. In particular, we focus on a class of alliance treaties known as *neutrality pacts*. Broadly, such alliances specify that a signatory will remain neutral in the event of war rather than joining one of the combatants to shape the eventual outcome. We will see that neutrality pacts often occur as a product of negotiations to prevent an impending alliance from being implemented.

Before turning to specific examples, it is useful to discuss neutrality pacts broadly, clarifying the general connections we draw between this class of treaties and the logic of anti-alliance deals. First, what characterizes a neutrality pact? The main difference between these and other types of alliances (e.g., offensive or defensive) is that neutrality pacts commit signatories to *inaction* in the event of war. This stands in stark contrast to the defensive and offensive obligations that are typically the focus of the alliance literature.[17] The concepts and processes governing neutrality and nonaggression agreements are so different from those governing offensive and defensive alliances that empirical studies of the causes and consequences of alliances typically exclude pure neutrality pacts (Mattes and Vonnahme 2010). More specifically, neutrality agreements often resemble peace deals in specifying a settlement in exchange for a guarantee of neutrality or nonaggression by a potential rival. In this way, neutrality pacts are connected to the logic of anti-alliance deals as outlined in Proposition 6.1.

Below, we make these connections concrete by discussing specific historical examples in which a neutrality pact came into force to stop impending military cooperation. In each case, we aim to illustrate the model's logic by providing evidence (1) that each pact was designed with the express purpose of preventing a new cooperative military relationship and (2) that each was supported by a *quid pro quo* arrangement in which the neutral party received compensation in exchange for its commitment to neutrality.

[17] Of course, these categories are not mutually exclusive and many alliances involve a mixture of these obligations. In this discussion we focus on treaties that are exclusively for the purpose of guaranteeing a party's neutrality in the event of war.

6.4.1 The Molotov–Ribbentrop Pact

The secret agreement between Nazi Germany and the Soviet Union to divide eastern Europe in the prelude to World War II is perhaps one of the best-known examples of a neutrality pact. In this agreement, signed on August 23, 1939, the two parties promised not to take aggressive action towards each other. In the discussion that follows, we connect the logic of this pact to the theoretical argument developed earlier in this chapter. In particular, we argue that the Molotov–Ribbentrop Pact was primarily designed to stifle the possibility of a cooperative security relationship between the Soviet Union, France, and Britain.

To connect the case to the model, we first trace the development of the Soviet Union's relationships with Germany, France, and Britain. In particular, we focus on the deterioration of the German–Soviet relationship following the Nazi Party's rise, and the consequent possibility of a tripartite alliance with the Soviets, Britain, and France. A clear picture of this relationship is crucial to understanding German decision-making at the time. In particular, we establish that Germany's pursuit of a neutrality agreement with the Soviets was primarily driven by a desire to forestall the formation of an opposing security bloc

Prior to the Nazi party's rise to power, the German–Soviet relationship saw relatively little conflict, with both sides inclined towards peaceful relations (Haslam 1997, 6). Weakened by the First World War, they enjoyed relatively peaceful relations throughout the 1920s. Though they had stood on opposite sides of the 1914 July Crisis and fought fiercely during the ensuing world war, these former rivals sought to formalize more peaceful relations beginning in 1922. The Treaty of Rapallo, signed April 16, 1922, initiated a rapprochement. The two signatories abandoned their territorial and economic claims against one another. The relationship warmed further with the signing of the 1926 Treaty of Berlin. This agreement built on the foundation of the Rapallo Treaty, adding an explicit guarantee of military neutrality, with each nation pledging to remain neutral in the event that either came under attack by a non-signatory state

However, with Hitler's rise came tension. The primary point of contention came from the Nazi Party's territorial aims. Hitler had repeatedly spoken of impending conflict in the east, driven by a need for *Lebensraum* for the German people (Kershaw 2000). This directly pointed to conflict with the Soviet Union, which was no secret to Stalin, and trade between Germany and the Soviet Union sharply declined throughout the 1930s. As restrictions on German economic activity under the Treaty of Versailles lapsed, domestic military production sharply increased, and imports from the Soviet Union to Germany consequently declined (Ericson III 1999, 13–18).

The outbreak of the Spanish Civil War accelerated the deterioration of the Nazi–Soviet relationship. Indeed, many of the tensions that would give rise to Germany's desire for the neutrality agreement became visible at the beginning of this conflict. At the outbreak of the war, France and Britain immediately committed to nonintervention. A nonintervention plan designed to limit the conflict was then proposed widely, and the German and Soviet governments each paid lip service to honoring such an arrangement. However, both nations continued to quietly provide the combatants with material support.

Recognizing this duplicity, the British and French led an effort to organize principles of nonintervention, hoping to prevent the conflict from spreading outside the Spanish border (Beevor 1982, 372–374). With representatives of 27 European nations in attendance, a committee on nonintervention met in London on September 9, 1936. In the weeks to come, the committee formulated a plan to formalize relations between the warring parties in Spain and external actors. In spite of the international commitment to nonintervention, both Republican and Nationalist forces in Spain continued to receive significant material assistance from external actors, including Germany and the Soviet Union. Importantly, this placed Hitler and Stalin on opposite sides of the conflict. Nazi Germany lent support to the Spanish Nationalists, while the Soviets sided with the Spanish government.

Here we can see cracks emerging between Hitler's Germany and Stalin's Soviet Union. In the years leading up to the signing of the 1939 neutrality pact, tensions continued to build. The main area of conflict was set up by Hitler's goal to expand eastward, pursuing his anti-Semitic and anti-Bolshevist agenda. Clearly, Hitler's aims were incompatible with Stalin's. Indeed, for Hitler, foreclosing the possibility of a two-front war by neutralizing the eastern threat posed by Stalin was essential (Weinberg 1989, 186). Recognizing this, Hitler sought to smooth relations with the Soviet Union (Roberts 1992).

But that pursuit was complicated by British and French efforts. As Hitler began to consider a strategy for eliminating the constraint imposed by the Soviet Union, the British and French were also engaged in negotiations with Stalin, pursuing a possible tripartite alliance to balance against Hitler.

In fact, Stalin made the first overture, floating the possibility of such a tripartite agreement in April 1939 (Carley 1993). The initial proposal was rejected, and negotiations quickly became bogged down in disagreements over the specific wording of a potential military pact. Growing exhausted and also increasingly anxious over Hitler's recent invasion and occupation of Czechoslovakia, the British and French sent a diplomatic envoy to Russia to negotiate with Stalin in hopes of finalizing an agreement. Talks began in early August, and were initially marked by optimism. However, on August 23, 1939, Stalin and Hitler finalized their own agreement, guaranteeing Soviet neutrality with respect to Germany and quashing the British and French attempt to draw the Soviets in.

This discussion establishes that the strategic contours of European international relations in 1939 are well described by our dynamic model of alliance implementation. Germany played the role of State 2, engaged in bargaining with the Soviets, who played the role of State 1. As these negotiations went on, the British and French aimed to solidify their friendly relationship with the Soviets, so they can be taken as State 3. As in the formal model, Hitler anticipated that, if the budding French–British–Soviet relationship were to bear a formal security agreement, his ability to extract concessions from Stalin would be significantly undermined. Anticipating this, Hitler acted. As we will see, Hitler's negotiating strategy fits the logic of anti-alliance deals outlined in this chapter. Using concessions, Hitler essentially bribed the Soviets away from the British and French. Consequently, direct conflict between Germany and the Soviet Union was delayed.

How did Hitler draw Stalin away from a security partnership with Britain and France? Consistent with our theoretical analysis, the German strategy relied on an implicit *quid pro quo* with Stalin. Indeed, the Soviets recognized that this is exactly what the Germans were seeking to do. Reporting to Moscow in the weeks before the Nazi–Soviet pact was signed, Soviet Foreign Minister Astakhov wrote from Berlin that the Germans were "obviously worried by our negotiations with the British and French military and they have become unsparing in their arguments and promises in order to prevent a military agreement. For the sake of this they are now ready, I believe, to make the kind of declarations and gestures that would have been inconceivable six months ago. The Baltic, Bessarabia, Eastern Poland (not to speak of the Ukraine)—at the present time this is the minimum they would give up without much discussion in order to secure a promise from us not to intervene in their conflict with Poland. Quoted in" (Roberts, 1992, 68).

This provides direct evidence that the logic of anti-alliance deals was at play in the negotiation of the Molotov–Ribbentrop pact. Recognizing that the Soviets were considering a pact with the British and French, Hitler reached out, offering concessions to draw Stalin away. Stalin clearly understood this, and worked to leverage the threat of a tripartite agreement to secure a deal. Importantly, this evidence indicates that the negotiations were understood by all parties as driving towards a *quid pro quo* arrangement that would draw the Soviets away from Britain and France.

Of course, Hitler recognized that buying the Soviets away from a pact with two military powerhouses would not be cheap. Accordingly, German diplomats offered concessions in two forms: economic and territorial. The economic concessions were the result of back-channel negotiations that had been in progress since 1938. The decline in German import of Soviet products had been a sticking point in the Nazi–Soviet relationship throughout the 1930s. However, in 1939, as military tensions on the European continent increased following Germany's 1938 occupation of Czechoslovakia, both Germany and the Soviet Union were in need of an economic deal to support the ramping-up of their military production. Recognizing this, the Nazi Party initiated formal talks with the Soviets. Months of negotiation and false starts culminated with an informal agreement in early July 1939 (Ericson III 1999, 40–54). On August 19, the economic deal was finalized. Germany would receive much-needed raw materials from the Soviets, and in exchange provide their new economic partners with industrial goods (Wegner 1997, 99–100). While this deal delivered much-needed economic relief to both signatories, it was only a part of the picture.

Ultimately, the negotiation of this economic deal paved the way for a more meaningful political deal that addressed the core tension in German–Soviet relations (Ericson III 1999, 56). This was the territorial concession. A secret passage (only revealed after World War II) divided the east into German and Soviet spheres of influence: "In the event of a territorial and political rearrangement of the areas belonging to the Polish state, the spheres of influence of Germany and the U.S.S.R. shall be bounded approximately by the line of the rivers Narev, Vistula and San" (Molotov–Ribbentrop Pact, secret additional protocol, Article II).

With the signing of this agreement, a 1939 tripartite alliance between Britain, France, and the Soviets became impossible. The agreement bought Hitler time to make preparations for the next steps in his quest to dominate Europe. Importantly, and consistent with the logic of anti-alliance deals outlined in this chapter, the Molotov–Ribbentrop Pact delayed the seemingly inevitable direct military confrontation between Germany and the Soviet Union (Gorodetsky 1990).

Importantly, our interpretation of this case is broadly consistent with that of historians of the interwar period. For example, Roberts (1992) argues that "Nazi Germany began its quest for a pact with the USSR in the spring of 1939 and from the outset pursued two clear goals: the prevention of an Anglo-Soviet-French alliance and Soviet neutrality in the event of a Polish-German war" (1992, 56).

This comment is indicative of a broad consensus among historians as to the correct interpretation of the pact. In particular, historians of the period see Hitler's desire to stop the budding Soviet–British–French relationship as a primary driver of this agreement (see Watson (2000) and Wegner (1997) for further examples). Thus the Molotov–Ribbentrop Pact can be taken as a prime example of the logic of anti-alliance deals outlined in this chapter.

6.4.2 The Reichstadt Agreement

The Molotov–Ribbentrop Pact is but one example of a broader pattern. Indeed, neutrality pacts have been common throughout history, and were especially prominent before World War I. The 1876 Reichstadt Agreement, and the negotiations from which it emerged, illustrate the connection between neutrality pacts and anti-alliance deals in this earlier period.

The agreement was formed at a July 8, 1876, meeting of Austro–Hungarian and Russian diplomats and secured Austro–Hungarian neutrality in the event of future conflict between Russia and Turkey. Both the ends and means of this agreement are consistent with the logic of anti-alliance deals. Importantly, the arrangement of interests that preceded the Reichstadt Agreement bears a strong resemblance to the structure of our formal model. Though a number of states had interest and potential involvement in the rising tensions that led to the agreement, our discussion will focus on the behavior of Russia, Austria–Hungary, and the Ottoman Empire. Hoping to recover losses from the Crimean War, Russia had a dispute with the Ottomans over territory in the Balkans. Involvement of third parties, in particular Austria-Hungary, was a major concern of Russian decision-makers (Armour 2014, 270–272). Viewed in this way, the Ottoman Empire and Russia can be understood as playing roles similar to States 1 and 2, respectively.

Russia's main concern was that Austria–Hungary might become involved in some conflict, shaping the outcome in a way that would run counter to Russian interests. Thus, it is reasonable to understand Austria–Hungary's role as similar to that of State 3 in our model.

Consistent with the logic of our model, Russia sought to limit Austria–Hungary's involvement in any future dispute with the Ottomans (Heraclides and Dialla, 2015). To this end, Russia negotiated to formalize Austro–Hungarian neutrality, initiating a process that culminated in the Reichstadt Treaty of 1876. Thus, it is clear that the motivation for this treaty is in line with the motivation for anti-alliance deals. Russia wanted to head off any involvement of a state that would counter its interests in a hypothetical conflict with the Ottomans. More importantly, the *quid pro quo* arrangement that sustained the treaty is consistent with the logic we have outlined in this chapter. As discussed in our exposition of Proposition 6.1's logic, third parties can be bribed away from potential cooperative relationships through targeted concessions. This is precisely what Russia did to secure Austro–Hungarian neutrality. The key bargaining chip Russia had was control of Bosnia and Herzegovina (Armour 2014, 272). Describing the terms of the deal, Heraclides and Dialla, p. 158 write: "Austria-Hungary promised not only to preserve a benevolent neutrality, but actively to impede the collective mediation of other powers in a Russo-Turkish conflict. Andrássy also reluctantly accepted that Serbia and Montenegro could be called on by Russia to assist in the campaign if necessary. In return, the Monarchy was to be free to decide on when, and how, it occupied both Bosnia and the Herzegovina in their entirety"

Thus, per the logic of anti-alliance deals, Austria–Hungary received concessions from Russia in exchange for a promise of neutrality. In turn, Russia was happy to offer these concessions, as it benefitted from limiting the involvement of a third party in its impending conflict with the Ottoman Empire.

6.5 Conclusion

This chapter, like the one before it, provided insight into the tools of statecraft that allow states to avoid the provocative effects of new alliances. In particular, we have advanced a logic of anti-alliance deals. Like the deals discussed in the previous chapter, anti-alliance deals avoid war through the use of careful negotiation. However, unlike the previous chapter, the deals discussed in this chapter prevent the formation of an alliance altogether. By offering concessions to a pair of potential allies, a targeted state can prevent a budding military relationship from coming to fruition in the first place. Under certain conditions, this behavior can be sustained, and is even preferred by the players, to an equilibrium in which war occurs. However, unfortunately, anti-alliance deals are not a panacea. If an alliance would result in a sufficiently large and rapid power shift, then the temptation of a "lucky" outcome in which implementation is finalized before a preventive strike can occur is too tempting for the potential allies. As a result, the commitment to forgo an alliance is not credible and, realizing this, the target of the alliance does not offer an anti-alliance deal. In spite of this, we demonstrated that for a large range of parameters such deals do exist. Furthermore, the possibility of such deals shed light on important historical episodes. As our cases illustrate, one important implication of this chapter's analysis is that many of the most dangerous alliances throughout history may likely never have come into force. This points towards a number of avenues for future work, as our theory suggests that these "dogs that didn't bark" are an important component of understanding alliance politics, and security cooperation in general. The final chapter of the book follows. In it, we discuss a number of implications of our work for the future study of alliance politics. We also outline important policy implications of our work.

7
Conclusion

We opened this book by asking whether alliances lead to peace or war. We have argued that an understanding of the dynamic nature of security cooperation is crucial to answering this question. In particular, we highlighted a key feature of alliance politics that has been largely overlooked by scholars of international relations: Realizing the benefits of an alliance relationship takes time and effort. An understanding of this process, which we call *alliance implementation*, forms the bedrock of the theoretical argument we have developed throughout this book.

To conclude, we discuss three ways in which our findings have relevance for the future. First, we revisit the central question that prompted this book: Do alliances provoke conflict? We contend that our theory offers novel insights into this issue, reconciling competing findings in existing research. Second, much work remains to be done on the broader topic of alliance implementation; we set forth a research agenda that builds on existing work and paves a path forward incorporating the insights we have identified in this book. Lastly, we address the complexities of alliance politics in the twenty-first century, extracting a range of policy implications from our analysis to guide future decision-making.

7.1 Do Alliances Cause War?

The question of whether alliances cause war or peace is perhaps the most fiercely debated topic among scholars of security cooperation. One perspective is that alliances, especially defensive alliances, cause peace by deterring aggression (Leeds 2003; Benson 2011; Johnson and Leeds 2011; Benson 2012; Leeds and Johnson 2017). An alternative perspective argues that alliances cause war by increasing enemies' perception of threat (Kenwick, Vasquez, and Powers 2015; Kenwick and Vasquez 2017).

We have noted that both perspectives offer valuable insights into the alliance–war nexus, though they may not fully capture all the

The Window Before. Brett V. Benson and Bradley C. Smith, Oxford University Press.
 DOI: 10.1093/9780197806760.003.0007

complexities involved. While each perspective addresses certain aspects of alliance politics, there are additional dimensions that they do not fully account for. Previous work tends to simplify the relationship, framing alliances as either deterrent or provocative. In contrast, our approach, based on the logic of commitment problems, suggests that the connection between alliances and war is more conditional and nuanced. Our theory aims to provide a fresh viewpoint in this ongoing debate.

We have emphasized the significance of examining the entire life cycle of an alliance rather than viewing it as a static entity. Existing research often treats alliances as if they exist only at a specific moment, focusing primarily on whether an alliance treaty is in place as the key factor defining an alliance's presence or absence. Consequently, the deterrent benefits of an alliance have been largely attributed to the mere existence of a treaty. Our framework suggests that this approach overlooks a crucial aspect: the process of alliance implementation. According to our perspective, alliances become effective deterrents through their implementation, which includes, but is not limited to, formalizing the relationship with a treaty. Therefore, it is essential to distinguish between alliance treaties and the broader process of alliance implementation, as both are important but distinct factors influencing the deterrent value of alliances.

As we argued in Chapter 2, the signing of an alliance treaty is only one part of a complex, multi-step process that allies must navigate to realize the deterrent benefits of an alliance. To effectively deter, alliances must coordinate members' military forces. A comprehensive understanding of alliance implementation reveals that an alliance treaty is just one factor in achieving effective coordination among allies. In this view, while the presence of a treaty is correlated with the ability of allies to fight together, this correlation is imperfect and varies between alliances. The presence or absence of a treaty does not capture the entire picture. In some cases, potential allies might fight effectively together even without a formal treaty, while in other cases, allies may still struggle with military interoperability even after signing and ratifying a treaty. Thus, formal alliance treaties do not fully encompass the scope of cooperation among partners.

By focusing on the dynamic process of alliance implementation, our theory provides a unified framework for understanding why alliances might lead to either peace or war. As discussed in Chapters 3 through 6, the key factor determining whether alliances cause peace or war is the *expected strength* of an alliance. In our theory, states are forward-looking, anticipating how their current actions will influence future power dynamics. Our theory suggests that allies must strike a careful balance to avoid war. Implementing a new alliance holds future benefits, but these benefits come at a cost to the enemies of the alliance. Consequently, enemies might be incentivized to prevent an alliance's implementation through force.

These dynamic considerations set our work apart from previous scholarship on alliances. The dynamic nature of our argument addresses the ongoing debate on whether alliances deter or provoke conflict. Specifically, it highlights a key difference between the research designs of two studies with competing findings. Kenwick, Vasquez, and Powers (2015) find that alliances do not deter and, in some cases, increase the likelihood of conflict, whereas Leeds and Johnson (2017) challenge this finding, pointing out a significant difference between Kenwick, Vasquez, and Powers (2015)'s analysis and other studies that find a deterrent effect. Leeds and Johnson note that Kenwick, Vasquez, and Powers (2015) focus only on the period around alliance formation, including cases where a dyad transitions from having no alliance to having one, and examine short-term effects within five years of a new alliance's formation.

Proposition 3.3 directly addresses why alliances might be dangerous shortly after signing. The equilibrium path can result in either provocation or deterrence, depending on the outcome of the initial implementation attempt. If this initial attempt fails and implementation is delayed, the expectation of future implementation can be provocative, leading the target state to initiate a preventive war. Importantly, and consistent with Kenwick, Vasquez, and Powers (2015), this logic identifies the period around alliance formation as particularly perilous. Any delay in implementation creates a window of opportunity for the target and may lead to conflict.

However, our analysis also suggests that alliances are not solely provocative. The equilibrium behavior under Proposition 3.3 is also consistent with the idea that alliances can deter. In a scenario where alliance implementation is not instantaneous, deterrence can succeed only after the alliance is fully implemented. In this way, our model aligns with the notion that defensive alliances have long-term deterrent effects (Leeds and Johnson 2017). Under Proposition 3.3, if implementation is successful, the target of the alliance accepts the new distribution of power and is effectively deterred from making aggressive demands or initiating a preventive war. Our model suggests that alliances achieve their maximal deterrent benefits in the long run once they are fully implemented and no longer represent a potential future power shift.

Thus, our model provides a unified framework for understanding the conflicting findings in the empirical literature. The commitment–problem logic underscores the importance of timing in the effectiveness of alliances. Timing is crucial to the conflicting empirical findings, as Leeds and Johnson point out: "The consequential difference between Johnson and Leeds (2011) and Kenwick, Vasquez, and Powers (2015) is whether the effect of alliances should be observed throughout their existence or only for a short time after gaining a newally" (2017, 373). Given this, our theoretical model offers a compelling perspective on this debate.[1]

More precisely, our theory provides a possible explanation for why alliances might be associated with conflict shortly after they are signed, while also being linked to long-term deterrent benefits. Both Kenwick, Vasquez, and Powers (2015) and Kenwick and Vasquez (2017) find that alliances are associated with conflict in the immediate aftermath of signing. In contrast, Leeds and Johnson (2017) find that defensive alliances are associated with long-term deterrent benefits by analyzing data that spans all alliance years. Moreover, Leeds and Johnson (2017) argue that the test provided by Kenwick, Vasquez, and Powers (2015) is better suited to examining the steps-to-war argument rather than evaluating the deterrent effects of alliances. Our theory supports this view, suggesting that the anticipation of a new alliance might trigger war precisely because targeted states aim to prevent the realization of the deterrent benefits of alliance implementation.

As discussed in Chapter 2, alliances are often not fully implemented by the time the relevant alliance treaty is signed. Rather, allies must coordinate their military efforts, and this process frequently extends beyond the signing of the treaty. Kenwick, Vasquez, and Powers (2015) argue that their findings align with the logic of the security dilemma (Jervis, 2017), which suggests that alliances may heighten threat perceptions and provoke hostility from targeted states. However, this argument only partially explains

[1] Morrow (2017) also provides a model to reconcile this empirical debate, though his argument is distinct from ours and relies on incomplete information about allies' goals. We do not claim that our model's explanation is superior to Morrow's (2017), but rather view these explanations as complementary. In situations characterized by uncertainty about the conflict of interest between alliance members and their shared enemy, Morrow's model offers valuable insights. Conversely, in scenarios where the constellation of interests is common knowledge but alliance formation unfolds dynamically, our model is more applicable. An important task for future research will be to identify which cases align with the informational logic and which with the commitment–problem logic, guiding the design of targeted statistical tests to further evaluate the mechanisms linking alliances to war.

the conflicting findings of Kenwick, Vasquez, and Powers (2015) and other research such as Leeds (2003) and Leeds and Johnson (2017). The security dilemma does not fully address why perceptions of threat might be higher immediately after an alliance is signed but lower once the alliance has been established for several years.

These dynamics are at the heart of the theory offered here, and the competing findings in the literature are consistent with the logic of our dynamic theory of alliance formation and war. As Leeds and Johnson (2017) and Morrow (2017) detail, the competing findings in the literature stem from differences in the temporal scope of the relevant studies. Kenwick and Vasquez (2017) find that alliance formation is associated with a short-term increase in the probability of war, while Leeds (2003) and Leeds and Johnson (2017) show that alliances have long-term deterrent effects that lead to peace. The theoretical explanation for this finding offered by Kenwick, Vasquez, and Powers (2015) points to the steps to war argument (Senese and Vasquez 2008). The steps to war argument draws on the logic of the security dilemma, arguing that states fall back on realist policies to resolve territorial disputes, and that these policy choices trigger perceptions of threat, leading to escalating steps that culminate in war (Owsiak 2017). However, theories rooted in the logic of the security dilemma cannot speak to this discrepancy, as they do not make specific predictions about why perceptions of threat should be higher in the time immediately after an alliance is signed, but lower after an alliance has been in place for a number of years.

Our theory addresses this gap by explaining why the effects of alliances change over time. The key lies in understanding alliance formation as a dynamic process. Alliance treaties are just one part of the alliance implementation process. Since the deterrent benefits of an alliance are only realized once the alliance is fully implemented, it is necessary to measure these effects once the implementation is complete. The presence of an alliance treaty does not always align with the completion of implementation, which means that preventive war might occur when a treaty is present but the deterrent benefits have not yet materialized due to delays in full implementation. Thus, our theory offers an explanation for why alliances might be associated with war early in their lifetimes but not otherwise. A full, quantitative test of this theory is beyond the scope of this book, but we have provided in-depth case evidence supporting the mechanism we identify. Assessing the generality of this mechanism is an important task for future research, and some scope conditions should be considered. For instance, our explanation relies on the idea that the deterrent effect of alliances primarily stems from military coordination rather than the treaty itself. Evaluating the balance of these factors is crucial, and we will revisit this discussion in the following section.

Although a more thorough test of our argument within the alliance–war debate is needed, our theory offers implications for future research. These implications build on the existing debate, highlighting the importance of dynamic, temporal considerations in the study of security cooperation and alliance politics. Specifically, our theory suggests that temporal dynamics are more significant than previously recognized, indicating the necessity of considering the period *prior to the signing of an alliance treaty*. A key insight of our theory is that *attempts* at alliance formation, even if they do not result in a formal treaty, may trigger conflict. This is because enemies might strike before a treaty is signed to prevent its conclusion. We argued that this logic may explain Russia's 2014 annexation of Crimea and the 2022 invasion of Ukraine. In this case, the *expectation* of an alliance treaty, rather than its actual existence, appears to be the key factor driving conflict.

In summary, while a comprehensive quantitative test of our theory would require data on the full scope of alliance implementation, our theory suggests that dynamic, temporal factors play a crucial role in understanding alliances' effects on conflict and deterrence. The quantitative analysis provided in Chapter 4 is a preliminary step, but future research should focus on collecting data across a range of security cooperation efforts. This richer data set is necessary for a robust quantitative evaluation of the theory of alliance implementation and preventive war presented in this book.

7.2 Alliance Implementation: A Research Agenda

Highlighting the concept of alliance implementation is a core contribution of this book. As Chapter 2 demonstrated, the complexity of security cooperation is well understood by policymakers and practitioners. While alliance treaties are crucial, the politics of alliances neither begins nor ends with treaty ratification. Instead, realizing the deterrent benefits of a military alliance requires overcoming numerous political and military challenges both before and after the formal signing of a treaty. Treaty ratification is merely one of these hurdles. Understanding these hurdles is essential for grasping the full connection between alliances and war.

In emphasizing this point and exploring its implications, this book marks a significant departure from previous studies of alliance politics, which have predominantly focused on the credibility of alliance commitments (Morrow 2000). In contrast, our focus has been on the dynamics of alliance formation, particularly how alliances influence states' expectations regarding future power distributions in the international system. We do not consider these approaches as competing theories but rather as complementary. Integrating the signaling and credibility framework with the commitment–problem framework is an important avenue for future research. The remainder of this section outlines a future research agenda that builds on the insights presented in this book. Our proposed agenda places alliance implementation at its center, aiming to advance both theoretical and empirical understanding of alliance politics.

7.2.1 Theories of Alliance Implementation

A central contribution of this book is to connect the logic of dynamic commitment problems to the logic of alliance politics. By focusing on the inter-temporal effects of alliances and the power shifts they create, our theory provides a new perspective on many issues in alliance formation and management. However, the dynamic considerations we have focused on do not paint the full picture of alliance politics. Decades of theoretical and empirical research have shown the importance of what Morrow (2000) calls the "credibility problem" inherent in alliances—the difficulty allies face in convincing a shared enemy that they will fight on behalf of one another in the event of war. We believe that a full theory of alliance politics should incorporate *both* commitment–problem dynamics and the credibility problem.

As such, one important task for future work is to integrate the commitment–problem framework developed throughout this book with the traditional view of alliances, which focuses on questions of credibility. To gain analytical purchase, our analysis has largely abstracted away from credibility considerations. We view this simplifying assumption as a useful one, as abstracting away from these considerations has allowed us to isolate the commitment–problem mechanism[2] to deliver novel insights about alliance

[2] This places our model in the category of "experimental" theoretical models under the framework presented by Paine et al. (2020).

formation and its connection to crisis bargaining. However, we believe that neither perspective provides a complete accounting of the forces that drive alliance politics. The interaction of commitment problems and information asymmetries has received some attention in the literature previously. For example, Wolford, Reiter, and Carrubba (2011) show that when information asymmetries and commitment problems interact, many standard patterns from the crisis bargaining literature are upended. Illustrating this, Dong (2023) shows that information asymmetries can enhance peace when they interact with commitment problems.

The interaction of information asymmetries and commitment problems is especially relevant for understanding alliance politics. To wit, in Chapter 5, we showed how successful alliance implementation often requires secrecy. In the context of our model, secrecy allows states to implement an alliance before an adversary can react. We developed this argument by pointing to secrecy as an effective tool to speed up alliance implementation—if adversaries are unaware of an impending alliance, then its implementation effectively occurs instantaneously. However, this treatment of secrecy abstracts away from the possibility that states may invest effort into learning about their enemies' alignments and possible alliance relationships.[3] One promising avenue for future work is to develop a model of secret alliances that combines endogenous information exchange with the commitment problem dynamics studied here.

Future work might also consider an important strategic feature of dynamic alliance implementation that we have abstracted away from in this book: the possibility of counter-alliances. In Chapters 5 and 6, we studied two approaches to avoiding wars driven by commitment problems in alliance formation. A third approach deserves attention as well. In anticipation of a new opposing alliance, states may form their own alliances. This idea—that states form "balancing" coalitions—has been studied before (Walt 1990; Powell 1999; Krainin and Wiseman 2016). However, to our knowledge the existing literature has not considered how balancing alliances operate in a world in which alliance implementation is subject to delay. The closest study is Krainin and Wiseman (2016), who does consider alliances in a dynamic environment where states are forward-looking, considering how alliances will shape the future distribution of power. However, this study abstracts away from the implementation delays that are a crucial part of our argument.

[3] For a signaling-based model of secret alliances that abstracts away from commitment–problem dynamics, see Bils and Smith (2023).

As such, we believe that incorporating these ideas in a unified model of balancing behavior is likely to yield new insights about how alliances affect the stability of international politics.

The concept of alliance implementation also points to areas for theoretical development that reach past the crisis bargaining framework that we have explored in this book. In Chapter 2, we discussed many difficulties in alliance implementation. Understanding these challenges, and how allies overcome them, is a promising avenue for future inquiry. This is consistent with Snyder (1997), who argues that interactions between allies themselves are just as important as interactions between allies and a shared enemy.

Alliances are, of course, international organizations. However, the literature on alliance politics has often focused on the effects of alliances on international security politics rather than the day-to-day functioning of alliances themselves. The difficulty of alliance implementation reveals that there is much to be learned about the internal politics of military alliances. Our interviews revealed that NATO is a vast bureaucracy. As such, pursuing the study of alliances through the lens of bureaucratic politics is a natural next step for the literature. For example, future work might look to characterize the agency problems that arise in the internal politics of alliances. In our discussion of implementation in Chapter 2, many of the difficulties stemmed from difficulties arising from principal–agent relationships. For example, in an asymmetric alliance, the stronger state (the principal) wants to induce the weaker partner (the agent) to exert effort in the implementation process, perhaps by participating in joint military exercises. However, because such effort is costly, agents have an incentive to shirk. Studying this kind of problem, and how allies overcome it, is a promising direction for future work.

Overall, we believe that the arguments presented in this book present many opportunities for future work. Some of that work might explore additional implications of the bargaining framework we have explored, either by integrating commitment and information problems, by considering counter-alliances, or by offering a more nuanced treatment of the role of secrecy in dynamic alliance formation. Other studies might move past the bargaining framework altogether, focusing on interactions between allies by applying a principal–agent framework. In either case, our hope is that the arguments in this book, and the new perspective they bring, spur a revival in the study of alliance politics.

7.2.2 Empirical Studies of Alliance Implementation

The primary goal of this book has been to offer a new theoretical perspective on the politics of alliance formation and war. Though we offered quantitative empirical analysis in Chapter 4, the bulk of our empirical evidence has been qualitative. We believe this approach was appropriate, as it allowed us to offer direct evidence that the strategic mechanism in our theoretical model was present in important cases of alliance formation. In demonstrating the relevance of this logic to alliance politics, this book points to new areas for quantitative empirical work.

We believe that the most important next step for the empirical literature is data collection. A key development in the study of alliance politics was the creation of the ATOP data (Leeds, Long and Mitchell 2000). By systematically documenting the rich variation in alliance treaty content, the ATOP data project has enabled scholars of military cooperation to study how alliance content shapes international politics. Our arguments point to another aspect of alliance politics for which we do not currently have such a rich data source: alliance implementation.

Developing a systematic data set on alliance implementation is an important task for future work, as it would allow for a more thorough test of the arguments developed in this book. We have offered much qualitative evidence consistent with the commitment–problem logic embodied in our theory. Absent such data, however, it is not possible to evaluate the generality of the mechanism that we have presented. We believe that the evidence we have presented suffices to illustrate that this mechanism influences many of the most important cases of alliance formation across the last two centuries. However, our theory also offers a number of testable predictions that relate the expected strength of a new alliance to the probability of war. Performing these tests requires systematic data on alliance implementation.

What would such a data set look like? The key challenge here is that alliance implementation is a complex process involving both political and military factors. Often observable indicators of implementation attempts begin well before the signing of an alliance treaty. This presents a challenge for the generation of quantitative data, as the complex multidimensional concept of implementation must be operationalized in a way that is suitable for the collection of quantitative data. For this reason, we believe that the most productive first step for this empirical research program is to focus on specific aspects of the alliance implementation process. By doing this, the field can accumulate knowledge about the different aspects of implementation, building a fuller picture of how specific barriers to implementation operate in practice.

One guiding example is Poast (2019), who studies negotiations over alliance treaty content. As Poast (2019) notes, a key difficulty in this subject area is in identifying cases of failed negotiations. It is easy to identify cases that resulted in successful negotiations and a formal alliance treaty. But identifying cases of failed negotiations is more difficult. The solution Poast offers is a systematic reading of diplomatic history, which identified attempts at alliance formation, successful and unsuccessful. Though labor-intensive, this approach produced a full data set of both successful and failed alliance negotiations. In fact, we view the data set provided and analyzed by Poast (2019) as a highly relevant first step on the road to understanding the political dimension of alliance implementation.

Future work might take a similar approach to the collection of data on the military dimension of implementation. The universe of potential alliances identified by Poast (2019) might provide a starting point, allowing scholars to refine the temporal dimension of their search for data on military aspects of implementation. With the search narrowed, a number of factors might be quantified. We consider some possibilities below, though given the complexity of the military dimension of alliance implementation we have documented, these possibilities should not be viewed as exhaustive.

A first step towards developing quantitative data on the military dimension of implementation might focus on whether allies seek to integrate their militaries at all. As discussed in Chapter 2, alliances vary along this dimension. Some alliances, like NATO, place interoperability at the forefront, investing immense effort to effectively field multinational forces, aggregating the military capabilities of member states. We have called such alliances capability aggregators. In contrast, some alliances do not aim for this kind of interoperability. Rather, as was the case in many nineteenth-century alliances, some alliance partners simply hope to use their cooperation to divide the forces of an enemy. In these alliances, a power shift comes from the fact that the alliance opens a second front to the war, rather than by introducing forces from multiple nations across a single front. As we discussed in Chapter 5, these two alliances face very different hurdles in terms of military implementation. Capability-aggregating alliances must deal with myriad challenges to achieve interoperability, while capability-dividing alliances do not. As such, the development of quantitative data that determines whether alliances fall into one category or the other will prove useful for future studies that build on our work. Importantly, such data should be gathered not only on alliances that reached the point where a treaty was signed but also on alliances that never came to pass. This is crucial for testing our theory, which points to the time before an alliance is fully implemented as key.

Another critical factor that should be considered in data collection is timing. The majority of quantitative data used by scholars of international relations considers observations at the yearly level. For many research questions, this is appropriate. But our theory indicates that studies of alliance implementation should aim for more fine-grained temporal data. The process of alliance implementation evolves subtly over time, and so yearly observations will be unlikely to capture the full spectrum of alliance implementation, which is crucial for quantitatively evaluating our theory. Of course, data collection efforts must strike a pragmatic balance, as data that is too fine-grained will not be of practical use. A first effort at collecting data on the stages of alliance implementation over time might begin with a subset of alliances, tracing their development to identify when key hurdles of implementation were crossed. Based on this initial effort, common patterns in implementation might be identified that could guide a more systematic data collection effort.

The importance of temporal dynamics also points to important considerations for the analysis of quantitative data on alliance implementation. A key implication of our theory is that the *anticipation* of a new alliance is just as important as the *existence* of an alliance. This poses a challenge, as it requires scholars to measure states' expectations about which alliances might come into force in the future. Though this is a difficult problem, future work might follow in the footsteps of previous studies that measure such expectations. Bell and Johnson (2015) offer a quantitative theory of shifting-power commitment problems, introducing a technique to measure states' expectations about the future distribution of power in the international system. Future work might tailor this general approach to isolate the effect of alliance-driven power shifts.

There is also room for qualitative empirical inquiry to build on the insights of this book. In many cases, idiosyncratic exogenous constraints influence the timeline of alliance implementation. For example, as we discussed previously, an unrelated political scandal in France significantly delayed the implementation of the 1894 Franco–Russian Alliance. Similarly, the PRC's reaction to the impending 1954 US–Taiwan Mutual Defense Pact was constrained by the PRC's inability to rapidly mount a full-scale invasion of Taiwan. As these examples illustrate, though the speed of alliance implementation does depend on endogenous factors, it is also subject to exogenous constraints. Systematically categorizing these constraints is difficult, and at present we do not see a clear path towards conceptualizing them in a systematic fashion. We believe this presents an opportunity for future qualitative work to engage in in-depth historical analysis. Such analysis might uncover insights about exogenous constraints to implementation that would allow for further theory development towards a more systematic understanding of how these apparently idiosyncratic forces shape the politics of alliance implementation.

7.3 Predicting Outcomes in the Real World

In this section, we address a question introduced at the end of the previous section: What are the endogenous and exogenous factors that predict the different outcomes outlined in our theory? Throughout this book, we have predicted a range of potential outcomes that may arise in the period leading up to the implementation of an alliance. We have shown that targets of military alliances might engage in large-scale wars, small-scale aggression, or negotiate deals to prevent alliances. Additionally, prospective allies might offer concessions or manipulate the timing and scale of power shifts to persuade targets to accept the alliance peacefully. When can we expect to see these different outcomes in practice?

Models are simplified representations of reality, which makes answering this question challenging due to the many external factors influencing real-world decision-makers. Our model intentionally omits these specific external factors, focusing instead on the internal conditions within our theory that predict responses to potentially provocative alliances. However, actual responses often depend on the feasible, real-world options available to decision-makers. For example, negotiating with adversaries might be impractical due to high domestic political costs or significant logistical challenges. This section outlines the conditions specified in our theory and discusses the practical constraints faced by decision-makers, offering a foundation for researchers interested in systematically exploring these outcomes.

When might opponents of impending military alliances opt for small-scale aggression instead of large-scale war? As detailed in Chapter 4, the crucial conditions of our theory are the speed and size of a power shift from an alliance, the cost of small-scale aggression, and the probability that small-scale aggression can successfully block an alliance. Typically, targets of alliances prefer low-cost measures to block the alliance if there is a high enough chance that those measures can be successful.

Russia's approach has typically involved fostering separatist conflicts and small-scale military incursions rather than full-scale war. For example, Russia attacked Georgia in 2008, incited conflicts in Ukraine in 2014, and, in 2023, reportedly planned to destabilize Moldova to hinder NATO accession.[4] This strategy is cost-effective and effectively blocks NATO membership due to NATO's accession requirements, which demand resolution of various disputes before granting a membership action plan. This process allows adversaries like Putin to disrupt NATO bids with minimal interference, even when membership is not imminent. Therefore, Russia may use small-scale aggression in various scenarios, from imminent membership to less certain or distant accession.

The 2022 large-scale attack on Ukraine marks a deviation from Russia's typical use of smaller-scale interference. According to our theory, if the power shift is significant and the chance of blocking NATO membership with small-scale aggression is low, a large-scale attack may be chosen. Between 2014 and 2022, Ukraine increasingly unified around NATO membership, diminishing the effectiveness of small-scale aggression. Ukrainian domestic politics aligned more with Western priorities, and public opinion grew favorable towards NATO. The backlash against President Yanukovych's rejection of the EU–Ukraine Association Agreement and the Euromaidan protests marked a shift towards Europe. In response, Ukrainian leaders actively pursued NATO membership, culminating in a 2014 referendum and a 2019 constitutional amendment making NATO membership a formal government responsibility. These trends decreased the effectiveness of small-scale aggression and increased the urgency of NATO membership, leading Russia to opt for a large-scale conflict.

Real-world constraints can limit the application of theoretical predictions. Sometimes, a large-scale war might be predicted, but the target may lack the capacity to engage in such a conflict and only resort to small-scale aggression. For instance, during the 1954–55 Taiwan Strait Crisis, the Chinese

[4] https://www.cnn.com/2023/03/16/europe/russia-moldova-secret-document-intl-cmd/index.html

Communists, unable to launch an amphibious assault, opted for small-scale aggression on offshore islands. In a counterfactual scenario in which the PRC was considerably more powerful, they might have considered attacking Taiwan because the mutual defense pact with the United States had posed such a significant power shift.

Our theory also addresses scenarios where countries might negotiate rather than resort to preventive war. Does our theory offer any guidance for predicting peaceful negotiations? The results of our analysis show that a peaceful negotiated deal to abandon an alliance is possible whenever preventive war is an option, unless the power shift from the alliance is extremely high. In such high-risk scenarios, preventive war is preferred, though many alliances will still be implemented peacefully due to the speed of implementation.

Even when both peaceful negotiations and preventive war are theoretically viable, real-world constraints often influence the choice between them. Generally, opponents are likely to prefer a peaceful solution to war, which may explain the prevalence of pre-alliance negotiations and neutrality pacts throughout history. Additionally, countries might pursue both strategies simultaneously. For example, as explained in Chapter 6, the United States employed small-scale aggression alongside peaceful negotiations during the Cuban Missile Crisis to persuade the Soviet Union to abandon its alliance with Cuba.

If peaceful deals are generally preferred over preventive war, why might preventive action still occur? Practical constraints often determine which equilibrium is selected. In many cases, negotiations between adversaries may be impractical or prohibitively costly, making war the only viable option. Many of the historical cases highlight the variation in outcomes depending on what is feasible. During the Cuban Missile Crisis, for example, a secret deal was negotiated because a public negotiation would have been politically costly for the Kennedy administration. Conversely, the Louisiana Purchase was negotiated openly due to established diplomatic relations between the United States and France. In contrast, negotiations during the 1954–55 Taiwan Strait Crisis were challenging due to the lack of diplomatic relations between the United States and the PRC, compounded by ongoing tensions from the Korean War. The lack of diplomatic channels made such negotiations difficult.

Finally, our theory examines strategies for manipulating the speed of alliance implementation. Slowing implementation allows allies to make concessions to targets to bring about peaceful implementation, while accelerating implementation aims to achieve the power shift before the target can launch preventive attacks. Accelerating implementation is generally preferred, which is why secret implementation is a popular strategy. However, if speeding up implementation is not feasible, allies may choose to slow it down to appease the target and gradually achieve the power shift. Practical constraints, such as the difficulty of concealing military integration, often influence these decisions. For example, NATO has deliberately adopted rules to slow the membership process due to the intense interoperability required among its members, which is challenging to conceal.

Here again, practical constraints in the real world determine which direction allies choose to go. If secrecy is an option, then allies will choose this strategy. However, certain types of alliances are difficult to conceal. Alliances that require military integration are especially difficult to hide. NATO requires intense interoperability across its membership. Unable to conceal such efforts, NATO has deliberately adopted rules that slow the membership accession process.

The discussion in this section highlights the complexities of applying theoretical conditions to the range of political maneuvers countries might employ before an alliance is implemented. This book aims to clarify a previously overlooked issue in alliance studies: The time-consuming nature of alliance implementation creates incentives for states to engage in various actions to either prevent or facilitate power shifts from alliances. While our theory offers valuable predictions about the conditions under which these actions occur, real-world constraints often shape the feasible options. For example, military capacity constraints affect whether targets engage in full-scale or small-scale aggression, diplomatic constraints impact the feasibility of negotiations, and technological factors determine the viability of secret implementation. Future empirical research can further uncover systematic real-world constraints that predict when states choose different political actions in the lead-up to alliance implementation.

7.4 Commitment Problems in Alliance Formation in the Twenty-First Century

Our theory provides many implications for contemporary security cooperation policy. As we discussed in Chapter 4, alliance politics are crucial to understanding the Russian decision to invade Ukraine in February 2022. At the time of writing, the war has raged for over two years. What lessons can be drawn from our theory about the course of the war, and how it might end? War termination is an important topic that has been widely studied (see, for example, Reiter (2010), Slantchev (2003), and Goemans (2000)) and though war termination is not the main focus of this chapter, the commitment problem's logic can still be used to deliver insights about the likely duration of the war.[5] An unfortunate implication of the commitment problem logic is that the war is unlikely to end until either Russia or Ukraine achieves a fairly decisive victory. This is consistent with Wolford's (2019) description of preventive war; such wars are pursued because they "solve" the underlying commitment problem. As we highlighted in our case analysis of the Ukraine War, a key driving factor was the inability of Ukraine to commit to remain outside of NATO indefinitely.

Applying this to the Russian invasion of Ukraine implies that Russia will not stop until Ukraine's westward turn is reversed, and its path not only to NATO but also to EU membership and friendship with the West is reversed and halted for good. Given NATO's open-door policy, and Ukraine's constitutional commitment to seek membership, it seems unlikely that a peaceful commitment to remain outside the alliance will materialize. This unfortunately implies that if Russia's goal is to prevent Ukrainian NATO membership, war may be the only option.

Though many unknowns remain about the logic of key decision-makers in both Russia and Ukraine, this interpretation is consistent with the length of the conflict, which has persisted even though fighting has largely settled into a territorial stalemate at the time of writing. As Powell (2006) notes, the logic of commitment problems can be more readily applied to lengthy wars, in which information about battlefield effectiveness has likely been resolved through informative fighting (Slantchev 2003). At this point, it is reasonable to speculate that a primary Russian motivation for continuing the war is to prevent Ukraine from moving further towards NATO and EU membership.

This consideration points to a broader policy lesson for alliances like NATO that impose high barriers to entry for aspirational members. NATO's stringent membership requirements served to delay Ukraine's membership quest. These requirements are key to the design of the alliance, as one of its major goals is to create incentives for domestic political stability among members (Sayle 2019). However, our arguments show that this

[5] For a treatment of the interaction of information and commitment problems, and the implications of this interaction for war duration, see Wolford, Reiter, and Carrubba (2011).

comes with a cost. By placing barriers to membership, NATO throws wide open the window of opportunity for states like Russia to meddle in the affairs of aspirational members to block their entry. Telegraphing the possibility of a military commitment can trigger a dangerous race between efforts to implement and to block the alliance. NATO is likely to face these crises again, because its transparent and drawn-out membership processes exacerbate the dangers caused by potential alliances. Not every conflict will be as cataclysmic as the Ukraine invasion, but the negative incentive remains. As the United States and its allies punish Russia with sanctions, and otherwise pressure Putin to withdrawn from Ukraine, they should also be thinking about how to change these structural flaws. In particular, the alliance might consider replacing its road map for future members with a more opaque, private, deliberative process, so that adversaries cannot so clearly see the window of opportunity, and when it is closing.

Our argument also has significant implications for China–Taiwan relations, particularly regarding the delicate balance third parties must strike in supporting Taiwan against potential hostility from China. Previous research has emphasized the need for the United States to carefully design its commitments to Taiwan, aiming to balance deterrence of China with avoiding the emboldening of Taiwan (Benson 2012). This prior work highlights moral hazard concerns, where the United States might worry that Taiwan could use US assistance to adopt a more aggressive stance towards China, potentially leading to conflict. Our model introduces an additional layer of complexity by incorporating dynamic considerations.

Since 1980, when the United States abrogated its mutual defense treaty with Taiwan as part of normalizing relations with China, the United States has supported Taiwan through ad hoc arms transfers and a policy of strategic ambiguity. This approach aims to deter China by creating the impression that the United States is likely to defend Taiwan, while simultaneously restraining Taiwan's provocative moves towards independence by suggesting that US intervention might not be guaranteed. Although the United States does not currently have a formal alliance treaty with Taiwan, our model still offers valuable insights for policymakers involved in supporting Taiwan.

In particular, our findings highlight the challenges associated with modifying the level of US support. According to our theory, maintaining a constant level of support is generally manageable. However, if the United States chooses to increase its level of support, such as by moving towards a more transparent and formal alliance with Taiwan, this could trigger a commitment–problem dynamic. If such a commitment could be implemented immediately, it might enhance peace and security in the Taiwan Strait through a stronger military commitment to Taiwan. However, as demonstrated by our theory and various historical cases discussed in this book, implementing such a commitment will likely take time. This delay could prompt China to take aggressive action during the implementation period before Taiwan can benefit from the increased support. As a result, in attempting to bolster security through greater commitment, the United States might instead provoke preventive conflict. Our research cautions policymakers to account for these dynamic considerations in considering how to navigate security challenges in the Taiwan Strait.

Another emerging challenge in foreign affairs is the no-limits partnership between Russia and China. This relationship raises significant concerns for US policymakers and NATO allies. In our interviews with NATO officers, one noted that NATO is closely monitoring this partnership and, at this point, it is still early in the implementation phase. He indicated that NATO will begin to take the partnership seriously if there are observable moves towards military integration between the two countries.

Our theory suggests several considerations for understanding and responding to this partnership. It predicts that targets of alliances may resort to various forms of aggression, including full-scale war and also more limited but yet costly forms of aggression to prevent the formation of enemy alliances while they are still being implemented. Initially, this could manifest as economic sanctions aimed at disrupting the partnership. At the time of writing, little has been revealed about the intentions of this partnership. Other states' responses to the Russia–China no-limits partnership will reveal a great deal about how threatening it is perceived to be.

Our theory also predicts that allies will take steps to avoid preventive aggression target. We posit that secrecy is one tool for expediting the implementation process and avoiding interference. Unfortunately, Russia's and China's respective tensions with the United States preclude the possibility that negotiations can bring about peaceful alliance implementation or abandonment of the alliance. As a result, we might expect that the partnership will move forward in secret.

Given the opacity of the Russia–China partnership, our theory provides cautionary notes on the potential for escalation. If more explicit military cooperation arises, the risk of a direct military confrontation will increase.

Additionally, the theory suggests that elements of the partnership may be intentionally concealed to evade preventive actions by other global actors.

To conclude, our findings have important implications for alliance politics in the twenty-first century. Policymakers have long focused on issues of credibility and deterrence in alliance politics. However, a sole focus on credibility is not sufficient to address the challenges ahead. Our arguments suggest that security cooperation can trigger commitment problems, and that care is needed. To be clear, careful alliance management is a central part of addressing future challenges in international relations. A central lesson of this book is that addressing these challenges without an eye towards the potential for unintended consequences due to commitment problems may be destabilizing.

Appendix

Here we collect proof of all mathematical propositions that appear in the main text. For convenience, the propositions are reproduced here.

A.1 Proofs for Chapter 3

Before proving the results in the main text, it is necessary to establish several preliminary results.

Lemma A.1. *If σ is a stationary MPE, then in every period in which $s^t = A$, States 1 and 2 use the following strategies:*

1. *State 1 offers $x^t = 1 - w_2'$*
2. *State 2 accepts x^t if and only if $x^t \leq 1 - w_2'$.*

Proof. First, we show that State 1 may profitably deviate from any value x^t other than $x^t = 1 - w_2'$. To begin, suppose that State 1 is offering some value $x^t > 1 - w_2'$ in every period in which $s^t = A$. If State 1 is using such a strategy, then State 2 must be rejecting x^t, as

$$w_2' > 1 - x^t.$$

Now, consider a deviation to offering $1 - w_2' - \epsilon$ for some small $\epsilon > 0$. State 2 will accept this in period t, as

$$(1 - \delta)(w_2' + \epsilon) + \delta w_2' > w_2.$$

This deviation is profitable for State 1 if

$$(1 - \delta)(1 - w_2' - \epsilon) + \delta w_1' > w_1',$$

which holds for sufficiently small $\epsilon > 0$.

Next, suppose that State 1 is offering some $x^t < 1 - w_2'$ in equilibrium. State 2 must accept this offer, as it yields a strictly higher payoff than war. Now, consider a one-shot deviation from x^t to $x' = (x^t + 1 - w_2')/2$. State 2 will accept, as

$$(1 - \delta)(1 - x') + \delta(1 - x^t) > 1 - x^t > w_2'.$$

Because State 2 accepts and $x' > x^t$, this deviation is profitable for State 1. Therefore, State 1 cannot offer $x^t < 1 - w_2'$ in equilibrium. As State 1 cannot offer $x^t < 1 - w_2'$ or $x^t > 1 - w_2'$, it follows that State 1 must be offering $x^t = 1 - w_2'$. □

Lemma A.2. *If $a \leq r(w_2 - w_2')/(1 - \delta)$, then in every equilibrium, State 3 extends an alliance in every period in which $s^t = N$ and State 1 always joins if State 3 extends.*

Proof. We proceed in two steps. First, we show that if $a < a^*$, then State 1 must join if State 3 extends an alliance. Second, we show that State 3 must extend an alliance.

We prove the first step by contradiction. Suppose that σ is a stationary MPE in which State 1 does not join if State 3 extends an alliance and that $a < a^*$. Under σ, the payoff of war in every period for State 1 is w_1. Standard arguments establish that, under such a σ, in every period in which $s^t = N$, State 1 offers $1 - w_2$ and State 2 accepts x^t if and only if $x^t \leq 1 - w_2$. Now, consider State 1's reaction to State 3's (potentially off-path) extension of an alliance in a period in which $s^t = N$. As σ is an equilibrium, State 2 cannot profitably deviate to joining. Therefore, it must be that

$$r(1 - w_2') + (1 - r)(1 - w_2) - (1 - \delta)a \geq 1 - w_2 \implies a > r(w_2 - w_2')/(1 - \delta) \equiv a^*,$$

a contradiction. Therefore, in equilibrium, State 1 must join after State 3 extends an alliance.

Our second step is to show that State 3 must extend an alliance. Again, we proceed by contradiction. Suppose that σ is a stationary MPE in which State 3 never extends in a period in which $s^t = N$ and that $a < a^*$. As State 1 must join, State 3 does not have a profitable deviation if

$$r(1 - w_2') + (1 - r)(1 - w_2) - (1 - \delta)a \geq 1 - w_2 \implies a > r(w_2 - w_2')/(1 - \delta) \equiv a^*,$$

a contradiction. This completes the proof. □

Lemma A.3. *Suppose that $w_2' \geq w_2 - (1 - \delta)(1 - w_2)/\delta r$. If σ is a stationary MPE in which State 3 extends and State 1 joins in every period in which $s^t = N$, then in every period in which $s^t = N$ and an alliance was not successfully implemented, State 1 offers $x^t = \max\{0, 1 - w_2 - \delta r(w_2 - w_2')/(1 - \delta)\}$.*

Proof. First, suppose that $w_2' \geq w_2 - (1 - \delta)(1 - w_2)/\delta r$.

Let σ be a stationary MPE in which State 3 extends an alliance in every period in which $s^t = N$ and State 1 always joins in response.

We show that State 1 must be offering $x^t = \max\{0, 1 - w_2 - \delta r(w_2 - w_2')/(1 - \delta)\} \equiv x^N$. To do this, we show that if State 1 uses any other stationary strategy in such a period, offering $x^t < x^N$ or $x^t > x^N$, there exists a profitable deviation. As a preliminary step, we form State 2's continuation value under σ of accepting x^t if State 1 offers x^t in every period in which $s^t = N$. Denoting this continuation value V^2, we have

$$V^2 = (1 - \delta)(1 - x^t) + \delta[rw_2' + (1 - r)V^2].$$

Rearranging this expression yields

$$V^2 = \frac{(1 - \delta)(1 - x^t) + \delta r w_2'}{1 - \delta + \delta r}.$$

It is optimal for State 2 to accept x^t in a period in which $s^t = N$ under σ if $V^2 \geq w_2$. Substituting and solving for x^t, we find that State 2 will accept if

$$x^t \leq 1 - w_2 - \delta r(w_2 - w_2')/(1 - \delta).$$

Note that our assumption that $w_2' \geq w_2 - (1 - \delta)(1 - w_2)/\delta r$ implies that $1 - w_2 - \delta r(w_2 - w_2')/(1 - \delta) \geq 0$.

Now suppose that State 1 offers some $x^t < x^N$ in a period in which an alliance has not been implemented and $s^t = N$. By the argument above, State 2 will accept x^t. As before, let V^2 be State 2's continuation value of accepting x^t under σ. Consider a deviation to $x^t + \epsilon$ for some arbitrarily small value $\epsilon > 0$. State 2 must accept this offer if

$$(1 - \delta)(1 - x^t - \epsilon) + \delta[rw_2' + (1 - r)V^2] > w_2.$$

Recall that $x^t < x^N \implies V^2 > w_2$. Therefore, it suffices to show that

$$(1 - \delta)(1 - x^t - \epsilon) + \delta[rw_2' + (1 - r)w_2] > w_2.$$

This holds if

$$x^t + \epsilon < 1 - w_2 - \delta r(w_2 - w_2')/(1 - \delta),$$

which holds for sufficiently small $\epsilon > 0$ as $x^t < x^N$. This contradicts the assumption that σ is an equilibrium, and so State 1 cannot offer $x^t < x^N$ in equilibrium.

Next, suppose that in every period in which $s^t = N$, State 1 offers some $x^t > x^N$ after an alliance fails to be implemented under σ. Consider a one-shot deviation from x^t to $x^N - \epsilon$ for some arbitrarily small $\epsilon > 0$. As we have assumed that σ is an equilibrium, State 2 must react optimally to this deviation, accepting if

$$(1 - \delta)(1 - x^N - \epsilon) + \delta[rw_2' + (1 - r)w_2] > w_2.$$

Rearranging this, we find that State 2 must accept after such a deviation if

$$x^N - \epsilon < 1 - w_2 - \delta r(w_2 - w_2')/(1 - \delta),$$

which holds by definition of x^N. This deviation is profitable for State 1 if

$$w_1 - (1 - \delta)a < (1 - \delta)(x^N - \epsilon - a) + \delta[r(1 - w_2') + (1 - r)w_1 - (1 - \delta)a],$$

which holds as long as

$$a < (1 - \delta)(1 - w_2 - w_1 - \epsilon) + \delta r(1 - w_2 - w_1).$$

Recall that we have assumed that $a < 1 - w_2 - w_1$, and that the limit of the right-hand side of the above inequality as $\epsilon \to 0$ is equal to $1 - w_2 - w_1$. Therefore, by continuity, there exists sufficiently small $\epsilon > 0$ such that the above inequality is satisfied. As this deviation is profitable, State 1 cannot be using $x^t > x^N$ under σ. This completes the proof. □

Proposition 3.1. *If $a > r\Delta/(1 - \delta)$, then there is a unique equilibrium. Strategies in this equilibrium are as follows:*

1. *If $s^t = N$ and an alliance has not been successfully implemented in the current period, State 1 offers $x^t = 1 - w_2$. Otherwise, State 1 offers $x^t = 1 - w_2'$.*
2. *State 2 does not join after State 3 invites. If $s^t = N$ and an alliance has not been implemented, State 2 accepts any $x^t \leq 1 - w_2$ and rejects otherwise. If $s^t = A$, State 2 accepts any $x^t \leq 1 - w_2'$ and rejects otherwise.*

3. *State 3 never extends an alliance.*

Proof. Uniqueness of strategies is implied by lemmas A.1, A.2, and A.3.

Next, we proceed to show that the strategy profile is an equilibrium by demonstrating that no player has a profitable one-shot deviation.

To begin, consider State 3's choice to extend an alliance in every period in which $s^t = N$. To do this, we first compute State 3's continuation value of extending under σ. First, note that under σ, with probability $1-r$, the alliance is not implemented after 3 extends and 1 joins. If this occurs, then State 3's continuation payoff once implementation fails, denoted V^3, is given by

$$V^3 = (1-\delta)(1 - w_2 - \delta r(w_2 - w_2')/(1-\delta)) + \delta[r(1 - w_2' - a(1-\delta)) + (1-r)V^3,$$

which implies

$$V^3 = 1 - w_2 - a\frac{(1-\delta)(1+\delta r)}{1-\delta+\delta r}.$$

Continuing to form 3's continuation payoff of extending under σ, note that with probability r the alliance is implemented after State 1 joins, leading to a continuation payoff of $1 - w_2' - a(1-\delta)$. Pulling these together, the continuation value of extending under σ for player 3 is

$$(1-r)\left(1 - w_2 - a\frac{(1-\delta)(1+\delta r)}{1-\delta+\delta r}\right) + r(1 - w_2' - a(1-\delta)),$$

which simplifies to

$$1 - w_2 + r(w_2 - w_2') - \frac{a(1-\delta)}{1-\delta+\delta r}.$$

With this, under σ, a deviation to not extending is not profitable if

$$1 - w_2 + r(w_2 - w_2') - \frac{a(1-\delta)}{1-\delta+\delta r} \geq (1-\delta)\left[1 - w_2 - \frac{\delta r(w_2 - w_2')}{1-\delta}\right]$$
$$+ \delta\left[1 - w_2 + r(w_2 - w_2') - \frac{a(1-\delta)}{1-\delta+\delta r}\right].$$

This inequality is satisfied if

$$\left(\frac{1-\delta+\delta r}{1-\delta}\right)\left(\frac{a(w_2 - w_2')}{1-\delta}\right),$$

which holds as we have assumed that $a \leq r(w_2 - w_2')/(1-\delta)$. Therefore, State 3 cannot profitably deviate to not extend. Next, note that the same argument above establishes that State 1 cannot profitably deviate from joining after State 3 extends under σ.

Next, we show that State 1 cannot profitably deviate from offering $x^t = x^N$ in a period in which $s^t = N$ and an alliance was not successfully implemented in the current period. First, consider a deviation to some $x' > x^N$. In response to such a deviation, State 2 will reject. Comparing this to the continuation value of offering x^N derived above, we find that this deviation is not profitable if

$$1 - w_2 + r(w_2 - w_2') - \frac{a(1-\delta)}{1-\delta+\delta r}. \geq w_1,$$

which holds if

$$a \leq \left(\frac{1-\delta+\delta r}{1-\delta}\right)(1 - w_2 - w_1 + r(w_2 - w_2')).$$

The above inequality is satisfied as we have assumed that $a < 1 - w_2 - w_1$. Therefore, State 1 cannot profitably deviate to offer some x^N.

Next, consider a deviation by State 1 to offer some $x' > x^N$. Denoting the value of the game beginning in an arbitrary period under σ in which $s^t = N$ as V^1, such a deviation is not profitable as long as

$$(1-\delta)(x' - a(1-\delta) + \delta V^1 \leq (1-\delta)(x^N - a(1-\delta) + \delta V^1,$$

which holds as $x' < x^N$ and $\delta \in (0, 1)$.

Finally, note that by construction of State 1's offer, State 2 weakly prefers to accept x^N in a period in which $s^t = N$ and an alliance has not been implemented. Similarly, in a period in which $s^t = A$ or an alliance has been implemented, State 2's payoff of rejecting is w_2', and so State 2 cannot profitably deviate from the proposed strategy in response to an offer by State 1. □

Proposition 3.3. *If $a \leq r\Delta/(1-\delta)$ and $\Delta > (1-\delta)(1-w_2)/\delta r$, then all equilibria are equivalent in outcome distribution to the equilibrium in which players use the following strategies:*

1. *State 1 joins an alliance after State 3 invites in every period in which $s^t = N$. State 1 offers $x^t = 0$ in every period in which $s^t = N$ and an alliance has not been implemented. Otherwise, State 1 offers $x^t = 1 - w_2'$.*
2. *If $s^t = N$ and an alliance was not implemented in the current period, State 2 rejects all offers x^t. Otherwise, State 2 accepts x^t if and only if $x^t \leq 1 - w_2'$.*
3. *State 3 extends an alliance in every period in which $s^t = N$.*

Proof. To begin, note that lemma A.2 implies that, under the conditions of the proposition, in every equilibrium, in period 1 State 3 extends and State 1 joins, and with probability r and alliance is implemented and play proceeds according to lemma A.1, and with probability $1 - r$ State 2 rejects any offer and the game concludes with war in period 1. This establishes that, under the parameter values indicated in the proposition, every equilibrium is equivalent in outcome distribution. Finally, note that the equilibrium strategies outlined in the proposition produce precisely this outcome distribution.

Next, we establish that this strategy profile is indeed an equilibrium by demonstrating that no player has a profitable one-shot deviation.

First consider a deviation by State 3 to not extend an alliance in a period in which $s^t = N$. Such a deviation is not profitable if

$$w_3 \leq r(1 - w_2') + (1 - r)w_3 - a(1 - \delta),$$

which holds if

$$a \leq \frac{r(1 - w_2' - w_3)}{1 - \delta}.$$

This holds, as we have assumed that $a \leq r(w_2 - w_2')/(1 - \delta)$ and

$$a \leq \frac{a(w_2 - w_2')}{1 - \delta} < \frac{r(1 - w_2' - w_3)}{1 - \delta}.$$

Therefore, State 3 cannot profitably deviate from extending an alliance in such a period. Next, we demonstrate that State 1 cannot profitably deviate from joining after State 3 extends in a period in which $s^t = N$. Such a deviation is not profitable if

$$w_1 \leq r(1 - w_2') + (1 - r)w_1 - a(1 - \delta),$$

which holds if

$$a \leq \frac{r(1 - w_2' - w_1)}{1 - \delta}.$$

This holds, as we have assumed that $a \leq r(w_2 - w_2')/(1 - \delta)$ and

$$a \leq \frac{a(w_2 - w_2')}{1 - \delta} < \frac{r(1 - w_2' - w_1)}{1 - \delta}.$$

Next, consider a deviation by State 1 to offer some $x^t \neq 0$ in a period in which $s^t = N$ and an alliance was not implemented in the current period. Given State 2's strategy, any such offer will be rejected, yielding a payoff of $w_1 - a(1 - \delta)$. This is equivalent to the payoff of offering $x^t = 0$ in such a period, therefore no such deviation is profitable.

Next, consider a deviation from State 2's acceptance strategy in response to an offer x^t in a period in which $s^t = N$ and an alliance has not been implemented in the current period. Such a deviation is profitable if $(1 - \delta)(1 - x^t) + \delta[rw_2' + (1 - r)w_2]$. Note that if this inequality holds for $x^t = 0$, it will also hold for all $x^t \in (0, 1]$. Substituting $x^t = 0$ and rearranging reveals that the inequality is satisfied if

$$w_2' \leq w_2 - \frac{(1 - \delta)(w_2 - 1)}{\delta r},$$

which holds as we have assumed that $w_2' \leq w_2 - (1 - \delta)(1 - w_2)/\delta r$, and

$$w_2' \leq w_2 - \frac{(1 - \delta)(1 - w_2)}{\delta r} < w_2 - \frac{(1 - \delta)(w_2 - 1)}{\delta r}.$$

Therefore, State 2 cannot profitably deviate from rejecting all offers x^t in a period in which $s^t = N$ and an alliance was not implemented in the current period.

Finally, the same argument employed in the proof of proposition 3.2 establishes that no player has a profitable deviation from the proposed strategies in a period in which an alliance has been successfully implemented or $s^t = A$. □

Proposition 3.4. *Suppose that $a \leq r\Delta/(1-\delta)$. The equilibrium probability of war is*

1. *0 if $\Delta \leq \Delta^*$*
2. *$1-r$ otherwise.*

Proof. Follows from the equilibrium strategies outlined in Propositions 3.2 and 3.3. □

Proposition 3.5. *Suppose that $a \leq r\Delta/(1-\delta)$. The equilibrium probability of war is*

1. *0 if $r \leq r^*$*
2. *$1-r$ otherwise.*

Proof. Follows from the equilibrium strategies outlined in Propositions 3.2 and 3.3. □

Proposition 3.6. *In the defensive alliance extension, an equilibrium in which State 2 engages in coercive bargaining and initiates a preventive war with positive probability on the path of play exists if (1) $q \geq 1-w_2+r\Delta$ and (2) $\Delta > (1-\delta)(1-w_2)/\delta r$.*

Proof. First, suppose that (1) $q \geq 1-w_2+r(w_2-w_2')$ and (2) $w_2' < w_2-(1-\delta)(1-w_2)/\delta r$. We construct an equilibrium with the desired features. First, we show that under the conditions of the proposition, players have no profitable deviation from the strategies outlined in Proposition 3.3 in any subgame after State 2 has chosen to engage in coercive bargaining. Recall that if $w_2' < w_2-(1-\delta)(1-w_2)/\delta r$, then in any subgame in which State 2 has chosen to engage in coercive bargaining, arguments from proof of Proposition 3.3 imply the strategies outlined in Proposition 3.3 are consistent with equilibrium play. With this, all that remains to establish the result is to demonstrate that if $q \geq 1-w_2+r(w_2-w_2')$, then it is optimal for State 2 to engage in coercive bargaining.

As players use strategies outlined in Proposition 3.3 after State 2 revises the status quo, if State 2 chooses to engage in coercive bargaining, it receives a (dynamic) payoff of $rw_2'+(1-r)w_2$. In contrast, if State 2 chooses to maintain the status quo it receives a (dynamic) payoff of $1-q$. Therefore, State 2 cannot profitably deviate from engaging in coercive bargaining to instead maintain the status quo if

$$rw_2'+(1-r)w_2 \geq 1-q,$$

which holds if and only if

$$q \geq 1-w_2+r(w_2-w_2'),$$

as required.

Therefore, an equilibrium exists in which State 2 engages in coercive bargaining and in all following subgames players use the strategies outlined in Proposition 3.3. Note that this strategy profile generates a positive probability of preventive war on the path of play (in particular, war occurs with probability $(1-r)$. This completes the proof. □

A.2 Proofs for Chapter 4

Proposition 4.1. *Consider an equilibrium in which State 3 extends an alliance and State 1 joins on the path of play in every period in which* $s^t = N$. *If* $c < \frac{\delta br\Delta}{1-\delta}$, *then State 2 does not accept an offer of* x^t *on the path of play in any such equilibrium.*

Proof. For a proof by contradiction, suppose not. That is, assume that $c < \frac{\delta br\Delta}{1-\delta}$, in which State 2 accepts an offer on the path of play in every period. Recall that in a stationary equilibrium, State 1 makes the same offer in each period in which $s^t = N$ and an alliance has not yet been implemented. Call this offer x^N, and denote the continuation payoff to State 2 of accepting such an offer as V^N. Applying arguments from our analysis of the baseline model, we know that V^N and x^N must satisfy

$$V^N = \frac{(1-\delta)(1-x^N) + \delta r w_2'}{1-\delta+\delta r} = w_2.$$

This implies that $1 - x^N = w_2 + \delta r\Delta/(1-\delta)$. Given this, note that a deviation to block is profitable for State 2 when faced with an offer of x^N if

$$V^N = w_2 < (1-\delta)(\delta r\Delta/(1-\delta) - c) + \delta[bw_2 + (1-b)(w_2 - r\Delta)],$$

which holds if and only if

$$c < \frac{\delta br\Delta}{1-\delta},$$

a contradiction. □

Proposition 4.2. *If*

$$c \leq \frac{\delta br\Delta}{1-\delta} \tag{4.1}$$

and

$$\Delta \leq \frac{(1-\delta)(1-w_2-c)}{\delta r(1-b)} \equiv \overline{\Delta}, \tag{4.2}$$

then there exists an equilibrium in which blocking occurs on the path of play. Strategies in this equilibrium are as follows:

1. *State 1 joins an alliance after State 3 invites in every period in which* $s^t = N$. *State 1 offers* $x^t = 1 - w_2 - c - \frac{\delta r(1-b)\Delta}{1-\delta}$ *in every period in which* $s^t = N$ *and an alliance has not been implemented. In any period in which* $s^t = A$ *or an alliance has been implemented in the current period, State 1 offers* $x^t = 1 - w_2'$. *In any period in which* $s^t = B$, *State 1 offers* $x^t = 1 - w_2$.
2. *If* $s^t = N$ *and an alliance was not implemented in the current period, State 2 blocks if and only if* $x^t \leq 1 - w_2 - c - \frac{\delta r(1-b)\Delta}{1-\delta}$, *and rejects otherwise. If* $s^t = A$ *or an alliance has been implemented in the current period, State 2 accepts if and only if* $x^t \leq 1 - w_2'$ *and rejects otherwise. If* $s^t = B$, *then State 2 accepts if and only if* $x^t \leq 1 - w_2$.
3. *State 3 chooses to extend every period in which* $s^t = N$.

Proof. We demonstrate that no player has a profitable one-shot deviation from the strategies described in the proposition.

First, note that subgames beginning in periods in which $s^t = A$ are covered by the arguments above, and so we do not reproduce them here. Similarly, because state B is absorbing, play in periods in which $s^t = B$ are covered by standard arguments that are analogous to those for $s^t = A$. The only difference is that in such periods State 1 offers $x^t = 1 - w_2$ and State 2 accepts all offers such that $x^t \leq 1 - w_2$.

Now, consider a period in which $s^t = N$. By the arguments from Chapter 3's analysis, States 1 and 3 cannot profitably deviate from offering and joining an alliance, as we assume that a is sufficiently low.

Now consider State 2's strategy after observing an offer of x^t in a period in which $s^t = N$. First, recall that by the previous result, given that

$$c < \frac{\delta br\Delta}{1-\delta},$$

a deviation to accept is not profitable.

Furthermore, note that by construction, following an offer of

$$x^t = 1 - w_2 - c - \frac{\delta r(1-b)\Delta}{1-\delta}$$

renders State 2 indifferent between blocking and rejecting. Therefore, State 2 cannot profitably deviate to reject such an offer.

Finally, given that State 2 is indifferent between blocking and fighting given the value of x^t offered on the path in this equilibrium, it follows that for strictly greater values of x^t State 2 has a strict preference to reject, and therefore cannot profitably deviate from her prescribed strategy.

This completes the proof. □

A.3 Proofs for Chapter 5

Proposition 5.1. *The equilibrium utilities of States 1 and 3 are*

1. *nonmonotonic in Δ, and*
2. *nonmonotonic in r.*

Proof. Recall that we have defined $\Delta = w_2 - w_2'$. We consider changes in w_2' to be changes in the size of the power shift for simplicity. We prove each component of the proposition in turn. First, note that the highest value of w_2' for which peace occurs with probability 1 in equilibrium is $w_2' = w_2 - (1-\delta)(1-w_2)/\delta r \equiv \overline{w}_2$. Note that for $w_2' > \overline{w}_2$, the equilibrium utility of States 1 and 3 is decreasing in w_2'. This follows from the proof of Proposition 3.2, which demonstrated that the equilibrium utilities of States 1 and 3 under these conditions are equal to

$$1 - w_2 + r(w_2 - w_2') - \frac{a(1-\delta)}{1-\delta+\delta r},$$

which is decreasing in w_2'.

Next, we show that, for sufficiently small ϵ, State 1's and State 3's equilibrium utilities are higher under $w_2' = \overline{w}_2$ than under $w_2' = \overline{w}_2 - \epsilon$. This is true for State 1 if

$$r(1-(\overline{w}_2-\epsilon))+(1-r)w_1-a(1-\delta)<1-w_2+r(w_2-\overline{w}_2)-\frac{a(1-\delta)}{1-\delta+\delta r}.$$

Algebra yields that this inequality holds if

$$\epsilon<\left(\frac{r}{1-r}\right)\left[1-w_1-w_2-\frac{a(1-\delta)\delta}{1-\delta+\delta r}\right].$$

Note that our assumption that $a < 1 - w_2 - w_1$ implies that the right-hand side of this inequality is strictly positive. Therefore, the inequality holds for sufficiently small $\epsilon > 0$, as required. A similar argument, replacing w_1 with w_3 in the previous inequality establishes the result for State 3's utility as well.

Finally, note that if $w_2' < \overline{w}_2$, the equilibrium utility of State 1 is

$$r(1-w_2')+(1-r)w_1-a(1-\delta),$$

which is decreasing in w_2'. Similarly, if $w_2' < \overline{w}_2$, the equilibrium utility of State 3 is

$$r(1-w_2')+(1-r)w_3-a(1-\delta),$$

which is decreasing in w_2'.

Finally, note that the preceding analysis implies that, for both States 1 and 3, equilibrium utility as a function of w_2' is decreasing for $w_2' < \overline{w}_2$. Then, equilibrium utility for both States 1 and 3 jumps up discontinuously at $w_2' = \overline{w}_2$, and decreases for $w_2' > \overline{w}_2$. Therefore, the equilibrium utility of both States 1 and 3 is nonmonotonic in w_2'.

To prove the second component of the proposition, note that the highest value of r for which peace occurs with probability 1 in equilibrium is $r = (1-\delta)(1-w_2)/\delta(w_2 - w_2') \equiv r^w$. Note that for $r > r^w$, the equilibrium utility of States 1 and 3 is increasing in r. This follows from the equilibrium strategies outlined in Proposition 3.3.

Next, we show that for sufficiently small ϵ, State 1 and State 3's equilibrium utilities are lower under $r = r^w + \epsilon$ than under $r = r^w$. This is true for State 1 if

$$(r^w+\epsilon)(1-w_2')+(1-r^w-\epsilon)w_1-a(1-\delta)<1-w_2+r(w_2-w_2')-\frac{a(1-\delta)}{1-\delta+\delta r}.$$

Algebra yields that this inequality holds if

$$\epsilon\left(\frac{1-w_2'-w_1}{1-r}\right)<1-w_1-w_2-\frac{a(1-\delta)\delta}{1-\delta+\delta r}.$$

Note that our assumption that $a < 1 - w_2 - w_1$ implies that the right-hand side of this inequality is strictly positive. Therefore, the inequality holds for sufficiently small $\epsilon > 0$, as required. A similar argument, replacing w_1 with w_3 in the previous inequality establishes the result for State 3's utility as well.

Finally, note that if $r < r^w$, the equilibrium utilities of States 1 and 3 are

$$1-w_2+r(w_2-w_2')-\frac{a(1-\delta)}{1-\delta+\delta r},$$

which is increasing in r. □

Proposition 5.2. *The conditions under which State 3 endogenously limits the size or speed of the shift in power from alliance are:*

1. *In the extension with endogenous w_2', there exists a unique $\hat{w}_2 < w_2 - \frac{(1-\delta)(1-w_2)}{\delta r}$ such that if $\overline{w}_2 > \hat{w}_2$, State 3 sets $w_2' = w_2 - \frac{(1-\delta)(1-w_2)}{\delta r}$, and war does not occur in equilibrium. Otherwise, the allies set $w_2' = \overline{w}_2$, and war occurs with positive probability.*
2. *In the extension with endogenous r, there exists a unique $\hat{r} > \frac{(1-\delta)(1-w_2)}{\delta(w_2-w_2')}$ such that if $\overline{r} < \hat{r}$, State 3 sets $r = \frac{(1-\delta)(1-w_2)}{\delta(w_2-w_2')}$, and war does not occur in equilibrium. Otherwise, the allies set $r = \overline{r}$, and war occurs with positive probability.*

Proof. This result follows from Proposition 5.1, along with the observation that in a peaceful equilibrium, the values of w_2' and r indicated in the proposition maximize the payoff of States 1 and 3. □

A.4 Proofs for Chapter 6

Proposition 6.1. *If $a < r(w_2 - w_2')/(1 - \delta)$ and w_2' lies in an intermediate range, then a deal equilibrium exists in which an alliance does not occur on the path of play.*

More precisely, if

$$\frac{w_2 - [(1-r)(1-w_1) + (1-\delta)a]}{r} \leq w_2' \leq w_2 - \frac{(1-\delta)(1-w_2)}{\delta r}, \tag{6.3}$$

then the following strategy profile constitutes an equilibrium:

1. *In any period in which $s_t = N$, State 3 does not offer an alliance and State 3 does not accept if an offer is made. State 1 offers $x^t = 1 - w_2$. State 2 accepts an offer if and only if two conditions are met: $x^t \leq 1 - w_2$ and no attempt to offer or form an alliance was made in the current period. In a period in which $s_t = N$, following an off-path deviation to form an alliance, if implementation fails then State 2 rejects all offers.*
2. *In any period in which $s_t = A$ or an alliance was implemented in the current period, the players use the strategies described in Proposition 3.3*

Proof. We show that no player has a profitable deviation from the proposed strategy profile.

First, note that in any subgame in which $s^t = A$, the strategies constitute a subgame perfect equilibrium by proof of Proposition 3.2.

Next, consider all subgames in which State 3 has offered an alliance and State 1 accepts (recall such subgames are off the path of play). If implementation succeeds, then arguments from the proof of Proposition 3.2 demonstrate that no player can profitably deviate. If implementation fails, then arguments contained in Proposition 3.3 suffice to demonstrate that no player has a profitable deviation.

Next, consider State 1's strategy at a subgame in which $s^t = N$ and State 3 has made an (off-path) offer to implement an alliance. A deviation to accept is not profitable if

$$1 - w_2 \geq r(1 - w_2') + (1 - r)w_1 - (1 - \delta)a. \tag{A.1}$$

This holds if and only if

$$\frac{w_2 - [(1 - r)(1 - w_1) - (1 - \delta)a]}{r} \leq w_2',$$

which we have assumed.

Now consider State 3's decision in a period in which $s^t = N$. A deviation to offer an alliance is not profitable if $1 - w_2 \geq w_3$, which holds if and only if $1 - w_2 - w_3 \geq 0$, which holds as we have assumed that $1 - w_1 - \max\{w_1, w_3\} > 0$. □

Bibliography

Alexander, Martin S., and William J. Philpott. 1998. "The Entente Cordiale and the Next War: Anglo-French Views on Future Military Cooperation, 1928-1939." In *Knowing Your Friends: Intelligence Inside Alliances and Coalitions from 1914 to the Cold War*, ed. Martin S. Alexander, 53–84. New York: Routledge Taylor & Francis.

Alexandroff, Alan and Richard Rosecrance. 1977. "Deterrence in 1939." *World Politics* 29(3):404–424.

Armour, Ian D. 2014. *Apple of Discord: The "Hungarian Factor" in Austro-Serbian Relations, 1867-1881*. Purdue University Press.

Asmus, Ronald. 2004. *Opening NATO's Door*. Columbia University Press.

Bamford, Tyler R. 2022. *Forging the Anglo-American Alliance: The British and American Armies, 1917-1941*. University Press of Kansas.

Barnett, Michael N., and Jack S. Levy. 1991. "Domestic Sources of Alliances and Alignments: The Case of Egypt, 1962–73." *International Organization* 45(3):369–395.

Bas, Muhammet and Robert Schub. 2016. "Mutual Optimism as a Cause of Conflict: Secret Alliances and Conflict Onset." *International Studies Quarterly* 60(3):552–564.

Beevor, Antony. 1982. *The Spanish Civil War*. Orbis London.

Bell, Sam R., and Jesse C. Johnson. 2015. "Shifting Power, Commitment Problems, and Preventive War." *International Studies Quarterly* 59(1):124–132.

Benson, Brett V. 2011. "Unpacking Alliances: Deterrent and Compellent Alliances and their Relationship with Conflict, 1816–2000." *The Journal of Politics* 73(4):1111–1127.

Benson, Brett V. 2012. *Constructing International Security: Alliances, Deterrence, and Moral Hazard*. Cambridge University Press.

Benson, Brett V., Adam Meirowitz, and Kristopher W. Ramsay. 2014. "Inducing Deterrence Through Moral Hazard in Alliance Contracts." *Journal of Conflict Resolution* 58(2):307–335.

Benson, Brett V., and Bradley C. Smith. 2021. "Commitment Problems in Alliance Formation." *American Journal of Political Science*.

Benson, Brett V, and Joshua D. Clinton Clinton. 2016. "Assessing the Variation of Formal Military Alliances." *Journal of Conflict Resolution* 60(5): 866–898.

Bils, Peter and Bradley C. Smith. 2023. "The Logic of Secret Alliances." *American Journal of Political Science* Forthcoming.

Blank, Stephen. 2008. "From Neglect to Duress: The West and the Georgian Crisis before the 2008 War." In *The Guns of August 2008. Russia's War in Georgia*, eds. Svante E. Cornell, and S. Frederick Starr, 104–121. ME Sharpe.

Buzo, Adrian. 2022. *The Making of Modern Korea*. Routledge.

CALL. N.d. "Multinational Interoperability Reference Guide: Lessons and Best Practices." *Center for Army Lessons Used Handbook*. Forthcoming.

Carley, Michael Jabara. 1993. "End of the 'low, dishonest decade': Failure of the Anglo-Franco-Soviet Alliance in 1939." *Europe-Asia Studies* 45(2):303–341.

Carley, Michael Jabara. 1999. *1939: The Alliances that Never was and the Coming of World War II*. Ivan R. Dee Publishing.

Chao, Zhongchen. 2016. *中国历代谋士传 (Strategists in the History of China)*. Liaoning, China: Liaoning People's Publishing House.

Christensen, Thomas J. 1996. *Useful Adversaries: Grand Strategy, Domestic Mobilization, and Sino-American Conflict, 1947-1958*. Princeton University Press.

Christensen, Thomas J. 2011. *Worse than a Monolith: Alliance Politics and Problems of Coercive Diplomacy in Asia*. Princeton University Press.

Clark, Christopher. 2012. *The Sleepwalkers: How Europe Went to War in 1914*. Allen Lane.

Copeland, Dale C. 2000. *The Origins of Major War*. Cornell University Press.

Crankshaw, Edward. 1970. *Khrushchev Remembers*. Bantam Book, & Little, Brown & Company.

Delcour, Laure and Kataryna Wolczuk. 2015. "Spoiler or Facilitator of Democratization?: Russia's Role in Georgia and Ukraine." *Democratization* 22(3):459–478.

DiNardo, Richard L. 1996. "The Dysfunctional Coalition: The Axis Powers and the Eastern Front in World War II." *Journal of Military History* 60(4): 711–730.

Dong, Haonan. 2023. "The Politics of Delay in Crisis Negotiations." *Journal of Conflict Resolution* 69(5): 711–730.

Ericson III, Edward E. 1999. *Feeding the German Eagle: Soviet Economic Aid to Nazi Germany, 1933-1941*. Bloomsbury Publishing USA.

Fang, Songying, Jesse C. Johnson, and Brett Ashley Leeds. 2014. "To Concede or to Resist? The Restraining Effect of Military Alliances." *International Organization* 68(4): 775–809.

Fast, Richard Charles. 1981. "The Politics of Weapons Standardization in NATO." PhD thesis. University of California at Santa Barbara.

Fearon, James D. 1995. "Rationalist Explanations for War." *International organization* 49(3):379–414.

Fearon, James D. 1997. "Signaling Foreign Policy Interests: Tying Hands Versus Sinking Costs." *Journal of Conflict Resolution* 41(1):68–90.

Fravel, M. Taylor. 2007. "Power Shifts and Escalation: Explaining China's Use of Force in Territorial Disputes." *International Security* 32(3):44–83.

Fursenko, Aleksandr and Timothy Naftali. 1997. *"One Hell of a Gamble": Khrushchev, Castro, and Kennedy, 1958-1964*. W.W. Norton & Company.

Gallup and Fortune Polls. 1949. *Public Opinion Quarterly* 4(1):102.

Gandhi, Jennifer, and Adam Przeworski. 2007. "Authoritarian Institutions and the Survival of Autocrats." *Comparative Political Studies* 40(11):1279–1301.

Gates, Robert M. 2011. *From the Shadows: The Ultimate Insider's Story of Five Presidents an*. Simon and Schuster.

Goemans, Hein Erich. 2000. *War and Punishment: The Causes of War Termination and the First World War*. Princeton University Press.

Goldgeier, James M. 2010. *Not Whether but When: The US Decision to Enlarge NATO*. Brookings Institution Press.

Gorbachev, Mikhail Sergeevich. 1996. *Mikhail Gorbachev: Memoirs*. Doubleday.

Gorodetsky, Gabriel. 1990. "The Impact of the Ribbentrop-Molotov Pact on the Course of Soviet Foreign Policy." *Cahiers du monde russe et soviétique* 30(1): 27–41.

Haslam, Jonathan. 1997. "Soviet-German Relations and the Origins of the Second World War: The Jury is Still Out." *The Journal of Modern History* 69(4):785–797.

Heraclides, Alexis and Ada Dialla. 2015. *Humanitarian Intervention in the Long Nineteenth Century: Setting the Precedent*. Manchester University Press.

Illarionov, Andrei. 2015. "The Russian Leadership's Preparation for War, 1999–2008." In *The Guns of August 2008*, eds. Svante E. Cornell and S. Frederick Starr, 73–108. Routledge.

Jervis, Robert. 2017. *Perception and Misperception in International Politics: New edition*. Princeton University Press.

Johnson, Jesse C., and Brett Ashley Leeds. 2011. "Defense Pacts: A Prescription for Peace?" *Foreign Policy Analysis* 7(1):45–65.

Jowett, Philip. 2013. *China's Wars: Rousing the Dragon 1894–1949*. Bloomsbury Publishing.

Kapstein, Ethan Barnaby. 1991. "International Collaboration in Armaments Production: A Second-Best Solution." *Political Science Quarterly* 106(4):657–675.

Kennedy, Robert F. 2015. *13 Days: The Cuban Missile Crisis October 1962*. Springer.

Kenwick, Michael R., and John A. Vasquez. 2017. "Defense Pacts and Deterrence: Caveat Emptor." *The Journal of Politics* 79(1):329–334.

Kenwick, Michael R., John A. Vasquez, and Matthew A. Powers. 2015. "Do Alliances Really Deter?" *The Journal of Politics* 77(4):943–954.

Kershaw, Ian. 2000. *Hitler: 1889-1936 Hubris*. WW Norton & Company.

Khan, Simbal. 2008. "Russia-Georgia War And NATO." *Strategic Studies* 28:1–14.

Kim, Tongfi. 2016. *The Supply Side of Security: A Market Theory of Military Alliances*. Stanford University Press.

Koremenos, Barbara, Charles Lipson, and Duncan Snidal. 2001. "The Rational Design of International Institutions." *International Organization* 55(4):761–799.

Krainin, Colin and Thomas Wiseman. 2016. "War and Stability in Dynamic International Systems." *The Journal of Politics* 78(4):1139–1152.

Kukla, J. 2009. *A Wilderness So Immense: The Louisiana Purchase and the Destiny of America*. Knopf Doubleday Publishing Group.

Kuo, Raymond. 2020. "Secrecy Among Friends: Covert Military Alliances and Portfolio Consistency." *Journal of Conflict Resolution* 64(1):63–89.

Lanoszka, Alexander. 2018. "Tangled up in rose? Theories of Alliance Entrapment and the 2008 Russo-Georgian War." *Contemporary Security Policy* 39(2):234–257.

Larsen, Kirk W. 2020. *Tradition, Treaties, and Trade: Qing Imperialism and Chosŏn Korea, 1850–1910*. Vol. 295. Brill.

Lebow, Richard Ned and Janice Gross Stein. 1994. *We All Lost the Cold War*. Princeton University Press.

Leeds, Brett Ashley. 2003. "Do Alliances Deter Aggression? The Influence of Military Alliances on the Initiation of Militarized Interstate Disputes." *American Journal of Political Science* 47(3):427–439.

Leeds, Brett Ashley, Andrew G. Long, and Sara McLaughlin Mitchell. 2000. "Reevaluating Alliance Reliability: Specific Threats, Specific Promises." *Journal of Conflict Resolution* 44(5):686–699.

Leeds, Brett Ashley, and Jesse C. Johnson. 2017. "Theory, Data, and Deterrence: A Response to Kenwick, Vasquez, and Powers." *The Journal of Politics* 79(1):335–340.

Leeds, Brett, Jeffrey Ritter, Sara Mitchell, and Andrew Long. 2002. "Alliance Treaty Obligations and Provisions, 1815-1944." *International Interactions* 28(3):237–260.

Li, Gong. 2001. "Tension across the Taiwan Strait in the 1950s Chinese Strategy and Tactics." In *Re-examining the Cold War: US-China Diplomacy, 1954–1973*, 141–172. Brill.

Maskin, Eric and Jean Tirole. 2001. "Markov Perfect Equilibrium: I. Observable Actions." *Journal of Economic Theory* 100(2):191–219.

Mattes, Michaela and Greg Vonnahme. 2010. "Contracting for Peace: Do Nonaggression Pacts Reduce Conflict?" *The Journal of Politics* 72(4):925–938.

Mattingly, Garrett. 1988. *Renaissance Diplomacy*. Courier Corporation.

May, Ernest R. 1997. *The Kennedy Tapes: Inside the White House During the Cuban Missile Crisis*. The Belknap Press of Harvard University Press.

Mearsheimer, John J. 2014. "Why the Ukraine Crisis is the West's Fault: The Liberal Delusions that Provoked Putin." *Foreign Affairs* 93:77.

Merjanski, Kiril Valtchev. 2007. "The Secret Serbian-Bulgarian *Treaty of Alliance* of 1904 and the Russian Policy in the Balkans Before the Bosnian Crisis." Master's thesis. Wright State University.

Moens, Alexander. 1991. "American Diplomacy and German Unification." *Survival* 33(6):531–545.

Morrow, James D. 1991. "Alliances and Asymmetry: An Alternative to the Capability Aggregation Model of Alliances." *American Journal of Political Science* 35(4): 904–933.

Morrow, James D. 1994. "Alliances, Credibility, and Peacetime Costs." *Journal of Conflict Resolution* 38(2):270–297.

Morrow, James D. 2000. "Alliances: Why Write Them Down?" *Annual Review of Political Science* 3(1):63–83.

Morrow, James D. 2017. "When Do Defensive Alliances Provoke Rather than Deter?" *The Journal of Politics* 79(1):341–345.

NATO AJP-01. 2017. *NATO Standard AJP-01 Allied Joint Doctrine*. E ed. NATO Standardization Office NATO/OTAN.

Newnham, Randall. 1999. "The Price of German Unity: The Role of Economic Aid in the German-Soviet Negotiations." *German Studies Review* 22(3):421–446.

Newnham, Randall E. 2002. *Deutsche Mark Diplomacy: Positive Economic Sanctions in German-Russian Relations*. Penn State Press.

Owsiak, Andrew P. 2017. "The Steps to War: Theory and Evidence." In *Oxford Research Encyclopedia of Politics*, ed. W. R. Thompson. Oxford.

Paine, Jack, Scott A. Tyson, Dirk Berg-Schlosser, Bertrand Badie, and Leonardo Morlino. 2020. "Uses and Abuses of Formal Models in Political Science." *The SAGE Handbook of Political Science* 3:188–202.

Paine, Sarah Crosby Mallory. 2002. *The Sino-Japanese War of 1894–1895: Perceptions, Power, and Primacy*. Cambridge University Press.

Paine, Sarah Crosby Mallory. 2017. *The Japanese Empire: Grand Strategy from the Meiji Restoration to the Pacific War*. Cambridge University Press.

Perkins, Bradford. 1955. "England and the Louisiana Question." *Huntington Library Quarterly* 18(3):279–295.

Phillips, Julianne and Scott Wolford. 2021. "Collective Deterrence in the Shadow of Shifting Power." *International Studies Quarterly* 65(1):136–145.

Poast, Paul. 2013. "Issue Linkage and International Cooperation: An Empirical Investigation." *Conflict Management and Peace Science* 30(3):286–303.

Poast, Paul. 2019. *Arguing About Alliances: The Art of Agreement in Military-Pact Negotiations*. Cornell University Press.

Powell, Robert. 1999. *In the Shadow of Power: States and Strategies in International Politics*. Princeton University Press.

Powell, Robert. 2004. "The Inefficient Use of Power: Costly Conflict with Complete Information." *American Political science review* 98(2):231–241.

Powell, Robert. 2006. "War as a Commitment Problem." *International Organization* 60(1):169–203.

Powell, Robert. 2012. "Commitment Problems and Shifting Powers a Cause of Conflict." In *The Oxford Handbook of the Economics of Peace and Conflict*. (online ed., Oxford Academic, November 21, 2012). https://doi.org/10.1093/oxfordhb/9780195392777.001.0001, accessed July 21, 2025.

Reiter, Dan. 2010. *How Wars End*. Princeton University Press.

Reynolds, David. 1981. *The Creation of the Anglo-American Alliance 1937–1941: A Study in Competitive Cooperation*. Europa Publications Limited.

Rice, Condoleezza, and Philip Zelikow. 1995. "Germany Unified and Europe Transformed." In *A Study in Statecraft*, eds. Philip Zelikow and Condoleeza Rice. Cambridge, MA: Cambridge Universtity Press.

Ritter, Jeffrey Munro. 2004. ""Silent Partners" and Other Essays on Alliance Politics." PhD thesis. Harvard University.

Roberts, Geoffrey. 1992. "The Soviet Decision for a Pact with Nazi Germany." *Soviet Studies* 44(1):57–78.

Sarkees, Meredith Reid, and Frank Wayman. 2010. *Resort to War: 1816–2007*. Washington, DC: CQ Press. 2010

Sarotte, Mary Elise. 2010. "Perpetuating US Preeminence: The 1990 Deals to "Bribe the Soviets Out" and Move NATO In." *International Security* 35(1):110–137.

Sarotte, Mary Elise. 2014*a*. *1989: The Struggle to Create Post-Cold War Europe-Updated Edition*. Vol. 147. Princeton University Press.

Sarotte, Mary Elise. 2014*b*. "A Broken Promise: What the West Really Told Moscow About NATO Expansion." *Foreign Affairs* 93:90.

Sayle, Timothy Andrews. 2019. *Enduring Alliance: A History of NATO and the Postwar Global Order*. Cornell University Press.

Schram, Peter. 2021. "Hassling: How States Prevent a Preventive War." *American Journal of Political Science* 65(2):294–308.

Scott, Willliam Evans. 1962. *Alliance Against Hitler: The Origins of the Franco-Soviet Pact.* Duke University Press.

Senese, Paul D., and John A. Vasquez. 2008. *The Steps to War: An Empirical Study.* Princeton University Press.

Shazly, Saad. 1980. *The Crossing of the Suez / Saad el Shazly.* 1st ed. San Francisco: American Mideast Research.

Shifrinson, Joshua R. Itzkowitz. 2016. "Deal or No Deal? The End of the Cold War and the US Offer to Limit NATO Expansion." *International Security* 40(4):7–44.

Skinner, Mark Watson. 1950. *Chief of Staff: Prewar Plans and Preparations.* Center of Military History United States Army.

Slantchev, Branislav L. 2003. "The Principle of Convergence in Wartime Negotiations." *American Political Science Review* 97(4):621–632.

Smith, Alastair. 1995. "Alliance Formation and War." *International Studies Quarterly* 39(4):405–425.

Smith, Bradley C. 2021. "Military Coalitions and the Politics of Information." *The Journal of Politics* 83(4):1369–1382.

Smith, David J. 2008. "The Saakashvili Administration's Reaction to Russian Policies Before the 2008 War." In *The Guns of August*, eds. Svante E. Cornell, and S. Frederick Starr, 122–142. ME Sharpe.

Snyder, Glenn H. 1984. "The Security Dilemma in Alliance Politics." *World Politics* 36(4):461–495.

Snyder, Glenn H. 1997. *Alliance Politics.* Cornell University Press.

Stent, Angela E. 2008. "Restoration and Revolution in Putin's Foreign Policy." *Europe-Asia Studies* 60(6):1089–1106.

Stolper, Thomas E. 1985. "China, Taiwan, and the Offshore Islands Together with an Implication for Outer Mongolia and Sino-Soviet Relations." *International Journal of Politics* 15(1/2):1–162.

Walt, Stephen M. 1990. *The Origins of Alliance.* Cornell University Press.

Wang, Tao. 2021. *Isolating the Enemy: Diplomatic Strategy in China and the United States, 1953–1956.* Columbia University Press.

Watson, Derek. 2000. "Molotov's Apprenticeship in Foreign Policy: The Triple Alliance Negotiations in 1939." *Europe-Asia Studies* 52(4):695–722.

Wegner, Bernd. 1997. *From Peace to War: Germany, Soviet Russia, and the World, 1939-1941.* Berghahn Books.

Weinberg, Gerhard L. 1989. "The Nazi-Soviet Pacts: A Half-Century Later." *Foreign Affairs* 68(4):175–189.

Weitsman, Patricia A. 2014. *Waging War: Alliances, Coalitions, and Institutions of Interstate Violence.* Stanford University Press.

Wettig, Gerhard. 1993. "Moscow's Acceptance of NATO: The Catalytic Role of German Unification." *Europe-Asia Studies* 45(6):953–972.

Wilson, Theodore A., et al. 1994. "Coalition: Structure, Strategy, and Statecraft." In *Allies at War: The Soviet, American, and British Experience, 1939-1945*, eds. Warren F. Kimball A. O. Chubarian, and David Reynolds., 79–111. New York, NY: St. Martin's Press.

Wolford, Scott. 2012. "Incumbents, Successors, and Crisis Bargaining: Leadership Turnover as a Commitment Problem." *Journal of Peace Research* 49(4):517–530.

Wolford, Scott. 2014. "Showing Restraint, Signaling Resolve: Coalitions, Cooperation, and Crisis Bargaining." *American Journal of Political Science* 58(1):144–156.

Wolford, Scott. 2018. "Wars of Succession." *International Interactions* 44(1):173–187.

Wolford, Scott. 2019. *The Politics of the First World War: A Course in Game Theory and International Security*. Cambridge University Press.

Wolford, Scott, Dan Reiter, and Clifford J. Carrubba. 2011. "Information, Commitment, and War." *Journal of Conflict Resolution* 55(4):556–579.

Zhang, Shu Guang. 1993. *Deterrence and Strategic Culture: Chinese-American Confrontations, 1949-1958*. Cornell University Press.

Zhou, Yi Le David. 2016. "NATO Infantry Weapons Standardization: Ideal or Possibility?" PhD thesis. University of Calgary.

Index